Cram101 Textbook Outlines to accompany:

Practical Financial Management

Lasher, 4th Edition

An Academic Internet Publishers (AIPI) publication (c) 2007.

You have a discounted membership at www.Cram101.com with this book.

Get all of the practice tests for the chapters of this textbook, and access in-depth reference material for writing essays and papers. Here is an example from a Cram101 Biology text:

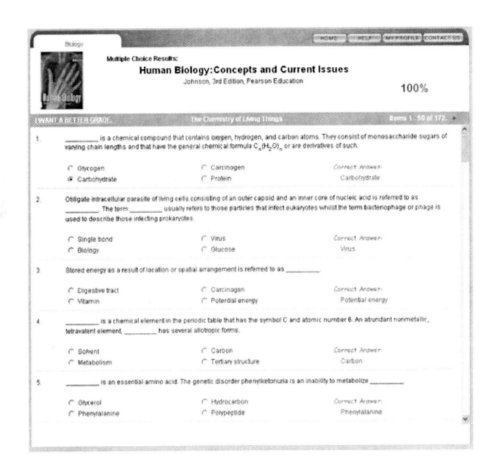

When you need problem solving help with math, stats, and other disciplines, www.Cram101.com will walk through the formulas and solutions step by step.

With Cram101.com online, you also have access to extensive reference material.

You will nail those essays and papers. Here is an example from a Cram101 Biology text:

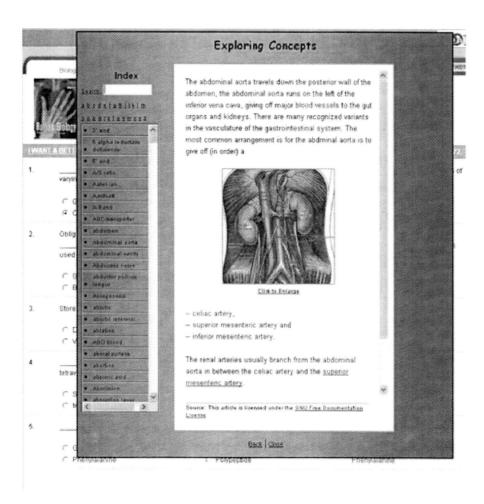

Learning System

Cram101 Textbook Outlines is a learning system. The notes in this book are the highlights of your textbook, you will never have to highlight a book again.

How to use this book. Take this book to class, it is your notebook for the lecture. The notes and highlights on the left hand side of the pages follow the outline and order of the textbook. All you have to do is follow along while your intructor presents the lecture. Circle the items emphasized in class and add other important information on the right side. With Cram101 Textbook Outlines you'll spend less time writing and more time listening. Learning becomes more efficient.

Cram101.com Online

Increase your studying efficiency by using Cram101.com's practice tests and online reference material. It is the perfect complement to Cram101 Textbook Outlines. Use self-teaching matching tests or simulate in-class testing with comprehensive multiple choice tests, or simply use Cram's true and false tests for quick review. Cram101.com even allows you to enter your in-class notes for an integrated studying format combining the textbook notes with your class notes.

Visit **www.Cram101.com**, click Sign Up at the top of the screen, and enter **DK73DW2840** in the promo code box on the registration screen. Access to www.Cram101.com is normally $9.95, but because you have purchased this book, your access fee is only $4.95. Sign up and stop highlighting textbooks forever.

Practical Financial Management
Lasher, 4th

CONTENTS

Enterprise	Enterprise refers to another name for a business organization. Other similar terms are business firm, sometimes simply business, sometimes simply firm, as well as company, and entity.
Financial assets	Financial assets refer to monetary claims or obligations by one party against another party. Examples are bonds, mortgages, bank loans, and equities.
Asset	An item of property, such as land, capital, money, a share in ownership, or a claim on others for future payment, such as a bond or a bank deposit is an asset.
Service	Service refers to a "non tangible product" that is not embodied in a physical good and that typically effects some change in another product, person, or institution. Contrasts with good.
Economics	The social science dealing with the use of scarce resources to obtain the maximum satisfaction of society's virtually unlimited economic wants is an economics.
Financial institution	A financial institution acts as an agent that provides financial services for its clients. Financial institutions generally fall under financial regulation from a government authority.
Financial management	The job of managing a firm's resources so it can meet its goals and objectives is called financial management.
Management	Management characterizes the process of leading and directing all or part of an organization, often a business, through the deployment and manipulation of resources. Early twentieth-century management writer Mary Parker Follett defined management as "the art of getting things done through people."
Stock	In financial terminology, stock is the capital raized by a corporation, through the issuance and sale of shares.
Bond	Bond refers to a debt instrument, issued by a borrower and promising a specified stream of payments to the purchaser, usually regular interest payments plus a final repayment of principal.
A share	In finance the term A share has two distinct meanings, both relating to securities. The first is a designation for a 'class' of common or preferred stock. A share of common or preferred stock typically has enhanced voting rights or other benefits compared to the other forms of shares that may have been created. The equity structure, or how many types of shares are offered, is determined by the corporate charter.
Holder	A person in possession of a document of title or an instrument payable or indorsed to him, his order, or to bearer is a holder.
Shareholder	A shareholder is an individual or company (including a corporation) that legally owns one or more shares of stock in a joined stock company.
Security	Security refers to a claim on the borrower future income that is sold by the borrower to the lender. A security is a type of transferable interest representing financial value.
Firm	An organization that employs resources to produce a good or service for profit and owns and operates one or more plants is referred to as a firm.
Principal	In agency law, one under whose direction an agent acts and for whose benefit that agent acts is a principal.
Interest	In finance and economics, interest is the price paid by a borrower for the use of a lender's money. In other words, interest is the amount of paid to "rent" money for a period of time.
Lender	Suppliers and financial institutions that lend money to companies is referred to as a lender.
Fund	Independent accounting entity with a self-balancing set of accounts segregated for the purposes of carrying on specific activities is referred to as a fund.
Buyer	A buyer refers to a role in the buying center with formal authority and responsibility to select the supplier and negotiate the terms of the contract.

Contribution	In business organization law, the cash or property contributed to a business by its owners is referred to as contribution.
Mutual fund	A mutual fund is a form of collective investment that pools money from many investors and invests the money in stocks, bonds, short-term money market instruments, and/or other securities. In a mutual fund, the fund manager trades the fund's underlying securities, realizing capital gains or loss, and collects the dividend or interest income.
Investment	Investment refers to spending for the production and accumulation of capital and additions to inventories. In a financial sense, buying an asset with the expectation of making a return.
Market	A market is, as defined in economics, a social arrangement that allows buyers and sellers to discover information and carry out a voluntary exchange of goods or services.
Financial market	In economics, a financial market is a mechanism which allows people to trade money for securities or commodities such as gold or other precious metals. In general, any commodity market might be considered to be a financial market, if the usual purpose of traders is not the immediate consumption of the commodity, but rather as a means of delaying or accelerating consumption over time.
Regulation	Regulation refers to restrictions state and federal laws place on business with regard to the conduct of its activities.
Stock market	An organized marketplace in which common stocks are traded. In the United States, the largest stock market is the New York Stock Exchange, on which are traded the stocks of the largest U.S. companies.
Stock exchange	A stock exchange is a corporation or mutual organization which provides facilities for stock brokers and traders, to trade company stocks and other securities.
Exchange	The trade of things of value between buyer and seller so that each is better off after the trade is called the exchange.
Stockbroker	A registered representative who works as a market intermediary to buy and sell securities for clients is a stockbroker.
Broker	In commerce, a broker is a party that mediates between a buyer and a seller. A broker who also acts as a seller or as a buyer becomes a principal party to the deal.
Debt security	Type of security acquired by loaning assets is called a debt security.
Bond market	The bond market refers to people and entities involved in buying and selling of bonds and the quantity and prices of those transactions over time.
Foundation	A Foundation is a type of philanthropic organization set up by either individuals or institutions as a legal entity (either as a corporation or trust) with the purpose of distributing grants to support causes in line with the goals of the foundation.
Dividend	Amount of corporate profits paid out for each share of stock is referred to as dividend.
Equity	Equity is the name given to the set of legal principles, in countries following the English common law tradition, which supplement strict rules of law where their application would operate harshly, so as to achieve what is sometimes referred to as "natural justice."
Portfolio	In finance, a portfolio is a collection of investments held by an institution or a private individual. Holding but not always a portfolio is part of an investment and risk-limiting strategy called diversification. By owning several assets, certain types of risk (in particular specific risk) can be reduced.
Financial manager	Managers who make recommendations to top executives regarding strategies for improving the financial strength of a firm are referred to as a financial manager.
Operation	A standardized method or technique that is performed repetitively, often on different materials resulting in different finished goods is called an operation.

Go to **Cram101.com** for the Practice Tests for this Chapter.
And, **NEVER** highlight a book again!

Chief financial officer	Chief financial officer refers to executive responsible for overseeing the financial operations of an organization.
Accounting	A system that collects and processes financial information about an organization and reports that information to decision makers is referred to as accounting.
Manufacturing	Production of goods primarily by the application of labor and capital to raw materials and other intermediate inputs, in contrast to agriculture, mining, forestry, fishing, and services a manufacturing.
Marketing	Promoting and selling products or services to customers, or prospective customers, is referred to as marketing.
Cash flow	In finance, cash flow refers to the amounts of cash being received and spent by a business during a defined period of time, sometimes tied to a specific project. Most of the time they are being used to determine gaps in the liquid position of a company.
Financial statement	Financial statement refers to a summary of all the transactions that have occurred over a particular period.
Controller	Controller refers to the financial executive primarily responsible for management accounting and financial accounting. Also called chief accounting officer.
Treasurer	In many governments, a treasurer is the person responsible for running the treasury. Treasurers are also employed by organizations to look after funds.
Preponderance	Preponderance of the evidence means that evidence, in the judgment of the juror, is entitled to the greatest weight, appears to be more credible, has greater force, and overcomes not only the opposing presumptions, but also the opposing evidence.
Insurance	Insurance refers to a system by which individuals can reduce their exposure to risk of large losses by spreading the risks among a large number of persons.
Industry	A group of firms that produce identical or similar products is an industry. It is also used specifically to refer to an area of economic production focused on manufacturing which involves large amounts of capital investment before any profit can be realized, also called "heavy industry".
Depreciation	Depreciation is an accounting and finance term for the method of attributing the cost of an asset across the useful life of the asset. Depreciation is a reduction in the value of a currency in floating exchange rate.
Income statement	Income statement refers to a financial statement that presents the revenues and expenses and resulting net income or net loss of a company for a specific period of time.
Fixed asset	Fixed asset, also known as property, plant, and equipment (PP&E), is a term used in accountancy for assets and property which cannot easily be converted into cash. This can be compared with current assets such as cash or bank accounts, which are described as liquid assets. In most cases, only tangible assets are referred to as fixed.
Expense	In accounting, an expense represents an event in which an asset is used up or a liability is incurred. In terms of the accounting equation, expenses reduce owners' equity.
Profit	Profit refers to the return to the resource entrepreneurial ability; total revenue minus total cost.
Financial transaction	A financial transaction involves a change in the status of the finances of two or more businesses or individuals.
Analyst	Analyst refers to a person or tool with a primary function of information analysis, generally with a more limited, practical and short term set of goals than a researcher.
Financial economics	That branch of economics which analyzes how rational investors should invest their funds to attain their objectives in the best possible manner is called financial economics.

Economic theory	Economic theory refers to a statement of a cause-effect relationship; when accepted by all economists, an economic principle.
Limited liability company	Limited liability company refers to a form of entity allowed by all of the states. The entity is taxed as a partnership in which all members or owners of the limited liability company are treated much like limited partners.
Limited liability	Limited liability is a liability that is limited to a partner or investor's investment. Shareholders in a corporation or in a limited liability company cannot lose more money than the value of their shares if the corporation runs into debt, as they are not personally responsible for the corporation's obligations.
Corporation	A legal entity chartered by a state or the Federal government that is distinct and separate from the individuals who own it is a corporation. This separation gives the corporation unique powers which other legal entities lack.
Liability	A liability is a present obligation of the enterprise arizing from past events, the settlement of which is expected to result in an outflow from the enterprise of resources embodying economic benefits.
Financial liability	A financial liability is something that is owed to another party. This is typically contrasted with an asset which is something of value that is owned.
Sole proprietorship	A sole proprietorship is a business which legally has no separate existence from its owner. Hence, the limitations of liability enjoyed by a corporation do not apply.
Partnership	In the common law, a partnership is a type of business entity in which partners share with each other the profits or losses of the business undertaking in which they have all invested.
Context	The effect of the background under which a message often takes on more and richer meaning is a context. Context is especially important in cross-cultural interactions because some cultures are said to be high context or low context.
Entrepreneur	The owner/operator. The person who organizes, manages, and assumes the risks of a firm, taking a new idea or a new product and turning it into a successful business is an entrepreneur.
Personal income tax	A tax levied on the taxable income of individuals, households, and unincorporated firms is referred to as personal income tax.
Collateral	Property that is pledged to the lender to guarantee payment in the event that the borrower is unable to make debt payments is called collateral.
Default	In finance, default occurs when a debtor has not met its legal obligations according to the debt contract, e.g. it has not made a scheduled payment, or violated a covenant (condition) of the debt contract.
Corporate tax	Corporate tax refers to a direct tax levied by various jurisdictions on the profits made by companies or associations. As a general principle, this varies substantially between jurisdictions.
Legal entity	A legal entity is a legal construct through which the law allows a group of natural persons to act as if it were an individual for certain purposes. The most common purposes are lawsuits, property ownership, and contracts.
Economy	The income, expenditures, and resources that affect the cost of running a business and household are called an economy.
Shares	Shares refer to an equity security, representing a shareholder's ownership of a corporation. Shares are one of a finite number of equal portions in the capital of a company, entitling the owner to a proportion of distributed, non-reinvested profits known as dividends and to a portion of the value of the company in case of liquidation.
Stockholder	A stockholder is an individual or company (including a corporation) that legally owns one or more

Go to **Cram101.com** for the Practice Tests for this Chapter.

shares of stock in a joined stock company. The shareholders are the owners of a corporation. Companies listed at the stock market strive to enhance shareholder value.

Gain

In finance, gain is a profit or an increase in value of an investment such as a stock or bond. Gain is calculated by fair market value or the proceeds from the sale of the investment minus the sum of the purchase price and all costs associated with it.

Damages

The sum of money recoverable by a plaintiff who has received a judgment in a civil case is called damages.

Personal property

Personal property is a type of property. In the common law systems personal property may also be called chattels. It is distinguished from real property, or real estate.

Property

Assets defined in the broadest legal sense. Property includes the unrealized receivables of a cash basis taxpayer, but not services rendered.

Incorporation

Incorporation is the forming of a new corporation. The corporation may be a business, a non-profit organization or even a government of a new city or town.

Double taxation

The taxation of both corporate net income and the dividends paid from this net income when they become the personal income of households a double taxation.

Revenue

Revenue is a U.S. business term for the amount of money that a company receives from its activities, mostly from sales of products and/or services to customers.

Joint venture

Joint venture refers to an undertaking by two parties for a specific purpose and duration, taking any of several legal forms.

Forming

The first stage of team development, where the team is formed and the objectives for the team are set is referred to as forming.

Renewable resource

A renewable resource is any natural resource that is depleted at a rate slower than the rate at which it regenerates.

Byproduct

A byproduct is a secondary or incidental product deriving from a manufacturing process or chemical reaction, and is not the primary product or service being produced.

Small business

Small business refers to a business that is independently owned and operated, is not dominant in its field of operation, and meets certain standards of size in terms of employees or annual receipts.

Incentive

An incentive is any factor (financial or non-financial) that provides a motive for a particular course of action, or counts as a reason for preferring one choice to the alternatives.

Profit maximization

Search by a firm for the product quantity, quality, and price that gives that firm the highest possible profit is profit maximization.

Research and development

The use of resources for the deliberate discovery of new information and ways of doing things, together with the application of that information in inventing new products or processes is referred to as research and development.

Short run

Short run refers to a period of time that permits an increase or decrease in current production volume with existing capacity, but one that is too short to permit enlargement of that capacity itself (eg, the building of new plants, training of additional workers, etc.).

Long run

In economic models, the long run time frame assumes no fixed factors of production. Firms can enter or leave the marketplace, and the cost (and availability) of land, labor, raw materials, and capital goods can be assumed to vary.

Stakeholder

A stakeholder is an individual or group with a vested interest in or expectation for organizational performance. Usually stakeholders can either have an effect on or are affected by an organization.

Shareholder

Shareholder wealth maximization refers to maximizing the wealth of the firm's shareholders through

Go to **Cram101.com** for the Practice Tests for this Chapter.

Go to **Cram101.com** for the Practice Tests for this Chapter.
And, **NEVER** highlight a book again!

wealth maximization	achieving the highest possible value for the firm in the marketplace. It is the overriding objective of the firm and should influence all decisions.
Conflict of interest	A conflict that occurs when a corporate officer or director enters into a transaction with the corporation in which he or she has a personal interest is a conflict of interest.
Authority	Authority in agency law, refers to an agent's ability to affect his principal's legal relations with third parties. Also used to refer to an actor's legal power or ability to do something. In addition, sometimes used to refer to a statute, case, or other legal source that justifies a particular result.
Agent	A person who makes economic decisions for another economic actor. A hired manager operates as an agent for a firm's owner.
Balance	In banking and accountancy, the outstanding balance is the amount of money owned, (or due), that remains in a deposit account (or a loan account) at a given date, after all past remittances, payments and withdrawal have been accounted for. It can be positive (then, in the balance sheet of a firm, it is an asset) or negative (a liability).
Management team	A management team is directly responsible for managing the day-to-day operations (and profitability) of a company.
Controlling	A management function that involves determining whether or not an organization is progressing toward its goals and objectives, and taking corrective action if it is not is called controlling.
Production	The creation of finished goods and services using the factors of production: land, labor, capital, entrepreneurship, and knowledge.
Advertising	Advertising refers to paid, nonpersonal communication through various media by organizations and individuals who are in some way identified in the advertising message.
Stock option	A stock option is a specific type of option that uses the stock itself as an underlying instrument to determine the option's pay-off and therefore its value.
Option	A contract that gives the purchaser the option to buy or sell the underlying financial instrument at a specified price, called the exercise price or strike price, within a specific period of time.
Privilege	Generally, a legal right to engage in conduct that would otherwise result in legal liability is a privilege. Privileges are commonly classified as absolute or conditional. Occasionally, privilege is also used to denote a legal right to refrain from particular behavior.
Creditor	A person to whom a debt or legal obligation is owed, and who has the right to enforce payment of that debt or obligation is referred to as creditor.
Valuation	In finance, valuation is the process of estimating the market value of a financial asset or liability. They can be done on assets (for example, investments in marketable securities such as stocks, options, business enterprises, or intangible assets such as patents and trademarks) or on liabilities (e.g., Bonds issued by a company).
Market price	Market price is an economic concept with commonplace familiarity; it is the price that a good or service is offered at, or will fetch, in the marketplace; it is of interest mainly in the study of microeconomics.
Business analysis	Business analysis is a structured methodology that is focused on completely understanding the customer's needs, identifying how best to meet those needs, and then "reinventing" the stream of processes to meet those needs.
Credit	Credit refers to a recording as positive in the balance of payments, any transaction that gives rise to a payment into the country, such as an export, the sale of an asset, or borrowing from abroad.
Budget	Budget refers to an account, usually for a year, of the planned expenditures and the expected receipts of an entity. For a government, the receipts are tax revenues.

Marginal tax rate	The percentage of an additional dollar of earnings that goes to taxes is referred to as the marginal tax rate.
Brokerage firm	A company that conducts various aspects of securities trading, analysis and advisory services is a brokerage firm.
Price index	A measure of the average prices of a group of goods relative to a base year. A typical price index for a vector of quantities q and prices pb, pg in the base and given years respectively would be I = 100 Pgq / Pbq.
Net income	Net income is equal to the income that a firm has after subtracting costs and expenses from the total revenue. Expenses will typically include tax expense.

Go to **Cram101.com** for the Practice Tests for this Chapter.

Accounting	A system that collects and processes financial information about an organization and reports that information to decision makers is referred to as accounting.
Financial transaction	A financial transaction involves a change in the status of the finances of two or more businesses or individuals.
Consideration	Consideration in contract law, a basic requirement for an enforceable agreement under traditional contract principles, defined in this text as legal value, bargained for and given in exchange for an act or promise. In corporation law, cash or property contributed to a corporation in exchange for shares, or a promise to contribute such cash or property.
Enterprise	Enterprise refers to another name for a business organization. Other similar terms are business firm, sometimes simply business, sometimes simply firm, as well as company, and entity.
Financial management	The job of managing a firm's resources so it can meet its goals and objectives is called financial management.
Management	Management characterizes the process of leading and directing all or part of an organization, often a business, through the deployment and manipulation of resources. Early twentieth-century management writer Mary Parker Follett defined management as "the art of getting things done through people."
Holding	The holding is a court's determination of a matter of law based on the issue presented in the particular case. In other words: under this law, with these facts, this result.
Financial statement	Financial statement refers to a summary of all the transactions that have occurred over a particular period.
Income statement	Income statement refers to a financial statement that presents the revenues and expenses and resulting net income or net loss of a company for a specific period of time.
Net income	Net income is equal to the income that a firm has after subtracting costs and expenses from the total revenue. Expenses will typically include tax expense.
Expense	In accounting, an expense represents an event in which an asset is used up or a liability is incurred. In terms of the accounting equation, expenses reduce owners' equity.
Accounts receivable	Accounts receivable is one of a series of accounting transactions dealing with the billing of customers which owe money to a person, company or organization for goods and services that have been provided to the customer. This is typically done in a one person organization by writing an invoice and mailing or delivering it to each customer.
Credit	Credit refers to a recording as positive in the balance of payments, any transaction that gives rise to a payment into the country, such as an export, the sale of an asset, or borrowing from abroad.
Credit sale	A credit sale occurs when a customer does not pay cash at the time of the sale but instead agrees to pay later. The sale occurs now, with payment from the customer to follow at a later time.
Firm	An organization that employs resources to produce a good or service for profit and owns and operates one or more plants is referred to as a firm.
Labor	People's physical and mental talents and efforts that are used to help produce goods and services are called labor.
Accounting income	The accountant's concept of income is generally based upon the realization principle. Financial accounting income may differ from taxable income. Differences are included in a reconciliation of taxable and accounting income on Schedule M-1 of Form 1120.

Go to **Cram101.com** for the Practice Tests for this Chapter.

Depreciation	Depreciation is an accounting and finance term for the method of attributing the cost of an asset across the useful life of the asset. Depreciation is a reduction in the value of a currency in floating exchange rate.
Asset	An item of property, such as land, capital, money, a share in ownership, or a claim on others for future payment, such as a bond or a bank deposit is an asset.
Proration	The spreading of underallocated or overallocated overhead among ending work in process, finished goods, and cost of goods sold is a proration. Also known as an allocation. A temporary limit on the amount of product customers can purchase at the terminal usually based on contracts and used to protect inventories in time of shortage.
Allocate	Allocate refers to the assignment of income for various tax purposes. A multistate corporation's nonbusiness income usually is distributed to the state where the nonbusiness assets are located; it is not apportioned with the rest of the entity's income.
Service	Service refers to a "non tangible product" that is not embodied in a physical good and that typically effects some change in another product, person, or institution. Contrasts with good.
Balance sheet	A statement of the assets, liabilities, and net worth of a firm or individual at some given time often at the end of its "fiscal year," is referred to as a balance sheet.
Cash flow	In finance, cash flow refers to the amounts of cash being received and spent by a business during a defined period of time, sometimes tied to a specific project. Most of the time they are being used to determine gaps in the liquid position of a company.
Interest	In finance and economics, interest is the price paid by a borrower for the use of a lender's money. In other words, interest is the amount of paid to "rent" money for a period of time.
Balance	In banking and accountancy, the outstanding balance is the amount of money owned, (or due), that remains in a deposit account (or a loan account) at a given date, after all past remittances, payments and withdrawal have been accounted for. It can be positive (then, in the balance sheet of a firm, it is an asset) or negative (a liability).
Statement of cash flow	Reports inflows and outflows of cash during the accounting period in the categories of operating, investing, and financing is a statement of cash flow.
Ledger	Ledger refers to a specialized accounting book in which information from accounting journals is accumulated into specific categories and posted so that managers can find all the information about one account in the same place.
Inventory	Tangible property held for sale in the normal course of business or used in producing goods or services for sale is an inventory.
Dividend	Amount of corporate profits paid out for each share of stock is referred to as dividend.
Wage	The payment for the service of a unit of labor, per unit time. In trade theory, it is the only payment to labor, usually unskilled labor. In empirical work, wage data may exclude other compenzation, which must be added to get the total cost of employment.
Fixed asset	Fixed asset, also known as property, plant, and equipment (PP&E), is a term used in accountancy for assets and property which cannot easily be converted into cash. This can be compared with current assets such as cash or bank accounts, which are described as liquid assets. In most cases, only tangible assets are referred to as fixed.
Debit	Debit refers to recording as negative in the balance of payments, any transaction that gives rise to a payment out of the country, such as an import, the purchase of an asset, or lending to foreigners. Opposite of credit.
Stock	In financial terminology, stock is the capital raized by a corporation, through the issuance

and sale of shares.

Revenue	Revenue is a U.S. business term for the amount of money that a company receives from its activities, mostly from sales of products and/or services to customers.
Creditor	A person to whom a debt or legal obligation is owed, and who has the right to enforce payment of that debt or obligation is referred to as creditor.
Estate	An estate is the totality of the legal rights, interests, entitlements and obligations attaching to property. In the context of wills and probate, it refers to the totality of the property which the deceased owned or in which some interest was held.
Cost of goods sold	In accounting, the cost of goods sold describes the direct expenses incurred in producing a particular good for sale, including the actual cost of materials that comprise the good, and direct labor expense in putting the good in salable condition.
Production	The creation of finished goods and services using the factors of production: land, labor, capital, entrepreneurship, and knowledge.
Manufacturing	Production of goods primarily by the application of labor and capital to raw materials and other intermediate inputs, in contrast to agriculture, mining, forestry, fishing, and services a manufacturing.
Manufacturing business	A business firm that makes the products it sells is called a manufacturing business.
Gross profit margin	Gross Profit Margin equals Gross Profit divided by Revenue, expressed as a percentage. The percentage represents the amount of each dollar of Revenue that results in Gross Profit.
Profit margin	Profit margin is a measure of profitability. It is calculated using a formula and written as a percentage or a number. Profit margin = Net income before tax and interest / Revenue.
Gross margin	Gross margin is an ambiguous phrase that expresses the relationship between gross profit and sales revenue as Gross Margin = Revenue - costs of good sold.
Gross profit	Net sales less cost of goods sold is called gross profit.
Profit	Profit refers to the return to the resource entrepreneurial ability; total revenue minus total cost.
Margin	A deposit by a buyer in stocks with a seller or a stockbroker, as security to cover fluctuations in the market in reference to stocks that the buyer has purchased but for which he has not paid is a margin. Commodities are also traded on margin.
Interest expense	The cost a business incurs to borrow money. With respect to bonds payable, the interest expense is calculated by multiplying the market rate of interest by the carrying value of the bonds on the date of the payment.
Interest payment	The payment to holders of bonds payable, calculated by multiplying the stated rate on the face of the bond by the par, or face, value of the bond. If bonds are issued at a discount or premium, the interest payment does not equal the interest expense.
Leverage	Leverage is using given resources in such a way that the potential positive or negative outcome is magnified. In finance, this generally refers to borrowing.
Earnings before interest and taxes	Income from operations before subtracting interest expense and income taxes is an earnings before interest and taxes.
Operation	A standardized method or technique that is performed repetitively, often on different materials resulting in different finished goods is called an operation.

Go to **Cram101.com** for the Practice Tests for this Chapter.

Equity	Equity is the name given to the set of legal principles, in countries following the English common law tradition, which supplement strict rules of law where their application would operate harshly, so as to achieve what is sometimes referred to as "natural justice."
Business operations	Business operations are those activities involved in the running of a business for the purpose of producing value for the stakeholders. The outcome of business operations is the harvesting of value from assets owned by a business.
Yield	The interest rate that equates a future value or an annuity to a given present value is a yield.
Deferred tax	Deferred tax is an accounting term, meaning future tax liability or asset, resulting from temporary differences between book (accounting) value of assets and liabilities, and their tax value.
Bottom line	The bottom line is net income on the last line of a income statement.
Short run	Short run refers to a period of time that permits an increase or decrease in current production volume with existing capacity, but one that is too short to permit enlargement of that capacity itself (eg, the building of new plants, training of additional workers, etc.).
Liability	A liability is a present obligation of the enterprise arizing from past events, the settlement of which is expected to result in an outflow from the enterprise of resources embodying economic benefits.
Equity investment	Equity investment generally refers to the buying and holding of shares of stock on a stock market by individuals and funds in anticipation of income from dividends and capital gain as the value of the stock rises.
Investment	Investment refers to spending for the production and accumulation of capital and additions to inventories. In a financial sense, buying an asset with the expectation of making a return.
Tangible	Having a physical existence is referred to as the tangible. Personal property other than real estate, such as cars, boats, stocks, or other assets.
Liquidity	Liquidity refers to the capacity to turn assets into cash, or the amount of assets in a portfolio that have that capacity.
Context	The effect of the background under which a message often takes on more and richer meaning is a context. Context is especially important in cross-cultural interactions because some cultures are said to be high context or low context.
Market	A market is, as defined in economics, a social arrangement that allows buyers and sellers to discover information and carry out a voluntary exchange of goods or services.
Security	Security refers to a claim on the borrower future income that is sold by the borrower to the lender. A security is a type of transferable interest representing financial value.
Marketable securities	Marketable securities refer to securities that are readily traded in the secondary securities market.
Allowance for doubtful accounts	Contra-asset account containing the estimated uncollectible accounts receivable is an allowance for doubtful accounts. Also called allowance for bad debts or allowance for uncollectible accounts.
Allowance	Reduction in the selling price of goods extended to the buyer because the goods are defective or of lower quality than the buyer ordered and to encourage a buyer to keep merchandise that would otherwise be returned is the allowance.
Bad debt	In accounting and finance, bad debt is the portion of receivables that can no longer be collected, typically from accounts receivable or loans. Bad debt in accounting is considered

	an expense.
Writing off	Writing off refers to the allocation of the cost of an asset over several accounting periods. Also, to expense a cost, that is, put it on the income statement as an expense.
Finished goods	Completed products awaiting sale are called finished goods. An item considered a finished good in a supplying plant might be considered a component or raw material in a receiving plant.
Raw material	Raw material refers to a good that has not been transformed by production; a primary product.
Factory overhead	Manufacturing costs that are not raw material or direct labor costs are factory overhead. Variable factory overhead is usually distinguished from factory overhead.
Shrinkage	Breakage and theft of merchandise by customers and employees is referred to as shrinkage.
Users	Users refer to people in the organization who actually use the product or service purchased by the buying center.
Current asset	A current asset is an asset on the balance sheet which is expected to be sold or otherwise used up in the near future, usually within one year.
Financial analysis	Financial analysis is the analysis of the accounts and the economic prospects of a firm.
Property	Assets defined in the broadest legal sense. Property includes the unrealized receivables of a cash basis taxpayer, but not services rendered.
Useful life	The length of service of a productive facility or piece of equipment is its useful life. The period of time during which an asset will have economic value and be usable.
Matching principle	The matching principle indictates that when it is reasonable to do so, expenses should be matched with revenues. When expenses are matched with revenues, they are not recognized until the associated revenue is also recognized.
Matching	Matching refers to an accounting concept that establishes when expenses are recognized. Expenses are matched with the revenues they helped to generate and are recognized when those revenues are recognized.
Argument	The discussion by counsel for the respective parties of their contentions on the law and the facts of the case being tried in order to aid the jury in arriving at a correct and just conclusion is called argument.
Accelerated depreciation	Methods that result in higher depreciation expense in the early years of an asset's life, and lower expense in the later years are referred to as accelerated depreciation.
Accumulated depreciation	Accumulated depreciation refers to the total depreciation that has been reported as depreciation expense for the entire life of a long-term tangible asset. It is a contra-asset account.
Depreciation expense	Depreciation expense refers to the amount recognized as an expense in one period resulting from the periodic recognition of the used portion of the cost of a long-term tangible asset over its life.
Market value	Market value refers to the price of an asset agreed on between a willing buyer and a willing seller; the price an asset could demand if it is sold on the open market.
Book value	The book value of an asset or group of assets is sometimes the price at which they were originally acquired, in many cases equal to purchase price.
Salvage value	In accounting, the salvage value of an asset is its remaining value after depreciation. The estimated value of an asset at the end of its useful life.

Depreciate	A nation's currency is said to depreciate when exchange rates change so that a unit of its currency can buy fewer units of foreign currency.
Operating income	Total revenues from operation minus cost of goods sold and operating costs are called operating income.
Incentive	An incentive is any factor (financial or non-financial) that provides a motive for a particular course of action, or counts as a reason for preferring one choice to the alternatives.
Trade credit	Trade credit refers to an amount that is loaned to an exporter to be repaid when the exports are paid for by the foreign importer.
Vendor	A person who sells property to a vendee is a vendor. The words vendor and vendee are more commonly applied to the seller and purchaser of real estate, and the words seller and buyer are more commonly applied to the seller and purchaser of personal property.
Buyer	A buyer refers to a role in the buying center with formal authority and responsibility to select the supplier and negotiate the terms of the contract.
Accounts payable	A written record of all vendors to whom the business firm owes money is referred to as accounts payable.
Discount	The difference between the face value of a bond and its selling price, when a bond is sold for less than its face value it's referred to as a discount.
Payables	Obligations to make future economic sacrifices, usually cash payments, are referred to as payables. Same as current liabilities.
Privilege	Generally, a legal right to engage in conduct that would otherwise result in legal liability is a privilege. Privileges are commonly classified as absolute or conditional. Occasionally, privilege is also used to denote a legal right to refrain from particular behavior.
Accrual	An accrual is an accounting event in which the transaction is recognized when the action takes place, instead of when cash is disbursed or received.
Closing	The finalization of a real estate sales transaction that passes title to the property from the seller to the buyer is referred to as a closing. Closing is a sales term which refers to the process of making a sale. It refers to reaching the final step, which may be an exchange of money or acquiring a signature.
Property tax	Property tax is an ad valorem tax that an owner of real estate or other property pays on the value of the thing taxed. The taxing authority requires and/or performs an appraisal of the monetary value of the property, and tax is assessed in proportion to that value.
Current liability	Current liability refers to a debt that can reasonably be expected to be paid from existing current assets or through the creation of other current liabilities, within one year or the operating cycle, whichever is longer.
Working capital	The dollar difference between total current assets and total current liabilities is called working capital.
Capital	Capital generally refers to financial wealth, especially that used to start or maintain a business. In classical economics, capital is one of four factors of production, the others being land and labor and entrepreneurship.
Bond	Bond refers to a debt instrument, issued by a borrower and promising a specified stream of payments to the purchaser, usually regular interest payments plus a final repayment of principal.
Interest rate	The rate of return on bonds, loans, or deposits. When one speaks of 'the' interest rate, it

is usually in a model where there is only one.

Fund	Independent accounting entity with a self-balancing set of accounts segregated for the purposes of carrying on specific activities is referred to as a fund.
Equity financing	Financing that consists of funds that are invested in exchange for ownership in the company is called equity financing.
Direct investment	Direct investment refers to a domestic firm actually investing in and owning a foreign subsidiary or division.
Entrepreneur	The owner/operator. The person who organizes, manages, and assumes the risks of a firm, taking a new idea or a new product and turning it into a successful business is an entrepreneur.
Retained earnings	Cumulative earnings of a company that are not distributed to the owners and are reinvested in the business are called retained earnings.
Common stock	Common stock refers to the basic, normal, voting stock issued by a corporation; called residual equity because it ranks after preferred stock for dividend and liquidation distributions.
Par value	The central value of a pegged exchange rate, around which the actual rate is permitted to fluctuate within set bounds is a par value.
Shares	Shares refer to an equity security, representing a shareholder's ownership of a corporation. Shares are one of a finite number of equal portions in the capital of a company, entitling the owner to a proportion of distributed, non-reinvested profits known as dividends and to a portion of the value of the company in case of liquidation.
Shareholder	A shareholder is an individual or company (including a corporation) that legally owns one or more shares of stock in a joined stock company.
Contribution	In business organization law, the cash or property contributed to a business by its owners is referred to as contribution.
Preferred stock	Stock that has specified rights over common stock is a preferred stock.
Common equity	The common stock or ownership capital of the firm is common equity. Common equity may be supplied through retained earnings or the sale of new common stock.
Corporation	A legal entity chartered by a state or the Federal government that is distinct and separate from the individuals who own it is a corporation. This separation gives the corporation unique powers which other legal entities lack.
Authority	Authority in agency law, refers to an agent's ability to affect his principal's legal relations with third parties. Also used to refer to an actor's legal power or ability to do something. In addition, sometimes used to refer to a statute, case, or other legal source that justifies a particular result.
Consumption	In Keynesian economics consumption refers to personal consumption expenditure, i.e., the purchase of currently produced goods and services out of income, out of savings (net worth), or from borrowed funds. It refers to that part of disposable income that does not go to saving.
Sales tax	A sales tax is a tax on consumption. It is normally a certain percentage that is added onto the price of a good or service that is purchased.
End user	End user refers to the ultimate user of a product or service.
User pays	User pays is a pricing approach based on the capitalist idea that the most economically efficient allocation of resources occurs when consumers pay the full cost of the goods that

they consume.

Federal government	Federal government refers to the government of the United States, as distinct from the state and local governments.
Effective tax rate	The effective tax rate is the amount of income tax an individual or firm pays divided by the individual or firm's total taxable income. This ratio is usually expressed as a percentage.
Deductible	The dollar sum of costs that an insured individual must pay before the insurer begins to pay is called deductible.
Progressive tax	A tax whose average tax rate increases as the taxpayer's income increases and decreases as the taxpayer's income decreases is a progressive tax.
Marginal tax rate	The percentage of an additional dollar of earnings that goes to taxes is referred to as the marginal tax rate.
Average tax rate	Total tax paid divided by total income, the average tax rate is expressed as a percentage. The ratio of taxes paid to the tax base.
Gross income	Income subject to the Federal income tax. Gross income does not include all economic income. That is, certain exclusions are allowed. For a manufacturing or merchandizing business, gross income usually means gross profit.
Capital gain	Capital gain refers to the gain in value that the owner of an asset experiences when the price of the asset rises, including when the currency in which the asset is denominated appreciates.
Gain	In finance, gain is a profit or an increase in value of an investment such as a stock or bond. Gain is calculated by fair market value or the proceeds from the sale of the investment minus the sum of the purchase price and all costs associated with it.
Capital loss	Capital loss refers to the loss in value that the owner of an asset experiences when the price of the asset falls, including when the currency in which the asset is denominated depreciates. Contrasts with capital gain.
Economy	The income, expenditures, and resources that affect the cost of running a business and household are called an economy.
Holding period	The period of time during which property has been held for income tax purposes. The holding period is significant in determining whether gain or loss from the sale or exchange of a capital asset is long term or short term.
Anticipation	In finance, anticipation is where debts are paid off early, generally in order to pay less interest.
Household	An economic unit that provides the economy with resources and uses the income received to purchase goods and services that satisfy economic wants is called household.
Points	Loan origination fees that may be deductible as interest by a buyer of property. A seller of property who pays points reduces the selling price by the amount of the points paid for the buyer.
Exempt	Employees who are not covered by the Fair Labor Standards Act are exempt. Exempt employees are not eligible for overtime pay.
Municipal bond	In the United States, a municipal bond is a bond issued by a state, city or other local government, or their agencies. Potential issuers of these include cities, counties, redevelopment agencies, school districts, publicly owned airports and seaports, and any other governmental entity (or group of governments) below the state level. They are guaranteed by a local government, a subdivision thereof, or a group of local governments, and are assessed

31

for risk and rated accordingly.

Mortgage	Mortgage refers to a note payable issued for property, such as a house, usually repaid in equal installments consisting of part principle and part interest, over a specified period.
Dependency exemption	The tax law provides an exemption for each individual taxpayer and an additional exemption for the taxpayer's spouse if a joint return is filed. An individual may also claim a dependency exemption for each dependent, provided certain tests are met.
Inflation	An increase in the overall price level of an economy, usually as measured by the CPI or by the implicit price deflator is called inflation.
Personal exemption	Personal exemption refers to the tax law provision of an exemption for each individual taxpayer and an additional exemption for the taxpayer's spouse if a joint return is filed.
Net capital gain	The excess of the net long-term capital gain for the tax year over the net short-term capital loss. The net capital gain of an individual taxpayer is eligible for the alternative tax.
Net capital loss	The excess of the losses from sales or exchanges of capital assets over the gains from sales or exchanges of such assets. Up to $3,000 per year of the net capital loss may be deductible by non-corporate taxpayers against ordinary income.
Corporate bond	A Corporate bond is a bond issued by a corporation, as the name suggests. The term is usually applied to longer term debt instruments, generally with a maturity date falling at least 12 months after their issue date (the term "commercial paper" being sometimes used for instruments with a shorter maturity).
Double taxation	The taxation of both corporate net income and the dividends paid from this net income when they become the personal income of households a double taxation.
Tax credit	Allows a firm to reduce the taxes paid to the home government by the amount of taxes paid to the foreign government is referred to as tax credit.
Debt financing	Obtaining financing by borrowing money is debt financing.
Industry	A group of firms that produce identical or similar products is an industry. It is also used specifically to refer to an area of economic production focused on manufacturing which involves large amounts of capital investment before any profit can be realized, also called "heavy industry".
Line of credit	Line of credit refers to a given amount of unsecured short-term funds a bank will lend to a business, provided the funds are readily available.
Overdraft	The withdrawal from a bank by a depositor of money in excess of the amount of money he or she has on deposit there is an overdraft.
Par value stock	Par value stock refers to capital stock that has been assigned a value per share in the corporate charter. .
Value stock	In financial terminology, a stock that appears attractive using the fundamental criteria of stock valuation because of valuable assets, particularly cash and real estate, owned by its company. A stock may be named a value stock if its earnings per share, cash per share or book value is high relative to the stock price
A share	In finance the term A share has two distinct meanings, both relating to securities. The first is a designation for a 'class' of common or preferred stock. A share of common or preferred stock typically has enhanced voting rights or other benefits compared to the other forms of shares that may have been created. The equity structure, or how many types of shares are offered, is determined by the corporate charter.
Small business	Small business refers to a business that is independently owned and operated, is not dominant

Go to **Cram101.com** for the Practice Tests for this Chapter.

	in its field of operation, and meets certain standards of size in terms of employees or annual receipts.
Principal	In agency law, one under whose direction an agent acts and for whose benefit that agent acts is a principal.
Interest income	Interest income refers to payments of income to those who supply the economy with capital.
Revenue bond	A revenue bond is a special type of municipal bond distinguished by its guarantee of repayment solely from revenues generated by a specified revenue-generating entity associated with the purpose of the bonds.
License	A license in the sphere of Intellectual Property Rights (IPR) is a document, contract or agreement giving permission or the 'right' to a legally-definable entity to do something (such as manufacture a product or to use a service), or to apply something (such as a trademark), with the objective of achieving commercial gain.
Regulation	Regulation refers to restrictions state and federal laws place on business with regard to the conduct of its activities.
Internal Revenue Service	In 1862, during the Civil War, President Lincoln and Congress created the office of Commissioner of Internal Revenue and enacted an income tax to pay war expenses. The position of Commissioner still exists today. The Commissioner is the head of the Internal Revenue Service.

Financial statement	Financial statement refers to a summary of all the transactions that have occurred over a particular period.
Cash flow	In finance, cash flow refers to the amounts of cash being received and spent by a business during a defined period of time, sometimes tied to a specific project. Most of the time they are being used to determine gaps in the liquid position of a company.
Firm	An organization that employs resources to produce a good or service for profit and owns and operates one or more plants is referred to as a firm.
Statement of cash flow	Reports inflows and outflows of cash during the accounting period in the categories of operating, investing, and financing is a statement of cash flow.
Business operations	Business operations are those activities involved in the running of a business for the purpose of producing value for the stakeholders. The outcome of business operations is the harvesting of value from assets owned by a business.
Operation	A standardized method or technique that is performed repetitively, often on different materials resulting in different finished goods is called an operation.
Management	Management characterizes the process of leading and directing all or part of an organization, often a business, through the deployment and manipulation of resources. Early twentieth-century management writer Mary Parker Follett defined management as "the art of getting things done through people."
Financial management	The job of managing a firm's resources so it can meet its goals and objectives is called financial management.
Conflict of interest	A conflict that occurs when a corporate officer or director enters into a transaction with the corporation in which he or she has a personal interest is a conflict of interest.
Interest	In finance and economics, interest is the price paid by a borrower for the use of a lender's money. In other words, interest is the amount of paid to "rent" money for a period of time.
Users	Users refer to people in the organization who actually use the product or service purchased by the buying center.
Creditor	A person to whom a debt or legal obligation is owed, and who has the right to enforce payment of that debt or obligation is referred to as creditor.
Analyst	Analyst refers to a person or tool with a primary function of information analysis, generally with a more limited, practical and short term set of goals than a researcher.
Lender	Suppliers and financial institutions that lend money to companies is referred to as a lender.
Stockholder	A stockholder is an individual or company (including a corporation) that legally owns one or more shares of stock in a joined stock company. The shareholders are the owners of a corporation. Companies listed at the stock market strive to enhance shareholder value.
Brokerage firm	A company that conducts various aspects of securities trading, analysis and advisory services is a brokerage firm.
Financial institution	A financial institution acts as an agent that provides financial services for its clients. Financial institutions generally fall under financial regulation from a government authority.
Credit	Credit refers to a recording as positive in the balance of payments, any transaction that gives rise to a payment into the country, such as an export, the sale of an asset, or borrowing from abroad.
Vendor	A person who sells property to a vendee is a vendor. The words vendor and vendee are more commonly applied to the seller and purchaser of real estate, and the words seller and buyer are more commonly applied to the seller and purchaser of personal property.

Service	Service refers to a "non tangible product" that is not embodied in a physical good and that typically effects some change in another product, person, or institution. Contrasts with good.
Fund	Independent accounting entity with a self-balancing set of accounts segregated for the purposes of carrying on specific activities is referred to as a fund.
Annual report	An annual report is prepared by corporate management that presents financial information including financial statements, footnotes, and the management discussion and analysis.
Stock	In financial terminology, stock is the capital raized by a corporation, through the issuance and sale of shares.
Financial analysis	Financial analysis is the analysis of the accounts and the economic prospects of a firm.
Accounting	A system that collects and processes financial information about an organization and reports that information to decision makers is referred to as accounting.
Generally accepted accounting principles	Generally accepted accounting principles refers to the standard framework of guidelines for financial accounting. It includes the standards, conventions, and rules accountants follow in recording and summarizing transactions, and in the preparation of financial statements.
Mistake	In contract law a mistake is incorrect understanding by one or more parties to a contract and may be used as grounds to invalidate the agreement. Common law has identified three different types of mistake in contract: unilateral mistake, mutual mistake, and common mistake.
Advertising	Advertising refers to paid, nonpersonal communication through various media by organizations and individuals who are in some way identified in the advertising message.
Exchange	The trade of things of value between buyer and seller so that each is better off after the trade is called the exchange.
NASDAQ	NASDAQ is an American electronic stock exchange. It was founded in 1971 by the National Association of Securities Dealers who divested it in a series of sales in 2000 and 2001.
Investment	Investment refers to spending for the production and accumulation of capital and additions to inventories. In a financial sense, buying an asset with the expectation of making a return.
General Motors	General Motors is the world's largest automaker. Founded in 1908, today it employs about 327,000 people around the world. With global headquarters in Detroit, it manufactures its cars and trucks in 33 countries.
Layout	Layout refers to the physical arrangement of the various parts of an advertisement including the headline, subheads, illustrations, body copy, and any identifying marks.
Pension	A pension is a steady income given to a person (usually after retirement). Pensions are typically payments made in the form of a guaranteed annuity to a retired or disabled employee.
Microsoft	Microsoft is a multinational computer technology corporation with 2004 global annual sales of US$39.79 billion and 71,553 employees in 102 countries and regions as of July 2006. It develops, manufactures, licenses, and supports a wide range of software products for computing devices.
Sherman Act	Federal antitrust act of 1890 that makes monopoly and conspiracies to restrain trade criminal offenses is the Sherman Act.
Monopoly	A monopoly is defined as a persistent market situation where there is only one provider of a kind of product or service.

Federal government	Federal government refers to the government of the United States, as distinct from the state and local governments.
Assessment	Collecting information and providing feedback to employees about their behavior, communication style, or skills is an assessment.
Litigation	The process of bringing, maintaining, and defending a lawsuit is litigation.
Notes to the financial statements	Notes that clarify information presented in the financial statements, as well as expand upon it where additional detail is needed are notes to the financial statements.
Corporation	A legal entity chartered by a state or the Federal government that is distinct and separate from the individuals who own it is a corporation. This separation gives the corporation unique powers which other legal entities lack.
Marketing	Promoting and selling products or services to customers, or prospective customers, is referred to as marketing.
Bid	A bid price is a price offered by a buyer when he/she buys a good. In the context of stock trading on a stock exchange, the bid price is the highest price a buyer of a stock is willing to pay for a share of that given stock.
Senior executive	Senior executive means a chief executive officer, chief operating officer, chief financial officer and anyone in charge of a principal business unit or function.
Shareholder	A shareholder is an individual or company (including a corporation) that legally owns one or more shares of stock in a joined stock company.
Shares	Shares refer to an equity security, representing a shareholder's ownership of a corporation. Shares are one of a finite number of equal portions in the capital of a company, entitling the owner to a proportion of distributed, non-reinvested profits known as dividends and to a portion of the value of the company in case of liquidation.
Short run	Short run refers to a period of time that permits an increase or decrease in current production volume with existing capacity, but one that is too short to permit enlargement of that capacity itself (eg, the building of new plants, training of additional workers, etc.).
Restructuring	Restructuring is the corporate management term for the act of partially dismantling and reorganizing a company for the purpose of making it more efficient and therefore more profitable.
Closing	The finalization of a real estate sales transaction that passes title to the property from the seller to the buyer is referred to as a closing. Closing is a sales term which refers to the process of making a sale. It refers to reaching the final step, which may be an exchange of money or acquiring a signature.
Balance sheet	A statement of the assets, liabilities, and net worth of a firm or individual at some given time often at the end of its "fiscal year," is referred to as a balance sheet.
Partnership	In the common law, a partnership is a type of business entity in which partners share with each other the profits or losses of the business undertaking in which they have all invested.
Revenue	Revenue is a U.S. business term for the amount of money that a company receives from its activities, mostly from sales of products and/or services to customers.
Balance	In banking and accountancy, the outstanding balance is the amount of money owned, (or due), that remains in a deposit account (or a loan account) at a given date, after all past remittances, payments and withdrawal have been accounted for. It can be positive (then, in the balance sheet of a firm, it is an asset) or negative (a liability).

Go to **Cram101.com** for the Practice Tests for this Chapter.

Profit	Profit refers to the return to the resource entrepreneurial ability; total revenue minus total cost.
Enron	Enron Corportaion's global reputation was undermined by persistent rumours of bribery and political pressure to secure contracts in Central America, South America, Africa, and the Philippines. Especially controversial was its $3 billion contract with the Maharashtra State Electricity Board in India, where it is alleged that Enron officials used political connections within the Clinton and Bush administrations to exert pressure on the board.
Bankruptcy	Bankruptcy is a legally declared inability or impairment of ability of an individual or organization to pay their creditors.
WorldCom	WorldCom was the United States' second largest long distance phone company (AT&T was the largest). WorldCom grew largely by acquiring other telecommunications companies, most notably MCI Communications. It also owned the Tier 1 ISP UUNET, a major part of the Internet backbone.
Deception	According to the Federal Trade Commission, a misrepresentation, omission, or practice that is likely to mislead the consumer acting reasonably in the circumstances to the consumer's detriment is referred to as deception.
Arthur Andersen	Arthur Andersen was once one of the Big Five accounting firms, performing auditing, tax, and consulting services for large corporations. In 2002 the firm voluntarily surrendered its licenses to practice as Certified Public Accountants in the U.S. pending the result of prosecution by the U.S. Department of Justice over the firm's handling of the auditing of Enron.
Audit	An examination of the financial reports to ensure that they represent what they claim and conform with generally accepted accounting principles is referred to as audit.
Investment banks	Investment banks, assist public and private corporations in raising funds in the capital markets (both equity and debt), as well as in providing strategic advisory services for mergers, acquisitions and other types of financial transactions. They also act as intermediaries in trading for clients. Investment banks differ from commercial banks, which take deposits and make commercial and retail loans.
Allegation	An allegation is a statement of a fact by a party in a pleading, which the party claims it will prove. Allegations remain assertions without proof, only claims until they are proved.
Long run	In economic models, the long run time frame assumes no fixed factors of production. Firms can enter or leave the marketplace, and the cost (and availability) of land, labor, raw materials, and capital goods can be assumed to vary.
Trust	An arrangement in which shareholders of independent firms agree to give up their stock in exchange for trust certificates that entitle them to a share of the trust's common profits.
Stock market	An organized marketplace in which common stocks are traded. In the United States, the largest stock market is the New York Stock Exchange, on which are traded the stocks of the largest U.S. companies.
Market	A market is, as defined in economics, a social arrangement that allows buyers and sellers to discover information and carry out a voluntary exchange of goods or services.
Wall Street Journal	Dow Jones & Company was founded in 1882 by reporters Charles Dow, Edward Jones and Charles Bergstresser. Jones converted the small Customers' Afternoon Letter into The Wall Street Journal, first published in 1889, and began delivery of the Dow Jones News Service via telegraph. The Journal featured the Jones 'Average', the first of several indexes of stock and bond prices on the New York Stock Exchange.
Journal	Book of original entry, in which transactions are recorded in a general ledger system, is

referred to as a journal.

Interest payment	The payment to holders of bonds payable, calculated by multiplying the stated rate on the face of the bond by the par, or face, value of the bond. If bonds are issued at a discount or premium, the interest payment does not equal the interest expense.
Holding	The holding is a court's determination of a matter of law based on the issue presented in the particular case. In other words: under this law, with these facts, this result.
Income statement	Income statement refers to a financial statement that presents the revenues and expenses and resulting net income or net loss of a company for a specific period of time.
Accounting income	The accountant's concept of income is generally based upon the realization principle. Financial accounting income may differ from taxable income. Differences are included in a reconciliation of taxable and accounting income on Schedule M-1 of Form 1120.
Depreciation	Depreciation is an accounting and finance term for the method of attributing the cost of an asset across the useful life of the asset. Depreciation is a reduction in the value of a currency in floating exchange rate.
Enterprise	Enterprise refers to another name for a business organization. Other similar terms are business firm, sometimes simply business, sometimes simply firm, as well as company, and entity.
Liability	A liability is a present obligation of the enterprise arizing from past events, the settlement of which is expected to result in an outflow from the enterprise of resources embodying economic benefits.
Dealer	People who link buyers with sellers by buying and selling securities at stated prices are referred to as a dealer.
Asset	An item of property, such as land, capital, money, a share in ownership, or a claim on others for future payment, such as a bond or a bank deposit is an asset.
Economy	The income, expenditures, and resources that affect the cost of running a business and household are called an economy.
Expense	In accounting, an expense represents an event in which an asset is used up or a liability is incurred. In terms of the accounting equation, expenses reduce owners' equity.
Net income	Net income is equal to the income that a firm has after subtracting costs and expenses from the total revenue. Expenses will typically include tax expense.
Accrual	An accrual is an accounting event in which the transaction is recognized when the action takes place, instead of when cash is disbursed or received.
Investing activities	Investing activities refers to cash flow activities that include purchasing and disposing of investments and productive long-lived assets using cash and lending money and collecting on those loans.
Fixed asset	Fixed asset, also known as property, plant, and equipment (PP&E), is a term used in accountancy for assets and property which cannot easily be converted into cash. This can be compared with current assets such as cash or bank accounts, which are described as liquid assets. In most cases, only tangible assets are referred to as fixed.
Financial assets	Financial assets refer to monetary claims or obligations by one party against another party. Examples are bonds, mortgages, bank loans, and equities.
Financing activities	Cash flow activities that include obtaining cash from issuing debt and repaying the amounts borrowed and obtaining cash from stockholders and paying dividends is referred to as financing activities.

Dividend	Amount of corporate profits paid out for each share of stock is referred to as dividend.
Operating activities	Cash flow activities that include the cash effects of transactions that create revenues and expenses and thus enter into the determination of net income is an operating activities.
Current account	Current account refers to a country's international transactions arising from current flows, as opposed to changes in stocks which are part of the capital account. Includes trade in goods and services plus inflows and outflows of transfers. A current account is a deposit account in the UK and countries with a UK banking heritage.
Equity	Equity is the name given to the set of legal principles, in countries following the English common law tradition, which supplement strict rules of law where their application would operate harshly, so as to achieve what is sometimes referred to as "natural justice."
Inventory	Tangible property held for sale in the normal course of business or used in producing goods or services for sale is an inventory.
Wage	The payment for the service of a unit of labor, per unit time. In trade theory, it is the only payment to labor, usually unskilled labor. In empirical work, wage data may exclude other compenzation, which must be added to get the total cost of employment.
Conversion	Conversion refers to any distinct act of dominion wrongfully exerted over another's personal property in denial of or inconsistent with his rights therein. That tort committed by a person who deals with chattels not belonging to him in a manner that is inconsistent with the ownership of the lawful owner.
Cash conversion cycle	Cash conversion cycle, also known as asset conversion cycle, net operating cycle, working capital cycle or just cash cycle, is a figure used in the financial analysis of a business. The higher the number, the longer a firm's money is tied up in operations of the business and unavailable for other activities such as investing.
Labor	People's physical and mental talents and efforts that are used to help produce goods and services are called labor.
Cash flow statement	A cash flow statement is a financial report that shows incoming and outgoing money during a particular period (often monthly or quarterly). The statement shows how changes in balance sheet and income accounts affected cash and cash equivalents and breaks the analysis down according to operating, investing, and financing activities.
Consideration	Consideration in contract law, a basic requirement for an enforceable agreement under traditional contract principles, defined in this text as legal value, bargained for and given in exchange for an act or promise. In corporation law, cash or property contributed to a corporation in exchange for shares, or a promise to contribute such cash or property.
Credit sale	A credit sale occurs when a customer does not pay cash at the time of the sale but instead agrees to pay later. The sale occurs now, with payment from the customer to follow at a later time.
Operating income	Total revenues from operation minus cost of goods sold and operating costs are called operating income.
Accounts receivable	Accounts receivable is one of a series of accounting transactions dealing with the billing of customers which owe money to a person, company or organization for goods and services that have been provided to the customer. This is typically done in a one person organization by writing an invoice and mailing or delivering it to each customer.
Purchasing	Purchasing refers to the function in a firm that searches for quality material resources, finds the best suppliers, and negotiates the best price for goods and services.
Accumulated	Accumulated depreciation refers to the total depreciation that has been reported as

Go to **Cram101.com** for the Practice Tests for this Chapter.

depreciation	depreciation expense for the entire life of a long-term tangible asset. It is a contra-asset account.
Cash from financing activities	Cash receipts and disbursements related to a company's financing-cash transactions related to debt and equity, shown together on the statement of cash flows is known as cash from financing activities.
Cash from investing activities	Cash receipts and disbursements related to a company's purchase and sale of long-term assets and investments, shown together on the statement of cash flows is known as cash from investing activities.
Capital	Capital generally refers to financial wealth, especially that used to start or maintain a business. In classical economics, capital is one of four factors of production, the others being land and labor and entrepreneurship.
Free cash flow	Cash provided by operating activities adjusted for capital expenditures and dividends paid is referred to as free cash flow.
Common stockholder	A person who owns common stock is referred to as common stockholder. They elect the members of the board of directors for the company, as well.
Distribution	Distribution in economics, the manner in which total output and income is distributed among individuals or factors.
Equity capital	Equity capital refers to money raized from within the firm or through the sale of ownership in the firm.
Acquisition	A company's purchase of the property and obligations of another company is an acquisition.
Financial ratio	A financial ratio is a ratio of two numbers of reported levels or flows of a company. It may be two financial flows categories divided by each other (profit margin, profit/revenue). It may be a level divided by a financial flow (price/earnings). It may be a flow divided by a level (return on equity or earnings/equity). The numerator or denominator may itself be a ratio (PEG ratio).
Ratio analysis	Ratio analysis refers to an analytical tool designed to identify significant relationships; measures the proportional relationship between two financial statement amounts.
Current liability	Current liability refers to a debt that can reasonably be expected to be paid from existing current assets or through the creation of other current liabilities, within one year or the operating cycle, whichever is longer.
Current ratio	The current ratio is a comparison of a firm's current assets to its current liabilities. The current ratio is an indication of a firm's market liquidity and ability to meet short-term debt obligations.
Current asset	A current asset is an asset on the balance sheet which is expected to be sold or otherwise used up in the near future, usually within one year.
Liquidity	Liquidity refers to the capacity to turn assets into cash, or the amount of assets in a portfolio that have that capacity.
Context	The effect of the background under which a message often takes on more and richer meaning is a context. Context is especially important in cross-cultural interactions because some cultures are said to be high context or low context.
Budget	Budget refers to an account, usually for a year, of the planned expenditures and the expected receipts of an entity. For a government, the receipts are tax revenues.
Trade association	An industry trade group or trade association is generally a public relations organization founded and funded by corporations that operate in a specific industry. Its purpose is

49

	generally to promote that industry through PR activities such as advertizing, education, political donations, political pressure, publishing, and astroturfing.
Industry	A group of firms that produce identical or similar products is an industry. It is also used specifically to refer to an area of economic production focused on manufacturing which involves large amounts of capital investment before any profit can be realized, also called "heavy industry".
Financial plan	The financial plan section of a business plan consists of three financial statements (the income statement, the cash flow projection, and the balance sheet) and a brief analysis of these three statements.
Controlling	A management function that involves determining whether or not an organization is progressing toward its goals and objectives, and taking corrective action if it is not is called controlling.
Alpha	Alpha is a risk-adjusted measure of the so-called "excess return" on an investment. It is a common measure of assessing active manager's performance as it is the return in excess of a benchmark index or "risk-free" investment.
Aid	Assistance provided by countries and by international institutions such as the World Bank to developing countries in the form of monetary grants, loans at low interest rates, in kind, or a combination of these is called aid. Aid can also refer to assistance of any type rendered to benefit some group or individual.
Cost of goods sold	In accounting, the cost of goods sold describes the direct expenses incurred in producing a particular good for sale, including the actual cost of materials that comprise the good, and direct labor expense in putting the good in salable condition.
Cost of sales	Cost of sales refers to the total costs of goods made or purchased and sold.
Cost ratio	An equality, the cost ratio shows the number of units of two products that can be produced with the same resources..
Return on sales	Return on sales refers to the percent of net income generated by each dollar of sales; computed by dividing net income before taxes by sales revenue.
Economies of scale	In economics, returns to scale and economies of scale are related terms that describe what happens as the scale of production increases. They are different terms and not to be used interchangeably.
Production	The creation of finished goods and services using the factors of production: land, labor, capital, entrepreneurship, and knowledge.
Markup	Markup is a term used in marketing to indicate how much the price of a product is above the cost of producing and distributing the product.
Trend	Trend refers to the long-term movement of an economic variable, such as its average rate of increase or decrease over enough years to encompass several business cycles.
Manufacturing	Production of goods primarily by the application of labor and capital to raw materials and other intermediate inputs, in contrast to agriculture, mining, forestry, fishing, and services a manufacturing.
Asset management	Asset management is the method that a company uses to track fixed assets, for example factory equipment, desks and chairs, computers, even buildings. Although the exact details of the task varies widely from company to company, asset management often includes tracking the physical location of assets, managing demand for scarce resources, and accounting tasks such as amortization.
Market value	Market value refers to the price of an asset agreed on between a willing buyer and a willing

seller; the price an asset could demand if it is sold on the open market.

Liquidity ratio	A financial ratio that indicates the organization's ability to meet its current debt obligations is referred to as liquidity ratio.
Solvency	The ability of a company to pay interest as it comes due and to repay the face value of debt at maturity is called solvency.
Line of credit	Line of credit refers to a given amount of unsecured short-term funds a bank will lend to a business, provided the funds are readily available.
Quick ratio	The Acid-test or quick ratio measures the ability of a company to use its "near cash" or quick assets to immediately extinguish its current liabilities. Quick assets include those current assets that presumably can be quickly converted to cash at close to their book values.
Average collection period	The average amount of time that a receivable is outstanding, calculated by dividing 365 days by the receivables turnover ratio is an average collection period.
Days Sales Outstanding	Days Sales Outstanding is a company's average collection period. A low figure indicates that the company collects its outstanding receivables quickly. Typically it is looked at either quarterly or yearly. It's a great leading indicator of impending trouble at a company particularly with product support and customer service.
Discount	The difference between the face value of a bond and its selling price, when a bond is sold for less than its face value it's referred to as a discount.
Allowance for doubtful accounts	Contra-asset account containing the estimated uncollectible accounts receivable is an allowance for doubtful accounts. Also called allowance for bad debts or allowance for uncollectible accounts.
Allowance	Reduction in the selling price of goods extended to the buyer because the goods are defective or of lower quality than the buyer ordered and to encourage a buyer to keep merchandise that would otherwise be returned is the allowance.
Turnover	Turnover in a financial context refers to the rate at which a provider of goods cycles through its average inventory. Turnover in a human resources context refers to the characteristic of a given company or industry, relative to rate at which an employer gains and loses staff.
Inventory turnover ratio	Inventory turnover ratio refers to a ratio that measures the number of times on average the inventory sold during the period; computed by dividing cost of goods sold by the average inventory during the period.
Raw material	Raw material refers to a good that has not been transformed by production; a primary product.
Trade credit	Trade credit refers to an amount that is loaned to an exporter to be repaid when the exports are paid for by the foreign importer.
Cash outflow	Cash flowing out of the business from all sources over a period of time is cash outflow.
Supply	Supply is the aggregate amount of any material good that can be called into being at a certain price point; it comprises one half of the equation of supply and demand. In classical economic theory, a curve representing supply is one of the factors that produce price.
Authority	Authority in agency law, refers to an agent's ability to affect his principal's legal relations with third parties. Also used to refer to an actor's legal power or ability to do something. In addition, sometimes used to refer to a statute, case, or other legal source that justifies a particular result.

Debt ratio	Debt ratio refers to the calculation of the total liabilities divided by the total liabilities plus capital. This results in the measurment of the debt level of the business (leverage).
Debt to equity ratio	The debt to equity ratio is a financial ratio debt divided by shareholders' equity. The two components are often taken from the firm's balance sheet, but they might also be calulated as market values if both the companiy's debt and equity are publicly traded. It is used to calculate a company's "financial leverage" and indicates what proportion of equity and debt the company is using to finance its assets.
Financial risk	The risk related to the inability of the firm to meet its debt obligations as they come due is called financial risk.
Lease	A contract for the possession and use of land or other property, including goods, on one side, and a recompense of rent or other income on the other is the lease.
Principal	In agency law, one under whose direction an agent acts and for whose benefit that agent acts is a principal.
Profitability ratios	Measures of the income or operating success of a company for a given period of time are called profitability ratios.
Profitability ratio	A financial ratio that describes the firm's profits is referred to as profitability ratio. It helps to explain the profitability of an entity during a defined period of time.
Profit margin	Profit margin is a measure of profitability. It is calculated using a formula and written as a percentage or a number. Profit margin = Net income before tax and interest / Revenue.
Net profit	Net profit is an accounting term which is commonly used in business. It is equal to the gross revenue for a given time period minus associated expenses.
Margin	A deposit by a buyer in stocks with a seller or a stockbroker, as security to cover fluctuations in the market in reference to stocks that the buyer has purchased but for which he has not paid is a margin. Commodities are also traded on margin.
Bottom line	The bottom line is net income on the last line of a income statement.
Return on Assets	The Return on Assets percentage shows how profitable a company's assets are in generating revenue.
Factoring	In mathematics, factorization or factoring is the decomposition of an object into a product of other objects, or factors, which when multiplied together give the original.
Earnings per share	Earnings per share refers to annual profit of the corporation divided by the number of shares outstanding.
Market price	Market price is an economic concept with commonplace familiarity; it is the price that a good or service is offered at, or will fetch, in the marketplace; it is of interest mainly in the study of microeconomics.
Common stock	Common stock refers to the basic, normal, voting stock issued by a corporation; called residual equity because it ranks after preferred stock for dividend and liquidation distributions.
P/E ratio	In finance, the P/E ratio of a stock is used to measure how cheap or expensive share prices are. It is probably the single most consistent red flag to excessive optimism and over-investment.
Book value	The book value of an asset or group of assets is sometimes the price at which they were originally acquired, in many cases equal to purchase price.
Book value per	Total shareholders' equity divided by the number of outstanding common shares is referred to

share	as book value per share.
Economic value added	After-tax operating income minus the weighted average cost of capital multiplied by total assets minus current liabilities is called economic value added.
Market value added	Market value added is the difference between the current market value of a firm and the capital contributed by investors. If market value added is positive, the firm has added value. If it is negative the firm has destroyed value.
Value added	The value of output minus the value of all intermediate inputs, representing therefore the contribution of, and payments to, primary factors of production a value added.
Cost of debt	The cost of debt is the cost of borrowing money (usually denoted by Kd). It is derived by dividing debt's interest payments on the total market value of the debts.
Cost of equity	In finance, the cost of equity is the minimum rate of return a firm must offer shareholders to compensate for waiting for their returns, and for bearing some risk.
Cost of capital	Cost of capital refers to the percentage cost of funds used for acquiring resources for an organization, typically a weighted average of the firms cost of equity and cost of debt.
Contribution	In business organization law, the cash or property contributed to a business by its owners is referred to as contribution.
Gain	In finance, gain is a profit or an increase in value of an investment such as a stock or bond. Gain is calculated by fair market value or the proceeds from the sale of the investment minus the sum of the purchase price and all costs associated with it.
Best Buy	Best Buy is the largest specialty retailer of consumer electronics, personal computers and related goods in North America. The company's subsidiaries include Geek Squad, Magnolia Audio Video, and Future Shop in Canada, which together operate over 700 stores in the United States and Canada. Best Buy is noted for being staffed with non-commissioned sales associates.
Equity multiplier	The amount of assets per dollar of equity capital is referred to as equity multiplier.
Leverage	Leverage is using given resources in such a way that the potential positive or negative outcome is magnified. In finance, this generally refers to borrowing.
Competitor	Other organizations in the same industry or type of business that provide a good or service to the same set of customers is referred to as a competitor.
Financial report	Financial report refers to a written statement-also called an accountant's certificate, accountant's opinion, or audit report-prepared by an independent accountant or auditor after an audit.
Commerce	Commerce is the exchange of something of value between two entities. It is the central mechanism from which capitalism is derived.
Disclosure	Disclosure means the giving out of information, either voluntarily or to be in compliance with legal regulations or workplace rules.
Scope	Scope of a project is the sum total of all projects products and their requirements or features.
Estate	An estate is the totality of the legal rights, interests, entitlements and obligations attaching to property. In the context of wills and probate, it refers to the totality of the property which the deceased owned or in which some interest was held.
Inflation	An increase in the overall price level of an economy, usually as measured by the CPI or by the implicit price deflator is called inflation.

Go to **Cram101.com** for the Practice Tests for this Chapter.

Go to **Cram101.com** for the Practice Tests for this Chapter.
And, **NEVER** highlight a book again!

Remainder	A remainder in property law is a future interest created in a transferee that is capable of becoming possessory upon the natural termination of a prior estate created by the same instrument.
Par value stock	Par value stock refers to capital stock that has been assigned a value per share in the corporate charter. .
Value stock	In financial terminology, a stock that appears attractive using the fundamental criteria of stock valuation because of valuable assets, particularly cash and real estate, owned by its company. A stock may be named a value stock if its earnings per share, cash per share or book value is high relative to the stock price
Par value	The central value of a pegged exchange rate, around which the actual rate is permitted to fluctuate within set bounds is a par value.
Working capital	The dollar difference between total current assets and total current liabilities is called working capital.
Total cost	The sum of fixed cost and variable cost is referred to as total cost.
Gross margin	Gross margin is an ambiguous phrase that expresses the relationship between gross profit and sales revenue as Gross Margin = Revenue - costs of good sold.
Retained earnings	Cumulative earnings of a company that are not distributed to the owners and are reinvested in the business are called retained earnings.
Capital account	The capital account is one of two primary components of the balance of payments. It tracks the movement of funds for investments and loans into and out of a country.
Financial manager	Managers who make recommendations to top executives regarding strategies for improving the financial strength of a firm are referred to as a financial manager.
Inputs	The inputs used by a firm or an economy are the labor, raw materials, electricity and other resources it uses to produce its outputs.
Return on equity	Net profit after taxes per dollar of equity capital is referred to as return on equity.
Starbucks	Although it has endured much criticism for its purported monopoly on the global coffee-bean market, Starbucks purchases only 3% of the coffee beans grown worldwide. In 2000 the company introduced a line of fair trade products and now offers three options for socially conscious coffee drinkers. According to Starbucks, they purchased 4.8 million pounds of Certified Fair Trade coffee in fiscal year 2004 and 11.5 million pounds in 2005.
Times interest earned	Times interest earned refers to net income before interest and taxes, divided by interest expense; describes a company's ability to make interest payments on its debt.

Consumption	In Keynesian economics consumption refers to personal consumption expenditure, i.e., the purchase of currently produced goods and services out of income, out of savings (net worth), or from borrowed funds. It refers to that part of disposable income that does not go to saving.
Production	The creation of finished goods and services using the factors of production: land, labor, capital, entrepreneurship, and knowledge.
Economy	The income, expenditures, and resources that affect the cost of running a business and household are called an economy.
Household	An economic unit that provides the economy with resources and uses the income received to purchase goods and services that satisfy economic wants is called household.
Service	Service refers to a "non tangible product" that is not embodied in a physical good and that typically effects some change in another product, person, or institution. Contrasts with good.
Wage	The payment for the service of a unit of labor, per unit time. In trade theory, it is the only payment to labor, usually unskilled labor. In empirical work, wage data may exclude other compenzation, which must be added to get the total cost of employment.
Debt security	Type of security acquired by loaning assets is called a debt security.
Corporation	A legal entity chartered by a state or the Federal government that is distinct and separate from the individuals who own it is a corporation. This separation gives the corporation unique powers which other legal entities lack.
Security	Security refers to a claim on the borrower future income that is sold by the borrower to the lender. A security is a type of transferable interest representing financial value.
Financial management	The job of managing a firm's resources so it can meet its goals and objectives is called financial management.
Management	Management characterizes the process of leading and directing all or part of an organization, often a business, through the deployment and manipulation of resources. Early twentieth-century management writer Mary Parker Follett defined management as "the art of getting things done through people."
Enterprise	Enterprise refers to another name for a business organization. Other similar terms are business firm, sometimes simply business, sometimes simply firm, as well as company, and entity.
Economic system	Economic system refers to a particular set of institutional arrangements and a coordinating mechanism for solving the economizing problem; a method of organizing an economy, of which the market system and the command system are the two general types.
Financial market	In economics, a financial market is a mechanism which allows people to trade money for securities or commodities such as gold or other precious metals. In general, any commodity market might be considered to be a financial market, if the usual purpose of traders is not the immediate consumption of the commodity, but rather as a means of delaying or accelerating consumption over time.
Financial assets	Financial assets refer to monetary claims or obligations by one party against another party. Examples are bonds, mortgages, bank loans, and equities.
Market	A market is, as defined in economics, a social arrangement that allows buyers and sellers to discover information and carry out a voluntary exchange of goods or services.
Buyer	A buyer refers to a role in the buying center with formal authority and responsibility to select the supplier and negotiate the terms of the contract.

Asset	An item of property, such as land, capital, money, a share in ownership, or a claim on others for future payment, such as a bond or a bank deposit is an asset.
Stock	In financial terminology, stock is the capital raized by a corporation, through the issuance and sale of shares.
Bond	Bond refers to a debt instrument, issued by a borrower and promising a specified stream of payments to the purchaser, usually regular interest payments plus a final repayment of principal.
Appreciation	Appreciation refers to a rise in the value of a country's currency on the exchange market, relative either to a particular other currency or to a weighted average of other currencies. The currency is said to appreciate. Opposite of 'depreciation.' Appreciation can also refer to the increase in value of any asset.
Dividend	Amount of corporate profits paid out for each share of stock is referred to as dividend.
Interest	In finance and economics, interest is the price paid by a borrower for the use of a lender's money. In other words, interest is the amount of paid to "rent" money for a period of time.
Labor	People's physical and mental talents and efforts that are used to help produce goods and services are called labor.
Normal profit	Normal profit refers to the payment made by a firm to obtain and retain entrepreneurial ability; the minimum income entrepreneurial ability must receive to induce it to perform entrepreneurial functions for a firm.
Profit	Profit refers to the return to the resource entrepreneurial ability; total revenue minus total cost.
Fund	Independent accounting entity with a self-balancing set of accounts segregated for the purposes of carrying on specific activities is referred to as a fund.
Firm	An organization that employs resources to produce a good or service for profit and owns and operates one or more plants is referred to as a firm.
Investment	Investment refers to spending for the production and accumulation of capital and additions to inventories. In a financial sense, buying an asset with the expectation of making a return.
Equity	Equity is the name given to the set of legal principles, in countries following the English common law tradition, which supplement strict rules of law where their application would operate harshly, so as to achieve what is sometimes referred to as "natural justice."
Termination	The ending of a corporation that occurs only after the winding-up of the corporation's affairs, the liquidation of its assets, and the distribution of the proceeds to the claimants are referred to as a termination.
Term loan	Term loan refers to an intermediate-length loan, in which credit is generally extended from one to seven years. The loan is usually repaid in monthly or quarterly installments over its life, rather than with one single payment.
Debt financing	Obtaining financing by borrowing money is debt financing.
Fixed asset	Fixed asset, also known as property, plant, and equipment (PP&E), is a term used in accountancy for assets and property which cannot easily be converted into cash. This can be compared with current assets such as cash or bank accounts, which are described as liquid assets. In most cases, only tangible assets are referred to as fixed.
Capital market	A financial market in which long-term debt and equity instruments are traded is referred to as a capital market. The capital market includes the stock market and the bond market.
Capital	Capital generally refers to financial wealth, especially that used to start or maintain a

63

business. In classical economics, capital is one of four factors of production, the others being land and labor and entrepreneurship.

Money market	The money market, in macroeconomics and international finance, refers to the equilibration of demand for a country's domestic money to its money supply; market for short-term financial instruments.
Operation	A standardized method or technique that is performed repetitively, often on different materials resulting in different finished goods is called an operation.
Commercial paper	Commercial paper is a money market security issued by large banks and corporations. It is generally not used to finance long-term investments but rather for purchases of inventory or to manage working capital. It is commonly bought by money funds (the issuing amounts are often too high for individual investors), and is generally regarded as a very safe investment.
Instrument	Instrument refers to an economic variable that is controlled by policy makers and can be used to influence other variables, called targets. Examples are monetary and fiscal policies used to achieve external and internal balance.
Federal government	Federal government refers to the government of the United States, as distinct from the state and local governments.
Budget deficit	A budget deficit occurs when an entity (often a government) spends more money than it takes
Federal budget	The annual statement of the expenditures and tax revenues of the government of the United States together with the laws and regulations that approve and support those expenditures and taxes is the federal budget.
Deficit	The deficit is the amount by which expenditure exceed revenue.
Budget	Budget refers to an account, usually for a year, of the planned expenditures and the expected receipts of an entity. For a government, the receipts are tax revenues.
Financial instrument	Formal or legal documents in writing, such as contracts, deeds, wills, bonds, leases, and mortgages is referred to as a financial instrument.
National debt	National debt refers to total of outstanding federal government bonds on which the federal government must pay interest.
Secondary market	Secondary market refers to the market for securities that have already been issued. It is a market in which investors trade back and forth with each other.
Stock market	An organized marketplace in which common stocks are traded. In the United States, the largest stock market is the New York Stock Exchange, on which are traded the stocks of the largest U.S. companies.
Financial manager	Managers who make recommendations to top executives regarding strategies for improving the financial strength of a firm are referred to as a financial manager.
Intermediaries	Intermediaries specialize in information either to bring together two parties to a transaction or to buy in order to sell again.
Primary market	The market for the raising of new funds as opposed to the trading of securities already in existence is called primary market.
Financial intermediary	Financial intermediary refers to a financial institution, such as a bank or a life insurance company, which directs other people's money into such investments as government and corporate securities.
Broker	In commerce, a broker is a party that mediates between a buyer and a seller. A broker who also acts as a seller or as a buyer becomes a principal party to the deal.

Go to **Cram101.com** for the Practice Tests for this Chapter.

Go to **Cram101.com** for the Practice Tests for this Chapter.
And, **NEVER** highlight a book again!

Possession	Possession refers to respecting real property, exclusive dominion and control such as owners of like property usually exercise over it. Manual control of personal property either as owner or as one having a qualified right in it.
Portfolio	In finance, a portfolio is a collection of investments held by an institution or a private individual. Holding but not always a portfolio is part of an investment and risk-limiting strategy called diversification. By owning several assets, certain types of risk (in particular specific risk) can be reduced.
Shares	Shares refer to an equity security, representing a shareholder's ownership of a corporation. Shares are one of a finite number of equal portions in the capital of a company, entitling the owner to a proportion of distributed, non-reinvested profits known as dividends and to a portion of the value of the company in case of liquidation.
Management control	That aspect of management concerned with the comparison of actual versus planned performance as well as the development and implementation of procedures to correct substandard performance is called management control.
Mutual fund	A mutual fund is a form of collective investment that pools money from many investors and invests the money in stocks, bonds, short-term money market instruments, and/or other securities. In a mutual fund, the fund manager trades the fund's underlying securities, realizing capital gains or loss, and collects the dividend or interest income.
Institutional investors	Institutional investors refers to large organizations such as pension funds, mutual funds, insurance companies, and banks that invest their own funds or the funds of others.
Trend	Trend refers to the long-term movement of an economic variable, such as its average rate of increase or decrease over enough years to encompass several business cycles.
Contribution	In business organization law, the cash or property contributed to a business by its owners is referred to as contribution.
Pension fund	Amounts of money put aside by corporations, nonprofit organizations, or unions to cover part of the financial needs of members when they retire is a pension fund.
Pension	A pension is a steady income given to a person (usually after retirement). Pensions are typically payments made in the form of a guaranteed annuity to a retired or disabled employee.
Estate	An estate is the totality of the legal rights, interests, entitlements and obligations attaching to property. In the context of wills and probate, it refers to the totality of the property which the deceased owned or in which some interest was held.
Insurance	Insurance refers to a system by which individuals can reduce their exposure to risk of large losses by spreading the risks among a large number of persons.
Premium	Premium refers to the fee charged by an insurance company for an insurance policy. The rate of losses must be relatively predictable: In order to set the premium (prices) insurers must be able to estimate them accurately.
Exchange	The trade of things of value between buyer and seller so that each is better off after the trade is called the exchange.
Brokerage firm	A company that conducts various aspects of securities trading, analysis and advisory services is a brokerage firm.
Grant	Grant refers to an intergovernmental transfer of funds . Since the New Deal, state and local governments have become increasingly dependent upon federal grants for an almost infinite variety of programs.
Specialist	A specialist is a trader who makes a market in one or several stocks and holds the limit

	order book for those stocks.
Auction	A preexisting business model that operates successfully on the Internet by announcing an item for sale and permitting multiple purchasers to bid on them under specified rules and condition is an auction.
Stock exchange	A stock exchange is a corporation or mutual organization which provides facilities for stock brokers and traders, to trade company stocks and other securities.
Standing	Standing refers to the legal requirement that anyone seeking to challenge a particular action in court must demonstrate that such action substantially affects his legitimate interests before he will be entitled to bring suit.
Securities market	The securities market is the market for securities, where companies and the government can raise long-term funds.
Regulation	Regulation refers to restrictions state and federal laws place on business with regard to the conduct of its activities.
Securities Act of 1933	An act that is sometimes referred to as the truth in securities act, because it requires detailed financial disclosures before securities may be sold to the public is called the Securities Act of 1933.
Securities and exchange commission	Securities and exchange commission refers to U.S. government agency that determines the financial statements that public companies must provide to stockholders and the measurement rules that they must use in producing those statements.
Securities Exchange Act of 1934	Legislation that established the Securities and Exchange Commission to supervise and regulate the securities markets is referred to as the Securities Exchange Act of 1934.
Disclosure	Disclosure means the giving out of information, either voluntarily or to be in compliance with legal regulations or workplace rules.
Entrepreneur	The owner/operator. The person who organizes, manages, and assumes the risks of a firm, taking a new idea or a new product and turning it into a successful business is an entrepreneur.
Stockholder	A stockholder is an individual or company (including a corporation) that legally owns one or more shares of stock in a joined stock company. The shareholders are the owners of a corporation. Companies listed at the stock market strive to enhance shareholder value.
Public company	A public company is a company owned by the public rather than by a relatively few individuals. There are two different meanings for this term: (1) A company that is owned by stockholders who are members of the general public and trade shares publicly, often through a listing on a stock exchange. Ownership is open to anyone that has the money and inclination to buy shares in the company. It is differentiated from privately held companies where the shares are held by a small group of individuals, who are often members of one or a small group of families or otherwise related individuals, or other companies. The variant of this type of company in the United Kingdom and Ireland is known as a public limited compan, and (2) A government-owned corporation. This meaning of a "public company" comes from the fact that government debt is sometimes referred to as "public debt" although there are no "public bonds", government finance is sometimes called "public finance", among similar uses. This is the less-common meaning.
Prospectus	Prospectus refers to a report detailing a future stock offering containing a set of financial statements; required by the SEC from a company that wishes to make an initial public offering of its stock.
Preparation	Preparation refers to usually the first stage in the creative process. It includes education

	and formal training.
Principal	In agency law, one under whose direction an agent acts and for whose benefit that agent acts is a principal.
Fraud	Tax fraud falls into two categories: civil and criminal. Under civil fraud, the IRS may impose as a penalty of an amount equal to as much as 75 percent of the underpayment.
Investment banker	Investment banker refers to a financial organization that specializes in selling primary offerings of securities. Investment bankers can also perform other financial functions, such as advising clients, negotiating mergers and takeovers, and selling secondary offerings.
Initial public offering	Firms in the process of becoming publicly traded companies will issue shares of stock using an initial public offering, which is merely the process of selling stock for the first time to interested investors.
NASDAQ	NASDAQ is an American electronic stock exchange. It was founded in 1971 by the National Association of Securities Dealers who divested it in a series of sales in 2000 and 2001.
Dealer	People who link buyers with sellers by buying and selling securities at stated prices are referred to as a dealer.
Jargon	Jargon is terminology, much like slang, that relates to a specific activity, profession, or group. It develops as a kind of shorthand, to express ideas that are frequently discussed between members of a group, and can also have the effect of distinguishing those belonging to a group from those who are not.
Industry	A group of firms that produce identical or similar products is an industry. It is also used specifically to refer to an area of economic production focused on manufacturing which involves large amounts of capital investment before any profit can be realized, also called "heavy industry".
Volatility	Volatility refers to the extent to which an economic variable, such as a price or an exchange rate, moves up and down over time.
A share	In finance the term A share has two distinct meanings, both relating to securities. The first is a designation for a 'class' of common or preferred stock. A share of common or preferred stock typically has enhanced voting rights or other benefits compared to the other forms of shares that may have been created. The equity structure, or how many types of shares are offered, is determined by the corporate charter.
Peak	Peak refers to the point in the business cycle when an economic expansion reaches its highest point before turning down. Contrasts with trough.
Browser	A program that allows a user to connect to the World Wide Web by simply typing in a URL is a browser.
Equity financing	Financing that consists of funds that are invested in exchange for ownership in the company is called equity financing.
Closing	The finalization of a real estate sales transaction that passes title to the property from the seller to the buyer is referred to as a closing. Closing is a sales term which refers to the process of making a sale. It refers to reaching the final step, which may be an exchange of money or acquiring a signature.
Warrant	A warrant is a security that entitles the holder to buy or sell a certain additional quantity of an underlying security at an agreed-upon price, at the holder's discretion.
Wall Street Journal	Dow Jones & Company was founded in 1882 by reporters Charles Dow, Edward Jones and Charles Bergstresser. Jones converted the small Customers' Afternoon Letter into The Wall Street Journal, first published in 1889, and began delivery of the Dow Jones News Service via

telegraph. The Journal featured the Jones 'Average', the first of several indexes of stock and bond prices on the New York Stock Exchange.

Journal	Book of original entry, in which transactions are recorded in a general ledger system, is referred to as a journal.
Efficient financial market	A financial market displaying the characteristics of an efficient market is called efficient financial market.
General Motors	General Motors is the world's largest automaker. Founded in 1908, today it employs about 327,000 people around the world. With global headquarters in Detroit, it manufactures its cars and trucks in 33 countries.
Analyst	Analyst refers to a person or tool with a primary function of information analysis, generally with a more limited, practical and short term set of goals than a researcher.
Bid	A bid price is a price offered by a buyer when he/she buys a good. In the context of stock trading on a stock exchange, the bid price is the highest price a buyer of a stock is willing to pay for a share of that given stock.
Efficient market hypothesis	The application of the theory of rational expectations to financial markets is referred to as efficient market hypothesis.
Efficient market	Efficient market refers to a market in which, at a minimum, current price changes are independent of past price changes, or, more strongly, price reflects all available information.
Dividend yield	Dividends per share divided by market price per share are called a dividend yield. Dividend yield indicates the percentage return that a stockholder will receive on dividends alone.
Yield	The interest rate that equates a future value or an annuity to a given present value is a yield.
P/E ratio	In finance, the P/E ratio of a stock is used to measure how cheap or expensive share prices are. It is probably the single most consistent red flag to excessive optimism and over-investment.
Interest rate	The rate of return on bonds, loans, or deposits. When one speaks of 'the' interest rate, it is usually in a model where there is only one.
Issuer	The company that borrows money from investors by issuing bonds is referred to as issuer. They are legally responsible for the obligations of the issue and for reporting financial conditions, material developments and any other operational activities as required by the regulations of their jurisdictions.
Maturity	Maturity refers to the final payment date of a loan or other financial instrument, after which point no further interest or principal need be paid.
Maturity date	The date on which the final payment on a bond is due from the bond issuer to the investor is a maturity date.
Mortgage	Mortgage refers to a note payable issued for property, such as a house, usually repaid in equal installments consisting of part principle and part interest, over a specified period.
Credit	Credit refers to a recording as positive in the balance of payments, any transaction that gives rise to a payment into the country, such as an export, the sale of an asset, or borrowing from abroad.
Government debt	The total of government obligations in the form of bonds and shorter-term borrowings.

Go to **Cram101.com** for the Practice Tests for this Chapter.

73

	Government debt held by the public excludes bonds held by quasi-governmental agencies such as the central bank.
Equity securities	Equity securities refer to representation of ownership rights to the corporation.
Expected return	Expected return refers to the return on an asset expected over the next period.
Price level	The overall level of prices in a country, as usually measured empirically by a price index, but often captured in theoretical models by a single variable is a price level.
Sales lead	A sales lead is the identity of a person or entity potentially interested in purchasing a product of service, and represents the first stage of a sales process.
Supply and demand	The partial equilibrium supply and demand economic model originally developed by Alfred Marshall attempts to describe, explain, and predict changes in the price and quantity of goods sold in competitive markets.
Supply	Supply is the aggregate amount of any material good that can be called into being at a certain price point; it comprises one half of the equation of supply and demand. In classical economic theory, a curve representing supply is one of the factors that produce price.
Economics	The social science dealing with the use of scarce resources to obtain the maximum satisfaction of society's virtually unlimited economic wants is an economics.
Demand curve	Demand curve refers to the graph of quantity demanded as a function of price, normally downward sloping, straight or curved, and drawn with quantity on the horizontal axis and price on the vertical axis.
Brief	Brief refers to a statement of a party's case or legal arguments, usually prepared by an attorney. Also used to make legal arguments before appellate courts.
Supply curve	Supply curve refers to the graph of quantity supplied as a function of price, normally upward sloping, straight or curved, and drawn with quantity on the horizontal axis and price on the vertical axis.
Lender	Suppliers and financial institutions that lend money to companies is referred to as a lender.
Equilibrium price	Equilibrium price refers to the price in a competitive market at which the quantity demanded and the quantity supplied are equal, there is neither a shortage nor a surplus, and there is no tendency for price to rise or fall.
Futures	Futures refer to contracts for the sale and future delivery of stocks or commodities, wherein either party may waive delivery, and receive or pay, as the case may be, the difference in market price at the time set for delivery.
Preference	The act of a debtor in paying or securing one or more of his creditors in a manner more favorable to them than to other creditors or to the exclusion of such other creditors is a preference. In the absence of statute, a preference is perfectly good, but to be legal it must be bona fide, and not a mere subterfuge of the debtor to secure a future benefit to himself or to prevent the application of his property to his debts.
Risk premium	In finance, the risk premium can be the expected rate of return above the risk-free interest rate.
Inflation	An increase in the overall price level of an economy, usually as measured by the CPI or by the implicit price deflator is called inflation.
Inflation rate	The percentage increase in the price level per year is an inflation rate. Alternatively, the inflation rate is the rate of decrease in the purchasing power of money.
Anticipated	Anticipated inflation is the expected or anticipated increase in the price level in the

Go to **Cram101.com** for the Practice Tests for this Chapter.
And, **NEVER** highlight a book again!

inflation	future.
Context	The effect of the background under which a message often takes on more and richer meaning is a context. Context is especially important in cross-cultural interactions because some cultures are said to be high context or low context.
Default	In finance, default occurs when a debtor has not met its legal obligations according to the debt contract, e.g. it has not made a scheduled payment, or violated a covenant (condition) of the debt contract.
Liquidity	Liquidity refers to the capacity to turn assets into cash, or the amount of assets in a portfolio that have that capacity.
Default risk	The chance that the issuer of a debt instrument will be unable to make interest payments or pay off the face value when the instrument matures is called default risk.
Creditworthiness	Creditworthiness indicates whether a borrower has in the past made loan payments when due.
Interest payment	The payment to holders of bonds payable, calculated by multiplying the stated rate on the face of the bond by the par, or face, value of the bond. If bonds are issued at a discount or premium, the interest payment does not equal the interest expense.
Holding	The holding is a court's determination of a matter of law based on the issue presented in the particular case. In other words: under this law, with these facts, this result.
Liquidity risk	Liquidity risk arises from situations in which a party interested in trading an asset cannot do it because nobody in the market wants to trade that asset. Liquidity risk becomes particularly important to parties who are about to hold or currently hold an asset, since it affects their ability to trade.
Variable	A variable is something measured by a number; it is used to analyze what happens to other things when the size of that number changes.
Interest rate risk	Interest rate risk is the risk that the relative value of a security, especially a bond, will worsen due to an interest rate increase. This risk is commonly measured by the bond's duration.
Allowance	Reduction in the selling price of goods extended to the buyer because the goods are defective or of lower quality than the buyer ordered and to encourage a buyer to keep merchandise that would otherwise be returned is the allowance.
Economic model	Economic model refers to a simplified picture of economic reality; an abstract generalization.
Aid	Assistance provided by countries and by international institutions such as the World Bank to developing countries in the form of monetary grants, loans at low interest rates, in kind, or a combination of these is called aid. Aid can also refer to assistance of any type rendered to benefit some group or individual.
Treasury bills	Short-term obligations of the federal government are treasury bills. They are like zero coupon bonds in that they do not pay interest prior to maturity; instead they are sold at a discount of the par value to create a positive yield to maturity.
Treasury security	A treasury security is a government bond issued by the United States Department of the Treasury through the Bureau of the Public Debt. They are the debt financing instruments of the U.S. Federal government, and are often referred to simply as Treasuries.
Real interest rate	The real interest rate is the nominal interest rate minus the inflation rate. It is a better measure of the return that a lender receives (or the cost to the borrower) because it takes into account the fact that the value of money changes due to inflation over the course of the loan period.

Go to **Cram101.com** for the Practice Tests for this Chapter.

Purchasing power	The amount of goods that money will buy, usually measured by the CPI is referred to as purchasing power.
Purchasing	Purchasing refers to the function in a firm that searches for quality material resources, finds the best suppliers, and negotiates the best price for goods and services.
Contract	A contract is a "promise" or an "agreement" that is enforced or recognized by the law. In the civil law, a contract is considered to be part of the general law of obligations.
Variable interest rate	Interest rate that fluctuates from period to period over the life of the loan is the variable interest rate. These rates are most often tied to the prime rate of a particular lending institution, the Consumer Price Index, Federal Funds rates or other money market measurements.
Nominal interest rate	The interest rate actually observed in the market, in contrast to the real interest rate is a nominal interest rate.
Treasurer	In many governments, a treasurer is the person responsible for running the treasury. Treasurers are also employed by organizations to look after funds.
Pure rate of interest	An essentially risk-free, long-term interest rate that is free of the influence of market imperfections is a pure rate of interest.
Term structure of interest rates	The relationship among interest rates on bonds with different terms to maturity is referred to as term structure of interest rates.
Yield curve	In finance, the yield curve is the relation between the interest rate (or cost of borrowing) and the maturity of the debt for a given borrower in a given currency.
Short rate	The balance advertisers have to pay if they estimated that they would run more ads in a year than they did and entered a contract to pay at a favorable rate is a short rate. The short rate is figured at the end of the year or sooner if advertisers fall behind schedule. It is calculated at a higher rate for the fewer insertions.
Slope	The slope of a line in the plane containing the x and y axes is generally represented by the letter m, and is defined as the change in the y coordinate divided by the corresponding change in the x coordinate, between two distinct points on the line.
Appeal	Appeal refers to the act of asking an appellate court to overturn a decision after the trial court's final judgment has been entered.
Expectations theory	The proposition that the interest rate on a long-term bond will equal the average of the short-term interest rates that people expect to occur over the life of the long-term bond is referred to as expectations theory.
Future interest	Future interest refers to an interest that will come into being at some future time. It is distinguished from a present interest, which already exists. Assume that Dan transfers securities to a newly created trust.
Normal yield curve	Normal yield curve refers to an upward-sloping yield curve. Long-term interest rates are higher than short-term rates.
Issued stock	The actual number of shares of stock currently classified as issued-comprises all the shares given in return for ownership in the corporation less any shares that have been retired is called issued stock.
Real rate of interest	The real rate of interest is the percentage increase in purchasing power that the borrower pays to the lender for the privilege of borrowing. It is the nominal rate of interest minus the inflation rate.

Corporate bond	A Corporate bond is a bond issued by a corporation, as the name suggests. The term is usually applied to longer term debt instruments, generally with a maturity date falling at least 12 months after their issue date (the term "commercial paper" being sometimes used for instruments with a shorter maturity).
Vendor	A person who sells property to a vendee is a vendor. The words vendor and vendee are more commonly applied to the seller and purchaser of real estate, and the words seller and buyer are more commonly applied to the seller and purchaser of personal property.
Market segmentation theory	Market segmentation theory refers to a theory that treasury securities are divided into market segments by various financial institutions investing in the market. The changing needs, desires, and strategies of these investors tend to strongly influence the nature and relationship of short-term and long-term interest rates.
Market segmentation	The process of dividing the total market into several groups whose members have similar characteristics is market segmentation.
Government bond	A government bond is a bond issued by a national government denominated in the country's own currency. Bonds issued by national governments in foreign currencies are normally referred to as sovereign bonds.
Consideration	Consideration in contract law, a basic requirement for an enforceable agreement under traditional contract principles, defined in this text as legal value, bargained for and given in exchange for an act or promise. In corporation law, cash or property contributed to a corporation in exchange for shares, or a promise to contribute such cash or property.
Analogy	Analogy is either the cognitive process of transferring information from a particular subject to another particular subject (the target), or a linguistic expression corresponding to such a process. In a narrower sense, analogy is an inference or an argument from a particular to another particular, as opposed to deduction, induction, and abduction, where at least one of the premises or the conclusion is general.

Interest	In finance and economics, interest is the price paid by a borrower for the use of a lender's money. In other words, interest is the amount of paid to "rent" money for a period of time.
Interest rate	The rate of return on bonds, loans, or deposits. When one speaks of 'the' interest rate, it is usually in a model where there is only one.
Discounted cash flow	In finance, the discounted cash flow approach describes a method to value a project or an entire company. The DCF methods determine the present value of future cash flows by discounting them using the appropriate cost of capital.
Present value	The value today of a stream of payments and/or receipts over time in the future and/or the past, converted to the present using an interest rate. If X t is the amount in period t and r the interest rate, then present value at time t=0 is V = ?T /t.
Future value	Future value measures what money is worth at a specified time in the future assuming a certain interest rate. This is used in time value of money calculations.
Cash flow	In finance, cash flow refers to the amounts of cash being received and spent by a business during a defined period of time, sometimes tied to a specific project. Most of the time they are being used to determine gaps in the liquid position of a company.
Security	Security refers to a claim on the borrower future income that is sold by the borrower to the lender. A security is a type of transferable interest representing financial value.
Yield	The interest rate that equates a future value or an annuity to a given present value is a yield.
Time value of money	Time value of money is the concept that the value of money varies depending on the timing of the cash flows, given any interest rate greater than zero.
Value of money	Value of money refers to the quantity of goods and services for which a unit of money can be exchanged; the purchasing power of a unit of money; the reciprocal of the price level.
Economics	The social science dealing with the use of scarce resources to obtain the maximum satisfaction of society's virtually unlimited economic wants is an economics.
Annuities	Financial contracts under which a customer pays an annual premium in exchange for a future stream of annual payments beginning at a set age, say 65, and ending when the person dies are annuities.
Annuity	A contract to make regular payments to a person for life or for a fixed period is an annuity.
Variable	A variable is something measured by a number; it is used to analyze what happens to other things when the size of that number changes.
Estate	An estate is the totality of the legal rights, interests, entitlements and obligations attaching to property. In the context of wills and probate, it refers to the totality of the property which the deceased owned or in which some interest was held.
Opportunity cost	The cost of something in terms of opportunity foregone. The opportunity cost to a country of producing a unit more of a good, such as for export or to replace an import, is the quantity of some other good that could have been produced instead.
Default	In finance, default occurs when a debtor has not met its legal obligations according to the debt contract, e.g. it has not made a scheduled payment, or violated a covenant (condition) of the debt contract.
Contract	A contract is a "promise" or an "agreement" that is enforced or recognized by the law. In the civil law, a contract is considered to be part of the general law of obligations.
Future value of an annuity	The sum of the future value of a series of consecutive equal payments is referred to as future value of an annuity.

Go to **Cram101.com** for the Practice Tests for this Chapter.

83

Industrial process	An industrial process is a procedure involving chemical or mechanical steps to aid in the manufacture of an item or items, usually carried out on a large scale.
Corporation	A legal entity chartered by a state or the Federal government that is distinct and separate from the individuals who own it is a corporation. This separation gives the corporation unique powers which other legal entities lack.
License	A license in the sphere of Intellectual Property Rights (IPR) is a document, contract or agreement giving permission or the 'right' to a legally-definable entity to do something (such as manufacture a product or to use a service), or to apply something (such as a trademark), with the objective of achieving commercial gain.
Patent	The legal right to the proceeds from and control over the use of an invented product or process, granted for a fixed period of time, usually 20 years. Patent is one form of intellectual property that is subject of the TRIPS agreement.
Management	Management characterizes the process of leading and directing all or part of an organization, often a business, through the deployment and manipulation of resources. Early twentieth-century management writer Mary Parker Follett defined management as "the art of getting things done through people."
Fund	Independent accounting entity with a self-balancing set of accounts segregated for the purposes of carrying on specific activities is referred to as a fund.
Capital	Capital generally refers to financial wealth, especially that used to start or maintain a business. In classical economics, capital is one of four factors of production, the others being land and labor and entrepreneurship.
Bond	Bond refers to a debt instrument, issued by a borrower and promising a specified stream of payments to the purchaser, usually regular interest payments plus a final repayment of principal.
Principal	In agency law, one under whose direction an agent acts and for whose benefit that agent acts is a principal.
Maturity	Maturity refers to the final payment date of a loan or other financial instrument, after which point no further interest or principal need be paid.
Lender	Suppliers and financial institutions that lend money to companies is referred to as a lender.
Financial market	In economics, a financial market is a mechanism which allows people to trade money for securities or commodities such as gold or other precious metals. In general, any commodity market might be considered to be a financial market, if the usual purpose of traders is not the immediate consumption of the commodity, but rather as a means of delaying or accelerating consumption over time.
Market	A market is, as defined in economics, a social arrangement that allows buyers and sellers to discover information and carry out a voluntary exchange of goods or services.
Sinking fund	A sinking fund is a method by which an organization sets aside money over time to retire its indebtedness. More specifically, it is a fund into which money can be deposited, so that over time its preferred stock, debentures or stocks can be retired.
Compound interest	Compound interest is interest computed on the sum of all past interest added as well as on the principal.
Balance	In banking and accountancy, the outstanding balance is the amount of money owned, (or due), that remains in a deposit account (or a loan account) at a given date, after all past remittances, payments and withdrawal have been accounted for. It can be positive (then, in the balance sheet of a firm, it is an asset) or negative (a liability).

Accumulation	The acquisition of an increasing quantity of something. The accumulation of factors, especially capital, is a primary mechanism for economic growth.
Frequency	Frequency refers to the speed of the up and down movements of a fluctuating economic variable; that is, the number of times per unit of time that the variable completes a cycle of up and down movement.
Future interest	Future interest refers to an interest that will come into being at some future time. It is distinguished from a present interest, which already exists. Assume that Dan transfers securities to a newly created trust.
Compounded semiannually	A compounding period of every six months is called compounded semiannually.
Nominal interest rate	The interest rate actually observed in the market, in contrast to the real interest rate is a nominal interest rate.
Advertisement	Advertisement is the promotion of goods, services, companies and ideas, usually by an identified sponsor. Marketers see advertising as part of an overall promotional strategy.
Credit	Credit refers to a recording as positive in the balance of payments, any transaction that gives rise to a payment into the country, such as an export, the sale of an asset, or borrowing from abroad.
Budget	Budget refers to an account, usually for a year, of the planned expenditures and the expected receipts of an entity. For a government, the receipts are tax revenues.
Rate of return	A rate of return is a comparison of the money earned (or lost) on an investment to the amount of money invested.
Investment	Investment refers to spending for the production and accumulation of capital and additions to inventories. In a financial sense, buying an asset with the expectation of making a return.
Discount	The difference between the face value of a bond and its selling price, when a bond is sold for less than its face value it's referred to as a discount.
Credit risk	The risk of loss due to a counterparty defaulting on a contract, or more generally the risk of loss due to some "credit event" is called credit risk.
Inputs	The inputs used by a firm or an economy are the labor, raw materials, electricity and other resources it uses to produce its outputs.
Consideration	Consideration in contract law, a basic requirement for an enforceable agreement under traditional contract principles, defined in this text as legal value, bargained for and given in exchange for an act or promise. In corporation law, cash or property contributed to a corporation in exchange for shares, or a promise to contribute such cash or property.
Authority	Authority in agency law, refers to an agent's ability to affect his principal's legal relations with third parties. Also used to refer to an actor's legal power or ability to do something. In addition, sometimes used to refer to a statute, case, or other legal source that justifies a particular result.
Tax accountant	An accountant trained in tax law and responsible for preparing tax returns or developing tax strategies is called a tax accountant.
Present value of an annuity	The sum of the present value of a series of consecutive equal payments is called present value of an annuity.
Mortgage	Mortgage refers to a note payable issued for property, such as a house, usually repaid in equal installments consisting of part principle and part interest, over a specified period.
Standing	Standing refers to the legal requirement that anyone seeking to challenge a particular action

in court must demonstrate that such action substantially affects his legitimate interests before he will be entitled to bring suit.

Amortization	Systematic and rational allocation of the acquisition cost of an intangible asset over its useful life is referred to as amortization.
Amortization schedule	An amortization schedule is a table detailing each periodic payment on a loan (typically a mortgage), as generated by an amortization calculator. They are calculated so that each periodic payment for the entirety of the loan is equal, making the repayment process somewhat simpler under amortization than with other models.
Composition	An out-of-court settlement in which creditors agree to accept a fractional settlement on their original claim is referred to as composition.
Financial transaction	A financial transaction involves a change in the status of the finances of two or more businesses or individuals.
Deductible	The dollar sum of costs that an insured individual must pay before the insurer begins to pay is called deductible.
Shares	Shares refer to an equity security, representing a shareholder's ownership of a corporation. Shares are one of a finite number of equal portions in the capital of a company, entitling the owner to a proportion of distributed, non-reinvested profits known as dividends and to a portion of the value of the company in case of liquidation.
Equity	Equity is the name given to the set of legal principles, in countries following the English common law tradition, which supplement strict rules of law where their application would operate harshly, so as to achieve what is sometimes referred to as "natural justice."
Interest payment	The payment to holders of bonds payable, calculated by multiplying the stated rate on the face of the bond by the par, or face, value of the bond. If bonds are issued at a discount or premium, the interest payment does not equal the interest expense.
Contribution	In business organization law, the cash or property contributed to a business by its owners is referred to as contribution.
Factoring	In mathematics, factorization or factoring is the decomposition of an object into a product of other objects, or factors, which when multiplied together give the original.
Perpetuity	A perpetuity is an annuity in which the periodic payments begin on a fixed date and continue indefinitely. Fixed coupon payments on permanently invested (irredeemable) sums of money are prime examples of perpetuities. Scholarships paid perpetually from an endowment fit the definition of perpetuity.
Holder	A person in possession of a document of title or an instrument payable or indorsed to him, his order, or to bearer is a holder.
Money market	The money market, in macroeconomics and international finance, refers to the equilibration of demand for a country's domestic money to its money supply; market for short-term financial instruments.
Dividend	Amount of corporate profits paid out for each share of stock is referred to as dividend.
Revenue	Revenue is a U.S. business term for the amount of money that a company receives from its activities, mostly from sales of products and/or services to customers.
Valuation	In finance, valuation is the process of estimating the market value of a financial asset or liability. They can be done on assets (for example, investments in marketable securities such as stocks, options, business enterprises, or intangible assets such as patents and trademarks) or on liabilities (e.g., Bonds issued by a company).

Go to **Cram101.com** for the Practice Tests for this Chapter.

89

Savings deposit	Savings deposit refers to a deposit that is interest-bearing and that the depositor can normally withdraw at any time.
National bank	A National bank refers to federally chartered banks. They are an ordinary private bank which operates nationally (as opposed to regionally or locally or even internationally).
Firm	An organization that employs resources to produce a good or service for profit and owns and operates one or more plants is referred to as a firm.
Brief	Brief refers to a statement of a party's case or legal arguments, usually prepared by an attorney. Also used to make legal arguments before appellate courts.
Cash discount	Cash discount refers to a discount offered on merchandise sold to encourage prompt payment; offered by sellers of merchandise and represents sales discounts to the seller when they are used and purchase discounts to the purchaser of the merchandise.
Property	Assets defined in the broadest legal sense. Property includes the unrealized receivables of a cash basis taxpayer, but not services rendered.
Corporate bond	A Corporate bond is a bond issued by a corporation, as the name suggests. The term is usually applied to longer term debt instruments, generally with a maturity date falling at least 12 months after their issue date (the term "commercial paper" being sometimes used for instruments with a shorter maturity).
Trust	An arrangement in which shareholders of independent firms agree to give up their stock in exchange for trust certificates that entitle them to a share of the trust's common profits.
Cash inflow	Cash coming into the company as the result of a previous investment is a cash inflow.
Evaluation	The consumer's appraisal of the product or brand on important attributes is called evaluation.
Net present value	Net present value is a standard method in finance of capital budgeting – the planning of long-term investments. Using this method a potential investment project should be undertaken if the present value of all cash inflows minus the present value of all cash outflows (which equals the net present value) is greater than zero.
Cash outflow	Cash flowing out of the business from all sources over a period of time is cash outflow.
Credit union	A credit union is a not-for-profit co-operative financial institution that is owned and controlled by its members, through the election of a volunteer Board of Directors elected from the membership itself.
Union	A worker association that bargains with employers over wages and working conditions is called a union.
Manufacturing	Production of goods primarily by the application of labor and capital to raw materials and other intermediate inputs, in contrast to agriculture, mining, forestry, fishing, and services a manufacturing.
Internal rate of return	Internal rate of return refers to a discounted cash flow method for evaluating capital budgeting projects. The internal rate of return is a discount rate that makes the present value of the cash inflows equal to the present value of the cash outflows.
Interest expense	The cost a business incurs to borrow money. With respect to bonds payable, the interest expense is calculated by multiplying the market rate of interest by the carrying value of the bonds on the date of the payment.
Financial plan	The financial plan section of a business plan consists of three financial statements (the income statement, the cash flow projection, and the balance sheet) and a brief analysis of these three statements.

Expense	In accounting, an expense represents an event in which an asset is used up or a liability is incurred. In terms of the accounting equation, expenses reduce owners' equity.
Liability	A liability is a present obligation of the enterprise arizing from past events, the settlement of which is expected to result in an outflow from the enterprise of resources embodying economic benefits.
Amortize	To provide for the payment of a debt by creating a sinking fund or paying in installments is to amortize.

Security	Security refers to a claim on the borrower future income that is sold by the borrower to the lender. A security is a type of transferable interest representing financial value.
Utility	Utility refers to the want-satisfying power of a good or service; the satisfaction or pleasure a consumer obtains from the consumption of a good or service.
Asset	An item of property, such as land, capital, money, a share in ownership, or a claim on others for future payment, such as a bond or a bank deposit is an asset.
Service	Service refers to a "non tangible product" that is not embodied in a physical good and that typically effects some change in another product, person, or institution. Contrasts with good.
Cash flow	In finance, cash flow refers to the amounts of cash being received and spent by a business during a defined period of time, sometimes tied to a specific project. Most of the time they are being used to determine gaps in the liquid position of a company.
Present value	The value today of a stream of payments and/or receipts over time in the future and/or the past, converted to the present using an interest rate. If X t is the amount in period t and r the interest rate, then present value at time t=0 is V = ?T /t.
Dividend	Amount of corporate profits paid out for each share of stock is referred to as dividend.
A share	In finance the term A share has two distinct meanings, both relating to securities. The first is a designation for a 'class' of common or preferred stock. A share of common or preferred stock typically has enhanced voting rights or other benefits compared to the other forms of shares that may have been created. The equity structure, or how many types of shares are offered, is determined by the corporate charter.
Stock	In financial terminology, stock is the capital raized by a corporation, through the issuance and sale of shares.
Return on investment	Return on investment refers to the return a businessperson gets on the money he and other owners invest in the firm; for example, a business that earned $100 on a $1,000 investment would have a ROI of 10 percent: 100 divided by 1000.
Investment	Investment refers to spending for the production and accumulation of capital and additions to inventories. In a financial sense, buying an asset with the expectation of making a return.
Valuation	In finance, valuation is the process of estimating the market value of a financial asset or liability. They can be done on assets (for example, investments in marketable securities such as stocks, options, business enterprises, or intangible assets such as patents and trademarks) or on liabilities (e.g., Bonds issued by a company).
Discounted cash flow	In finance, the discounted cash flow approach describes a method to value a project or an entire company. The DCF methods determine the present value of future cash flows by discounting them using the appropriate cost of capital.
Equity investment	Equity investment generally refers to the buying and holding of shares of stock on a stock market by individuals and funds in anticipation of income from dividends and capital gain as the value of the stock rises.
Equity	Equity is the name given to the set of legal principles, in countries following the English common law tradition, which supplement strict rules of law where their application would operate harshly, so as to achieve what is sometimes referred to as "natural justice."
Bond	Bond refers to a debt instrument, issued by a borrower and promising a specified stream of payments to the purchaser, usually regular interest payments plus a final repayment of principal.
Time value of	Time value of money is the concept that the value of money varies depending on the timing of

money	the cash flows, given any interest rate greater than zero.
Value of money	Value of money refers to the quantity of goods and services for which a unit of money can be exchanged; the purchasing power of a unit of money; the reciprocal of the price level.
Interest rate	The rate of return on bonds, loans, or deposits. When one speaks of 'the' interest rate, it is usually in a model where there is only one.
Principal	In agency law, one under whose direction an agent acts and for whose benefit that agent acts is a principal.
Interest	In finance and economics, interest is the price paid by a borrower for the use of a lender's money. In other words, interest is the amount of paid to "rent" money for a period of time.
Lender	Suppliers and financial institutions that lend money to companies is referred to as a lender.
Context	The effect of the background under which a message often takes on more and richer meaning is a context. Context is especially important in cross-cultural interactions because some cultures are said to be high context or low context.
Holding period	The period of time during which property has been held for income tax purposes. The holding period is significant in determining whether gain or loss from the sale or exchange of a capital asset is long term or short term.
Holding	The holding is a court's determination of a matter of law based on the issue presented in the particular case. In other words: under this law, with these facts, this result.
Discount rate	Discount rate refers to the rate, per year, at which future values are diminished to make them comparable to values in the present. Can be either subjective or objective .
Discount	The difference between the face value of a bond and its selling price, when a bond is sold for less than its face value it's referred to as a discount.
Yield	The interest rate that equates a future value or an annuity to a given present value is a yield.
Rate of return	A rate of return is a comparison of the money earned (or lost) on an investment to the amount of money invested.
Debt security	Type of security acquired by loaning assets is called a debt security.
Credit	Credit refers to a recording as positive in the balance of payments, any transaction that gives rise to a payment into the country, such as an export, the sale of an asset, or borrowing from abroad.
Firm	An organization that employs resources to produce a good or service for profit and owns and operates one or more plants is referred to as a firm.
Maturity	Maturity refers to the final payment date of a loan or other financial instrument, after which point no further interest or principal need be paid.
Issuer	The company that borrows money from investors by issuing bonds is referred to as issuer. They are legally responsible for the obligations of the issue and for reporting financial conditions, material developments and any other operational activities as required by the regulations of their jurisdictions.
Buyer	A buyer refers to a role in the buying center with formal authority and responsibility to select the supplier and negotiate the terms of the contract.
Promissory note	Commercial paper or instrument in which the maker promises to pay a specific sum of money to another person, to his order, or to bearer is referred to as a promissory note.
Face value	The nominal or par value of an instrument as expressed on its face is referred to as the face

	value.
Creditor	A person to whom a debt or legal obligation is owed, and who has the right to enforce payment of that debt or obligation is referred to as creditor.
Vendor	A person who sells property to a vendee is a vendor. The words vendor and vendee are more commonly applied to the seller and purchaser of real estate, and the words seller and buyer are more commonly applied to the seller and purchaser of personal property.
Seasoned issue	A stock issued for sale for which prior issues currently sell in the market is called a seasoned issue.
Coupon rate	In bonds, notes or other fixed income securities, the stated percentage rate of interest, usually paid twice a year is the coupon rate.
Coupon	In finance, a coupon is "attached" to a bond, either physically (as with old bonds) or electronically. Each coupon represents a predetermined payment promized to the bond-holder in return for his or her loan of money to the bond-issuer. .
Interest payment	The payment to holders of bonds payable, calculated by multiplying the stated rate on the face of the bond by the par, or face, value of the bond. If bonds are issued at a discount or premium, the interest payment does not equal the interest expense.
Bondholder	The individual or entity that purchases a bond, thus loaning money to the company that issued the bond is the bondholder.
Agent	A person who makes economic decisions for another economic actor. A hired manager operates as an agent for a firm's owner.
Bond valuation	Bond valuation is the process of determining the fair price of a bond. As with any security, the fair value of a bond is the present value of the stream of cash flows it is expected to generate.
Financial market	In economics, a financial market is a mechanism which allows people to trade money for securities or commodities such as gold or other precious metals. In general, any commodity market might be considered to be a financial market, if the usual purpose of traders is not the immediate consumption of the commodity, but rather as a means of delaying or accelerating consumption over time.
Market	A market is, as defined in economics, a social arrangement that allows buyers and sellers to discover information and carry out a voluntary exchange of goods or services.
Secondary market	Secondary market refers to the market for securities that have already been issued. It is a market in which investors trade back and forth with each other.
Primary market	The market for the raising of new funds as opposed to the trading of securities already in existence is called primary market.
Fund	Independent accounting entity with a self-balancing set of accounts segregated for the purposes of carrying on specific activities is referred to as a fund.
Option	A contract that gives the purchaser the option to buy or sell the underlying financial instrument at a specified price, called the exercise price or strike price, within a specific period of time.
Premium	Premium refers to the fee charged by an insurance company for an insurance policy. The rate of losses must be relatively predictable: In order to set the premium (prices) insurers must be able to estimate them accurately.
Par value	The central value of a pegged exchange rate, around which the actual rate is permitted to fluctuate within set bounds is a par value.

Go to **Cram101.com** for the Practice Tests for this Chapter.

At par	At equality refers to at par. Two currencies are said to be 'at par' if they are trading one-for-one.
Maturity date	The date on which the final payment on a bond is due from the bond issuer to the investor is a maturity date.
Annuity	A contract to make regular payments to a person for life or for a fixed period is an annuity.
Present value of an annuity	The sum of the present value of a series of consecutive equal payments is called present value of an annuity.
Future value	Future value measures what money is worth at a specified time in the future assuming a certain interest rate. This is used in time value of money calculations.
Yield to maturity	Yield to maturity refers to the required rate of return on a bond issue. It is the discount rate used in present-valuing future interest payments and the principal payment at maturity. The term is used interchangeably with market rate of interest.
Current yield	Current yield refers to the rate of return on a bond; the annual interest payment divided by the bond's price.
Inputs	The inputs used by a firm or an economy are the labor, raw materials, electricity and other resources it uses to produce its outputs.
Variable	A variable is something measured by a number; it is used to analyze what happens to other things when the size of that number changes.
Bond market	The bond market refers to people and entities involved in buying and selling of bonds and the quantity and prices of those transactions over time.
Operation	A standardized method or technique that is performed repetitively, often on different materials resulting in different finished goods is called an operation.
Gain	In finance, gain is a profit or an increase in value of an investment such as a stock or bond. Gain is calculated by fair market value or the proceeds from the sale of the investment minus the sum of the purchase price and all costs associated with it.
Corporation	A legal entity chartered by a state or the Federal government that is distinct and separate from the individuals who own it is a corporation. This separation gives the corporation unique powers which other legal entities lack.
Market price	Market price is an economic concept with commonplace familiarity; it is the price that a good or service is offered at, or will fetch, in the marketplace; it is of interest mainly in the study of microeconomics.
Interest rate risk	Interest rate risk is the risk that the relative value of a security, especially a bond, will worsen due to an interest rate increase. This risk is commonly measured by the bond's duration.
Points	Loan origination fees that may be deductible as interest by a buyer of property. A seller of property who pays points reduces the selling price by the amount of the points paid for the buyer.
Trial	An examination before a competent tribunal, according to the law of the land, of the facts or law put in issue in a cause, for the purpose of determining such issue is a trial. When the court hears and determines any issue of fact or law for the purpose of determining the rights of the parties, it may be considered a trial.
Call provision	Call provision refers to bonds and some preferred stock, in which a call allows the corporation to retire securities before maturity by forcing the bondholders to sell bonds back to it at a set price. The call provisions are included in the bond indenture.

Indenture	A bond contract that specifies the legal provisions of a bond issue is called an indenture.
Contract	A contract is a "promise" or an "agreement" that is enforced or recognized by the law. In the civil law, a contract is considered to be part of the general law of obligations.
Zero coupon bond	A zero coupon bond is a bond which do not pay periodic coupons, or so-called "interest payments." They are purchased at a discount from their value at maturity. The holder of a zero coupon bond is entitled to receive a single payment, usually of a specified sum of money at a specified time in the future.
Coupon bond	A credit market instrument, the coupon bond pays the owner a fixed interest payment every year until the maturity date, when a specified final amount is repaid.
Call premium	The call premium is the amount over par value an issuer must pay to redeem a callable bond on a call date.
Call price	Call price refers to specified price that must be paid for bonds that are called; usually higher than the face amount of the bonds.
Refunding	The process of retiring an old bond issue before maturity and replacing it with a new issue is refunding. Refunding will occur when interest rates have fallen and new bonds may be sold at lower interest rates.
Flotation cost	Flotation cost refers to the distribution cost of selling securities to the public. The cost includes the underwriter's spread and any associated fees.
Sinking fund	A sinking fund is a method by which an organization sets aside money over time to retire its indebtedness. More specifically, it is a fund into which money can be deposited, so that over time its preferred stock, debentures or stocks can be retired.
Mortgage	Mortgage refers to a note payable issued for property, such as a house, usually repaid in equal installments consisting of part principle and part interest, over a specified period.
Estate	An estate is the totality of the legal rights, interests, entitlements and obligations attaching to property. In the context of wills and probate, it refers to the totality of the property which the deceased owned or in which some interest was held.
Expected return	Expected return refers to the return on an asset expected over the next period.
Argument	The discussion by counsel for the respective parties of their contentions on the law and the facts of the case being tried in order to aid the jury in arriving at a correct and just conclusion is called argument.
Convertible bond	A convertible bond is type of bond that can be converted into shares of stock in the issuing company, usually at some pre-announced ratio.
Shares	Shares refer to an equity security, representing a shareholder's ownership of a corporation. Shares are one of a finite number of equal portions in the capital of a company, entitling the owner to a proportion of distributed, non-reinvested profits known as dividends and to a portion of the value of the company in case of liquidation.
Conversion ratio	Conversion ratio refers to the number of shares of common stock an investor will receive if he or she exchanges a convertible bond or convertible preferred stock for common stock.
Conversion	Conversion refers to any distinct act of dominion wrongfully exerted over another's personal property in denial of or inconsistent with his rights therein. That tort committed by a person who deals with chattels not belonging to him in a manner that is inconsistent with the ownership of the lawful owner.
Exchange	The trade of things of value between buyer and seller so that each is better off after the trade is called the exchange.

Go to **Cram101.com** for the Practice Tests for this Chapter.

Conversion price	The conversion ratio divided into the par value is the conversion price. The price of the common stock at which the security is convertible. An investor would usually not convert the security into common stock unless the market price was greater than the conversion price.
Appreciation	Appreciation refers to a rise in the value of a country's currency on the exchange market, relative either to a particular other currency or to a weighted average of other currencies. The currency is said to appreciate. Opposite of 'depreciation.' Appreciation can also refer to the increase in value of any asset.
Interest expense	The cost a business incurs to borrow money. With respect to bonds payable, the interest expense is calculated by multiplying the market rate of interest by the carrying value of the bonds on the date of the payment.
Expense	In accounting, an expense represents an event in which an asset is used up or a liability is incurred. In terms of the accounting equation, expenses reduce owners' equity.
Common stock	Common stock refers to the basic, normal, voting stock issued by a corporation; called residual equity because it ranks after preferred stock for dividend and liquidation distributions.
Unsecured bond	A bond backed only by the reputation of the issuer is an unsecured bond. A bond not backed by collateral, also called debentures.
Debenture	A debenture is a long-term debt instrument used by governments and large companies to obtain funds. It is similar to a bond except the securitization conditions are different.
Financial statement	Financial statement refers to a summary of all the transactions that have occurred over a particular period.
Accounting	A system that collects and processes financial information about an organization and reports that information to decision makers is referred to as accounting.
Cash outflow	Cash flowing out of the business from all sources over a period of time is cash outflow.
Balance sheet	A statement of the assets, liabilities, and net worth of a firm or individual at some given time often at the end of its "fiscal year," is referred to as a balance sheet.
Management	Management characterizes the process of leading and directing all or part of an organization, often a business, through the deployment and manipulation of resources. Early twentieth-century management writer Mary Parker Follett defined management as "the art of getting things done through people."
Balance	In banking and accountancy, the outstanding balance is the amount of money owned, (or due), that remains in a deposit account (or a loan account) at a given date, after all past remittances, payments and withdrawal have been accounted for. It can be positive (then, in the balance sheet of a firm, it is an asset) or negative (a liability).
Bond indenture	Bond contract that specifies the stated rate of interest and the face value of the bond as well as other contractual provisions is called the bond indenture. A company's bond indenture will cover all bonds issued by that company and also list all bond covenants.
Purchasing	Purchasing refers to the function in a firm that searches for quality material resources, finds the best suppliers, and negotiates the best price for goods and services.
Forced conversion	Forced conversion occurs when a company calls a convertible security that has a conversion value greater than the call price. Investors will take the higher of the two values and convert the security to common stock, rather than take a lower cash call price.
Market value	Market value refers to the price of an asset agreed on between a willing buyer and a willing seller; the price an asset could demand if it is sold on the open market.

Go to **Cram101.com** for the Practice Tests for this Chapter.

Conversion premium	The market price of a convertible bond or preferred stock minus the security's conversion value is referred to as conversion premium.
Earnings per share	Earnings per share refers to annual profit of the corporation divided by the number of shares outstanding.
Net income	Net income is equal to the income that a firm has after subtracting costs and expenses from the total revenue. Expenses will typically include tax expense.
Convertible security	A convertible security is a security that can be converted into another security, for example, a bond that under certain terms can be converted into equity.
Convertible securities	Securities giving their holders the power to exchange those securities for other securities without paying any additional consideration are convertible securities.
Holder	A person in possession of a document of title or an instrument payable or indorsed to him, his order, or to bearer is a holder.
Stockholder	A stockholder is an individual or company (including a corporation) that legally owns one or more shares of stock in a joined stock company. The shareholders are the owners of a corporation. Companies listed at the stock market strive to enhance shareholder value.
Extension	Extension refers to an out-of-court settlement in which creditors agree to allow the firm more time to meet its financial obligations. A new repayment schedule will be developed, subject to the acceptance of creditors.
Shareholder	A shareholder is an individual or company (including a corporation) that legally owns one or more shares of stock in a joined stock company.
Disclosure	Disclosure means the giving out of information, either voluntarily or to be in compliance with legal regulations or workplace rules.
Accounting Standards Board	The role of the Accounting Standards Board is to issue accounting standards in the United Kingdom. It is recognized for that purpose under the Companies Act 1985. It took over the task of setting accounting standards from the Accounting Standards Committee (ASC) in 1990.
Marginal tax rate	The percentage of an additional dollar of earnings that goes to taxes is referred to as the marginal tax rate.
Fixed price	Fixed price is a phrase used to mean that no bargaining is allowed over the price of a good or, less commonly, a service.
Warrant	A warrant is a security that entitles the holder to buy or sell a certain additional quantity of an underlying security at an agreed-upon price, at the holder's discretion.
Registered bond	A registered bond refers to a bond for which the issuing company keeps a record of the name and address of the bondholder and pays interest and principal payments directly to the registered owner.
Bearer bond	A bearer bond is a legal certificate that usually represents a bond obligation of, or stock in, a corporation or some other intangible property.
Bearer	A person in possession of a negotiable instrument that is payable to him, his order, or to whoever is in possession of the instrument is referred to as bearer.
Possession	Possession refers to respecting real property, exclusive dominion and control such as owners of like property usually exercise over it. Manual control of personal property either as owner or as one having a qualified right in it.
Default	In finance, default occurs when a debtor has not met its legal obligations according to the debt contract, e.g. it has not made a scheduled payment, or violated a covenant (condition) of the debt contract.

Go to **Cram101.com** for the Practice Tests for this Chapter.

Mortgage bond	Type of secured bond that conditionally transfers title of a designated piece of property to the bondholder until the bond is paid is referred to as mortgage bond.
Secured debt	A general category of debt that indicates the loan was obtained by pledging assets as collateral is secured debt. Secured debt has many forms and usually offers some protective features to a given class of bondholders.
Subordinated debenture	An unsecured bond, in which payment to the holder will occur only after designated senior debenture holders are satisfied is a subordinated debenture.
Junk bond	In finance, a junk bond is a bond that is rated below investment grade. These bonds have a higher risk of defaulting, but typically pay high yields in order to make them attractive to investors.
Recession	A significant decline in economic activity. In the U.S., recession is approximately defined as two successive quarters of falling GDP, as judged by NBER.
Economy	The income, expenditures, and resources that affect the cost of running a business and household are called an economy.
Bond ratings	Bond ratings refers to rating of bonds according to risk by Standard & Poor's and Moody's Investor Service. A bond that is rated A by Moody's has the lowest risk, while a bond with a C rating has the highest risk. Coupon rates are greatly influenced by a corporation's bond rating.
Default risk	The chance that the issuer of a debt instrument will be unable to make interest payments or pay off the face value when the instrument matures is called default risk.
Debt financing	Obtaining financing by borrowing money is debt financing.
Cost of debt	The cost of debt is the cost of borrowing money (usually denoted by Kd). It is derived by dividing debt's interest payments on the total market value of the debts.
Profit	Profit refers to the return to the resource entrepreneurial ability; total revenue minus total cost.
Institutional investors	Institutional investors refers to large organizations such as pension funds, mutual funds, insurance companies, and banks that invest their own funds or the funds of others.
Monopoly	A monopoly is defined as a persistent market situation where there is only one provider of a kind of product or service.
Wholesale	According to the United Nations Statistics Division Wholesale is the resale of new and used goods to retailers, to industrial, commercial, institutional or professional users, or to other wholesalers, or involves acting as an agent or broker in buying merchandise for, or selling merchandise, to such persons or companies.
Deregulation	The lessening or complete removal of government regulations on an industry, especially concerning the price that firms are allowed to charge and leaving price to be determined by market forces a deregulation.
Convergence	The blending of various facets of marketing functions and communication technology to create more efficient and expanded synergies is a convergence.
Conflict of interest	A conflict that occurs when a corporate officer or director enters into a transaction with the corporation in which he or she has a personal interest is a conflict of interest.
Business operations	Business operations are those activities involved in the running of a business for the purpose of producing value for the stakeholders. The outcome of business operations is the harvesting of value from assets owned by a business.
Controlling	A management function that involves determining whether or not an organization is progressing

	toward its goals and objectives, and taking corrective action if it is not is called controlling.
Bankruptcy	Bankruptcy is a legally declared inability or impairment of ability of an individual or organization to pay their creditors.
Dealer	People who link buyers with sellers by buying and selling securities at stated prices are referred to as a dealer.
Financial ratio	A financial ratio is a ratio of two numbers of reported levels or flows of a company. It may be two financial flows categories divided by each other (profit margin, profit/revenue). It may be a level divided by a financial flow (price/earnings). It may be a flow divided by a level (return on equity or earnings/equity). The numerator or denominator may itself be a ratio (PEG ratio).
Times interest earned	Times interest earned refers to net income before interest and taxes, divided by interest expense; describes a company's ability to make interest payments on its debt.
Trustee	An independent party appointed to represent the bondholders is referred to as a trustee.
Business analysis	Business analysis is a structured methodology that is focused on completely understanding the customer's needs, identifying how best to meet those needs, and then "reinventing" the stream of processes to meet those needs.
Analyst	Analyst refers to a person or tool with a primary function of information analysis, generally with a more limited, practical and short term set of goals than a researcher.
Capital	Capital generally refers to financial wealth, especially that used to start or maintain a business. In classical economics, capital is one of four factors of production, the others being land and labor and entrepreneurship.
Investment banker	Investment banker refers to a financial organization that specializes in selling primary offerings of securities. Investment bankers can also perform other financial functions, such as advising clients, negotiating mergers and takeovers, and selling secondary offerings.
Treasurer	In many governments, a treasurer is the person responsible for running the treasury. Treasurers are also employed by organizations to look after funds.
Consumer good	Products and services that are ultimately consumed rather than used in the production of another good are a consumer good.
Long run	In economic models, the long run time frame assumes no fixed factors of production. Firms can enter or leave the marketplace, and the cost (and availability) of land, labor, raw materials, and capital goods can be assumed to vary.
Industry	A group of firms that produce identical or similar products is an industry. It is also used specifically to refer to an area of economic production focused on manufacturing which involves large amounts of capital investment before any profit can be realized, also called "heavy industry".
Corporate bond	A Corporate bond is a bond issued by a corporation, as the name suggests. The term is usually applied to longer term debt instruments, generally with a maturity date falling at least 12 months after their issue date (the term "commercial paper" being sometimes used for instruments with a shorter maturity).
Alpha	Alpha is a risk-adjusted measure of the so-called "excess return" on an investment. It is a common measure of assessing active manager's performance as it is the return in excess of a benchmark index or "risk-free" investment.
Diluted earnings per	EPS adjusted for all potential dilution from the issuance of any new shares of common stock arising from convertible bonds, convertible preferred stock, warrants, or any other options

share	outstanding is referred to as the diluted earnings per share.
Effective tax rate	The effective tax rate is the amount of income tax an individual or firm pays divided by the individual or firm's total taxable income. This ratio is usually expressed as a percentage.
Volatility	Volatility refers to the extent to which an economic variable, such as a price or an exchange rate, moves up and down over time.
Brief	Brief refers to a statement of a party's case or legal arguments, usually prepared by an attorney. Also used to make legal arguments before appellate courts.
Lease	A contract for the possession and use of land or other property, including goods, on one side, and a recompense of rent or other income on the other is the lease.
Property	Assets defined in the broadest legal sense. Property includes the unrealized receivables of a cash basis taxpayer, but not services rendered.
Lessee	One who rents property from another. In the case of real estate, the lessee is also known as the tenant.
Lessor	The person who transfers the right of possession and use of goods under the lease is referred to as lessor.
Tenant	The party to whom the leasehold is transferred is a tenant. A leasehold estate is an ownership interest in land in which a lessee or a tenant holds real property by some form of title from a lessor or landlord.
Current liability	Current liability refers to a debt that can reasonably be expected to be paid from existing current assets or through the creation of other current liabilities, within one year or the operating cycle, whichever is longer.
Debt ratio	Debt ratio refers to the calculation of the total liabilities divided by the total liabilities plus capital. This results in the measurment of the debt level of the business (leverage).
Liability	A liability is a present obligation of the enterprise arizing from past events, the settlement of which is expected to result in an outflow from the enterprise of resources embodying economic benefits.
Bid	A bid price is a price offered by a buyer when he/she buys a good. In the context of stock trading on a stock exchange, the bid price is the highest price a buyer of a stock is willing to pay for a share of that given stock.
Collateral	Property that is pledged to the lender to guarantee payment in the event that the borrower is unable to make debt payments is called collateral.
Income statement	Income statement refers to a financial statement that presents the revenues and expenses and resulting net income or net loss of a company for a specific period of time.
Retained earnings	Cumulative earnings of a company that are not distributed to the owners and are reinvested in the business are called retained earnings.
Distortion	Distortion refers to any departure from the ideal of perfect competition that interferes with economic agents maximizing social welfare when they maximize their own.
Notes to the financial statements	Notes that clarify information presented in the financial statements, as well as expand upon it where additional detail is needed are notes to the financial statements.
Counterargument	A type of thought or cognitive response a receiver has that is counter or opposed to the position advocated in a message is referred to as counterargument.

Go to **Cram101.com** for the Practice Tests for this Chapter.

Financial accounting standards board	Financial accounting standards board refers to the private sector body given the primary responsibility to work out the detailed rules that become generally accepted accounting principles.
Financial accounting Standards	Financial Accounting Standards refers to a set of standards that dictate accounting rules concerning financial reporting; establish generally accepted accounting principles.
Financial accounting	Financial accounting is the branch of accountancy concerned with the preparation of financial statements for external decision makers, such as stockholders, suppliers, banks and government agencies. The fundamental need for financial accounting is to reduce principal-agent problem by measuring and monitoring agents' performance.
Bill of sale	A written agreement by which one person assigns or transfers interests or rights in personal property to another is referred to as the bill of sale.
Fair market value	Fair market value refers to the amount at which property would change hands between a willing buyer and a willing seller, neither being under any compulsion to buy or to sell, and both having reasonable knowledge of the relevant facts.
Capital lease	A type of lease whose characteristics make it similar to a debt-financed purchase and that is consequently accounted for in that fashion is called capital lease. A capital lease is usually used to finance equipment for the major part of its useful life, and there is a reasonable assurance that the lessee will obtain ownership of the equipment by the end of the lease term.
Insurance	Insurance refers to a system by which individuals can reduce their exposure to risk of large losses by spreading the risks among a large number of persons.
Acquisition	A company's purchase of the property and obligations of another company is an acquisition.
Operating lease	Operating lease refers to a contractual arrangement giving the lessee temporary use of the property with continued ownership of the property by the lessor. Accounted for as a rental.
Presentment	A demand for acceptance or payment of a negotiable instrument made on the maker, acceptor, drawee, or other payor by or on behalf of the holder is a presentment.
Depreciate	A nation's currency is said to depreciate when exchange rates change so that a unit of its currency can buy fewer units of foreign currency.
Depreciation	Depreciation is an accounting and finance term for the method of attributing the cost of an asset across the useful life of the asset. Depreciation is a reduction in the value of a currency in floating exchange rate.
Financial institution	A financial institution acts as an agent that provides financial services for its clients. Financial institutions generally fall under financial regulation from a government authority.
Ford	Ford is an American company that manufactures and sells automobiles worldwide. Ford introduced methods for large-scale manufacturing of cars, and large-scale management of an industrial workforce, especially elaborately engineered manufacturing sequences typified by the moving assembly lines.
Residual value	Residual value is one of the constituents of a leasing calculus or operation. It describes the future value of a good in terms of percentage of depreciation of its initial value.
Residual	Residual payments can refer to an ongoing stream of payments in respect of the completion of past achievements.
Negotiation	Negotiation is the process whereby interested parties resolve disputes, agree upon courses of action, bargain for individual or collective advantage, and/or attempt to craft outcomes which serve their mutual interests.

Credit risk	The risk of loss due to a counterparty defaulting on a contract, or more generally the risk of loss due to some "credit event" is called credit risk.
General Electric	In 1876, Thomas Alva Edison opened a new laboratory in Menlo Park, New Jersey. Out of the laboratory was to come perhaps the most famous invention of all—a successful development of the incandescent electric lamp. By 1890, Edison had organized his various businesses into the Edison General Electric Company.
Broker	In commerce, a broker is a party that mediates between a buyer and a seller. A broker who also acts as a seller or as a buyer becomes a principal party to the deal.
Users	Users refer to people in the organization who actually use the product or service purchased by the buying center.
Deductible	The dollar sum of costs that an insured individual must pay before the insurer begins to pay is called deductible.
Business opportunity	A business opportunity involves the sale or lease of any product, service, equipment, etc. that will enable the purchaser-licensee to begin a business
Layout	Layout refers to the physical arrangement of the various parts of an advertisement including the headline, subheads, illustrations, body copy, and any identifying marks.
Liquidity	Liquidity refers to the capacity to turn assets into cash, or the amount of assets in a portfolio that have that capacity.
Price competition	Price competition is where a company tries to distinguish its product or service from competing products on the basis of low price.
Regulation	Regulation refers to restrictions state and federal laws place on business with regard to the conduct of its activities.
Leverage	Leverage is using given resources in such a way that the potential positive or negative outcome is magnified. In finance, this generally refers to borrowing.
Operating profit	Operating profit is a measure of a company's earning power from ongoing operations, equal to earnings before the deduction of interest payments and income taxes.
Marketing	Promoting and selling products or services to customers, or prospective customers, is referred to as marketing.
Manufacturing	Production of goods primarily by the application of labor and capital to raw materials and other intermediate inputs, in contrast to agriculture, mining, forestry, fishing, and services a manufacturing.

116

Go to **Cram101.com** for the Practice Tests for this Chapter.

Common stock	Common stock refers to the basic, normal, voting stock issued by a corporation; called residual equity because it ranks after preferred stock for dividend and liquidation distributions.
Corporation	A legal entity chartered by a state or the Federal government that is distinct and separate from the individuals who own it is a corporation. This separation gives the corporation unique powers which other legal entities lack.
Holder	A person in possession of a document of title or an instrument payable or indorsed to him, his order, or to bearer is a holder.
Stock	In financial terminology, stock is the capital raized by a corporation, through the issuance and sale of shares.
Stockholder	A stockholder is an individual or company (including a corporation) that legally owns one or more shares of stock in a joined stock company. The shareholders are the owners of a corporation. Companies listed at the stock market strive to enhance shareholder value.
Board of directors	The group of individuals elected by the stockholders of a corporation to oversee its operations is a board of directors.
Investment	Investment refers to spending for the production and accumulation of capital and additions to inventories. In a financial sense, buying an asset with the expectation of making a return.
Equity	Equity is the name given to the set of legal principles, in countries following the English common law tradition, which supplement strict rules of law where their application would operate harshly, so as to achieve what is sometimes referred to as "natural justice."
Bond	Bond refers to a debt instrument, issued by a borrower and promising a specified stream of payments to the purchaser, usually regular interest payments plus a final repayment of principal.
Dividend	Amount of corporate profits paid out for each share of stock is referred to as dividend.
Gain	In finance, gain is a profit or an increase in value of an investment such as a stock or bond. Gain is calculated by fair market value or the proceeds from the sale of the investment minus the sum of the purchase price and all costs associated with it.
Valuation	In finance, valuation is the process of estimating the market value of a financial asset or liability. They can be done on assets (for example, investments in marketable securities such as stocks, options, business enterprises, or intangible assets such as patents and trademarks) or on liabilities (e.g., Bonds issued by a company).
Cash flow	In finance, cash flow refers to the amounts of cash being received and spent by a business during a defined period of time, sometimes tied to a specific project. Most of the time they are being used to determine gaps in the liquid position of a company.
Present value	The value today of a stream of payments and/or receipts over time in the future and/or the past, converted to the present using an interest rate. If X t is the amount in period t and r the interest rate, then present value at time t=0 is V = ?T /t.
Capital gain	Capital gain refers to the gain in value that the owner of an asset experiences when the price of the asset rises, including when the currency in which the asset is denominated appreciates.
Capital	Capital generally refers to financial wealth, especially that used to start or maintain a business. In classical economics, capital is one of four factors of production, the others being land and labor and entrepreneurship.
Yield	The interest rate that equates a future value or an annuity to a given present value is a yield.

Go to **Cram101.com** for the Practice Tests for this Chapter.
And, **NEVER** highlight a book again!

Dividend yield	Dividends per share divided by market price per share are called a dividend yield. Dividend yield indicates the percentage return that a stockholder will receive on dividends alone.
Shares	Shares refer to an equity security, representing a shareholder's ownership of a corporation. Shares are one of a finite number of equal portions in the capital of a company, entitling the owner to a proportion of distributed, non-reinvested profits known as dividends and to a portion of the value of the company in case of liquidation.
Discounted cash flow	In finance, the discounted cash flow approach describes a method to value a project or an entire company. The DCF methods determine the present value of future cash flows by discounting them using the appropriate cost of capital.
Security	Security refers to a claim on the borrower future income that is sold by the borrower to the lender. A security is a type of transferable interest representing financial value.
Stock valuation	There are several methods used for stock valuation. They try to give an estimate of their fair value, by using fundamental economic criteria. This theoretical valuation has to be perfected with market criteria, as the final purpose is to determine potential market prices.
Interest payment	The payment to holders of bonds payable, calculated by multiplying the stated rate on the face of the bond by the par, or face, value of the bond. If bonds are issued at a discount or premium, the interest payment does not equal the interest expense.
Interest	In finance and economics, interest is the price paid by a borrower for the use of a lender's money. In other words, interest is the amount of paid to "rent" money for a period of time.
Default	In finance, default occurs when a debtor has not met its legal obligations according to the debt contract, e.g. it has not made a scheduled payment, or violated a covenant (condition) of the debt contract.
Deed	A deed is a legal instrument used to grant a right. The deed is best known as the method of transferring title to real estate from one person to another.
Firm	An organization that employs resources to produce a good or service for profit and owns and operates one or more plants is referred to as a firm.
Annuity	A contract to make regular payments to a person for life or for a fixed period is an annuity.
Bondholder	The individual or entity that purchases a bond, thus loaning money to the company that issued the bond is the bondholder.
Face value	The nominal or par value of an instrument as expressed on its face is referred to as the face value.
Principal	In agency law, one under whose direction an agent acts and for whose benefit that agent acts is a principal.
Market price	Market price is an economic concept with commonplace familiarity; it is the price that a good or service is offered at, or will fetch, in the marketplace; it is of interest mainly in the study of microeconomics.
Market	A market is, as defined in economics, a social arrangement that allows buyers and sellers to discover information and carry out a voluntary exchange of goods or services.
Cash inflow	Cash coming into the company as the result of a previous investment is a cash inflow.
Interest rate	The rate of return on bonds, loans, or deposits. When one speaks of 'the' interest rate, it is usually in a model where there is only one.
Contract	A contract is a "promise" or an "agreement" that is enforced or recognized by the law. In the civil law, a contract is considered to be part of the general law of obligations.

Go to **Cram101.com** for the Practice Tests for this Chapter.

Maturity	Maturity refers to the final payment date of a loan or other financial instrument, after which point no further interest or principal need be paid.
Holding	The holding is a court's determination of a matter of law based on the issue presented in the particular case. In other words: under this law, with these facts, this result.
Option	A contract that gives the purchaser the option to buy or sell the underlying financial instrument at a specified price, called the exercise price or strike price, within a specific period of time.
Intrinsic value	Intrinsic value refers to as applied to a warrant, this represents the market value of common stock minus the exercise price. The difference is then multiplied by the number of shares each warrant entitles the holder to purchase.
Industry	A group of firms that produce identical or similar products is an industry. It is also used specifically to refer to an area of economic production focused on manufacturing which involves large amounts of capital investment before any profit can be realized, also called "heavy industry".
A share	In finance the term A share has two distinct meanings, both relating to securities. The first is a designation for a 'class' of common or preferred stock. A share of common or preferred stock typically has enhanced voting rights or other benefits compared to the other forms of shares that may have been created. The equity structure, or how many types of shares are offered, is determined by the corporate charter.
Fundamental analysis	Fundamental analysis is a security or stock valuation method that uses financial and economic analysis to predict the movement of security prices such as Bond prices, but more commonly stock prices. The fundamental information that is analyzed can include a company's financial reports, and non-finanical information such as estimates of the growth of demand for competing products, industry comparisons, analysis of the effects of new regulations or demographic changes, and economy-wide changes.
Planning horizon	The length of time it takes to conceive, develop, and complete a project and to recover the cost of the project on a discounted cash flow basis is referred to as planning horizon.
Value stock	In financial terminology, a stock that appears attractive using the fundamental criteria of stock valuation because of valuable assets, particularly cash and real estate, owned by its company. A stock may be named a value stock if its earnings per share, cash per share or book value is high relative to the stock price
Holding period	The period of time during which property has been held for income tax purposes. The holding period is significant in determining whether gain or loss from the sale or exchange of a capital asset is long term or short term.
Argument	The discussion by counsel for the respective parties of their contentions on the law and the facts of the case being tried in order to aid the jury in arriving at a correct and just conclusion is called argument.
Primary market	The market for the raising of new funds as opposed to the trading of securities already in existence is called primary market.
Variable	A variable is something measured by a number; it is used to analyze what happens to other things when the size of that number changes.
Analyst	Analyst refers to a person or tool with a primary function of information analysis, generally with a more limited, practical and short term set of goals than a researcher.
Expected return	Expected return refers to the return on an asset expected over the next period.
Wall Street	Dow Jones & Company was founded in 1882 by reporters Charles Dow, Edward Jones and Charles

Go to **Cram101.com** for the Practice Tests for this Chapter.
And, **NEVER** highlight a book again!

Journal	Bergstresser. Jones converted the small Customers' Afternoon Letter into The Wall Street Journal, first published in 1889, and began delivery of the Dow Jones News Service via telegraph. The Journal featured the Jones 'Average', the first of several indexes of stock and bond prices on the New York Stock Exchange.
Journal	Book of original entry, in which transactions are recorded in a general ledger system, is referred to as a journal.
Buyer	A buyer refers to a role in the buying center with formal authority and responsibility to select the supplier and negotiate the terms of the contract.
Inputs	The inputs used by a firm or an economy are the labor, raw materials, electricity and other resources it uses to produce its outputs.
Margin	A deposit by a buyer in stocks with a seller or a stockbroker, as security to cover fluctuations in the market in reference to stocks that the buyer has purchased but for which he has not paid is a margin. Commodities are also traded on margin.
Bond valuation	Bond valuation is the process of determining the fair price of a bond. As with any security, the fair value of a bond is the present value of the stream of cash flows it is expected to generate.
Future interest	Future interest refers to an interest that will come into being at some future time. It is distinguished from a present interest, which already exists. Assume that Dan transfers securities to a newly created trust.
Profit	Profit refers to the return to the resource entrepreneurial ability; total revenue minus total cost.
Management	Management characterizes the process of leading and directing all or part of an organization, often a business, through the deployment and manipulation of resources. Early twentieth-century management writer Mary Parker Follett defined management as "the art of getting things done through people."
Earnings per share	Earnings per share refers to annual profit of the corporation divided by the number of shares outstanding.
Broker	In commerce, a broker is a party that mediates between a buyer and a seller. A broker who also acts as a seller or as a buyer becomes a principal party to the deal.
Just price	The just price is a theory of ethics in economics that attempted to set standards of fairness in transactions. With intellectual roots in ancient Greek philosophy, it was advanced by Thomas Aquinas based on an argument against usury, which in his time referred to the making of any rate of interest on loans.
Stock market	An organized marketplace in which common stocks are traded. In the United States, the largest stock market is the New York Stock Exchange, on which are traded the stocks of the largest U.S. companies.
P/E ratio	In finance, the P/E ratio of a stock is used to measure how cheap or expensive share prices are. It is probably the single most consistent red flag to excessive optimism and over-investment.
Senior management	Senior management is generally a team of individuals at the highest level of organizational management who have the day-to-day responsibilities of managing a corporation.
Points	Loan origination fees that may be deductible as interest by a buyer of property. A seller of property who pays points reduces the selling price by the amount of the points paid for the buyer.
Merger	Merger refers to the combination of two firms into a single firm.

Outside director	A member of the board of directors who is not an officer of the corporation is called outside director.
Shareholder	A shareholder is an individual or company (including a corporation) that legally owns one or more shares of stock in a joined stock company.
Enterprise	Enterprise refers to another name for a business organization. Other similar terms are business firm, sometimes simply business, sometimes simply firm, as well as company, and entity.
Corporate governance	Corporate governance is the set of processes, customs, policies, laws and institutions affecting the way a corporation is directed, administered or controlled.
Accounting	A system that collects and processes financial information about an organization and reports that information to decision makers is referred to as accounting.
Preemptive right	Preemptive right refers to a shareholder's option to purchase new issuances of shares in proportion to the shareholder's current ownership of the corporation.
Common stockholder	A person who owns common stock is referred to as common stockholder. They elect the members of the board of directors for the company, as well.
Outstanding shares	Total number of shares of stock that are owned by stockholders on any particular date is referred to as outstanding shares.
Financial statement	Financial statement refers to a summary of all the transactions that have occurred over a particular period.
Proactive	To be proactive is to act before a situation becomes a source of confrontation or crisis. It is the opposite of "retroactive," which refers to actions taken after an event.
Stock exchange	A stock exchange is a corporation or mutual organization which provides facilities for stock brokers and traders, to trade company stocks and other securities.
Disclosure	Disclosure means the giving out of information, either voluntarily or to be in compliance with legal regulations or workplace rules.
Exchange	The trade of things of value between buyer and seller so that each is better off after the trade is called the exchange.
Regulation	Regulation refers to restrictions state and federal laws place on business with regard to the conduct of its activities.
Conflict of interest	A conflict that occurs when a corporate officer or director enters into a transaction with the corporation in which he or she has a personal interest is a conflict of interest.
Committee	A long-lasting, sometimes permanent team in the organization structure created to deal with tasks that recur regularly is the committee.
Business Week	Business Week is a business magazine published by McGraw-Hill. It was first published in 1929 under the direction of Malcolm Muir, who was serving as president of the McGraw-Hill Publishing company at the time. It is considered to be the standard both in industry and among students.
Enron	Enron Corportaion's global reputation was undermined by persistent rumours of bribery and political pressure to secure contracts in Central America, South America, Africa, and the Philippines. Especially controversial was its $3 billion contract with the Maharashtra State Electricity Board in India, where it is alleged that Enron officials used political connections within the Clinton and Bush administrations to exert pressure on the board.
Charter	Charter refers to an instrument or authority from the sovereign power bestowing the right or power to do business under the corporate form of organization. Also, the organic law of a

city or town, and representing a portion of the statute law of the state.

Authority	Authority in agency law, refers to an agent's ability to affect his principal's legal relations with third parties. Also used to refer to an actor's legal power or ability to do something. In addition, sometimes used to refer to a statute, case, or other legal source that justifies a particular result.
Proxy	Proxy refers to a person who is authorized to vote the shares of another person. Also, the written authorization empowering a person to vote the shares of another person.
Proxy fight	Proxy fight is an event that may occur when opposition develops to a corporation management among its stockholders. Corporate activists may attempt to persuade shareholders to use their proxy votes to install new management for any of a variety of reasons.
Mergers and acquisitions	The phrase mergers and acquisitions refers to the aspect of corporate finance strategy and management dealing with the merging and acquiring of different companies as well as other assets. Usually mergers occur in a friendly setting where executives from the respective companies participate in a due diligence process to ensure a successful combination of all parts.
Acquisition	A company's purchase of the property and obligations of another company is an acquisition.
Residual	Residual payments can refer to an ongoing stream of payments in respect of the completion of past achievements.
Asset	An item of property, such as land, capital, money, a share in ownership, or a claim on others for future payment, such as a bond or a bank deposit is an asset.
Expense	In accounting, an expense represents an event in which an asset is used up or a liability is incurred. In terms of the accounting equation, expenses reduce owners' equity.
Residual income	Residual income is the term used to describe income received based on the production of those others who have become members of one's organization.
Retained earnings	Cumulative earnings of a company that are not distributed to the owners and are reinvested in the business are called retained earnings.
Liquidated	Damages made certain by the prior agreement of the parties are called liquidated.
Preferred stock	Stock that has specified rights over common stock is a preferred stock.
Return on investment	Return on investment refers to the return a businessperson gets on the money he and other owners invest in the firm; for example, a business that earned $100 on a $1,000 investment would have a ROI of 10 percent: 100 divided by 1000.
Perpetuity	A perpetuity is an annuity in which the periodic payments begin on a fixed date and continue indefinitely. Fixed coupon payments on permanently invested (irredeemable) sums of money are prime examples of perpetuities. Scholarships paid perpetually from an endowment fit the definition of perpetuity.
Secondary market	Secondary market refers to the market for securities that have already been issued. It is a market in which investors trade back and forth with each other.
Dividends in arrears	Dividends on cumulative preferred stock that have not been declared in prior years are called dividends in arrears.
Maturity date	The date on which the final payment on a bond is due from the bond issuer to the investor is a maturity date.
Bankruptcy	Bankruptcy is a legally declared inability or impairment of ability of an individual or organization to pay their creditors.

Go to **Cram101.com** for the Practice Tests for this Chapter.

Stock dividend	Stock dividend refers to pro rata distributions of stock or stock rights on common stock. They are usually issued in proportion to shares owned.
Deductible	The dollar sum of costs that an insured individual must pay before the insurer begins to pay is called deductible.
Appreciation	Appreciation refers to a rise in the value of a country's currency on the exchange market, relative either to a particular other currency or to a weighted average of other currencies. The currency is said to appreciate. Opposite of 'depreciation.' Appreciation can also refer to the increase in value of any asset.
Exempt	Employees who are not covered by the Fair Labor Standards Act are exempt. Exempt employees are not eligible for overtime pay.
Institutional investors	Institutional investors refers to large organizations such as pension funds, mutual funds, insurance companies, and banks that invest their own funds or the funds of others.
Microsoft	Microsoft is a multinational computer technology corporation with 2004 global annual sales of US$39.79 billion and 71,553 employees in 102 countries and regions as of July 2006. It develops, manufactures, licenses, and supports a wide range of software products for computing devices.
Technical analysis	Uses price and volume data to determine past trends, which are expected to continue into the future is called technical analysis.
Efficient market hypothesis	The application of the theory of rational expectations to financial markets is referred to as efficient market hypothesis.
Efficient market	Efficient market refers to a market in which, at a minimum, current price changes are independent of past price changes, or, more strongly, price reflects all available information.
Financial market	In economics, a financial market is a mechanism which allows people to trade money for securities or commodities such as gold or other precious metals. In general, any commodity market might be considered to be a financial market, if the usual purpose of traders is not the immediate consumption of the commodity, but rather as a means of delaying or accelerating consumption over time.
Bid	A bid price is a price offered by a buyer when he/she buys a good. In the context of stock trading on a stock exchange, the bid price is the highest price a buyer of a stock is willing to pay for a share of that given stock.
Warrant	A warrant is a security that entitles the holder to buy or sell a certain additional quantity of an underlying security at an agreed-upon price, at the holder's discretion.
Fixed price	Fixed price is a phrase used to mean that no bargaining is allowed over the price of a good or, less commonly, a service.
Estate	An estate is the totality of the legal rights, interests, entitlements and obligations attaching to property. In the context of wills and probate, it refers to the totality of the property which the deceased owned or in which some interest was held.
Stock option	A stock option is a specific type of option that uses the stock itself as an underlying instrument to determine the option's pay-off and therefore its value.
Call option	Call option refers to an option contract that provides the right to buy a security at a specified price within a certain time period.
Grant	Grant refers to an intergovernmental transfer of funds . Since the New Deal, state and local governments have become increasingly dependent upon federal grants for an almost infinite

	variety of programs.
Financial assets	Financial assets refer to monetary claims or obligations by one party against another party. Examples are bonds, mortgages, bank loans, and equities.
Derivative	A derivative is a generic term for specific types of investments from which payoffs over time are derived from the performance of assets (such as commodities, shares or bonds), interest rates, exchange rates, or indices (such as a stock market index, consumer price index (CPI) or an index of weather conditions).
Leverage	Leverage is using given resources in such a way that the potential positive or negative outcome is magnified. In finance, this generally refers to borrowing.
Strike price	The strike price is a key variable in a derivatives contract between two parties. Where the contract requires delivery of the underlying instrument, the trade will be at the strike price, regardless of the spot price of the underlying at that time.
Strike	The withholding of labor services by an organized group of workers is referred to as a strike.
Slope	The slope of a line in the plane containing the x and y axes is generally represented by the letter m, and is defined as the change in the y coordinate divided by the corresponding change in the x coordinate, between two distinct points on the line.
Premium	Premium refers to the fee charged by an insurance company for an insurance policy. The rate of losses must be relatively predictable: In order to set the premium (prices) insurers must be able to estimate them accurately.
Volatility	Volatility refers to the extent to which an economic variable, such as a price or an exchange rate, moves up and down over time.
Mistake	In contract law a mistake is incorrect understanding by one or more parties to a contract and may be used as grounds to invalidate the agreement. Common law has identified three different types of mistake in contract: unilateral mistake, mutual mistake, and common mistake.
Purchasing	Purchasing refers to the function in a firm that searches for quality material resources, finds the best suppliers, and negotiates the best price for goods and services.
Put option	An option contract that provides the right to sell a security at a specified price within a specified period of time is a put option.
Exercise price	Exercise price refers to the price at which the purchaser of an option has the right to buy or sell the underlying financial instrument. Also known as the strike price.
Instrument	Instrument refers to an economic variable that is controlled by policy makers and can be used to influence other variables, called targets. Examples are monetary and fiscal policies used to achieve external and internal balance.
Lender	Suppliers and financial institutions that lend money to companies is referred to as a lender.
Political economy	Early name for the discipline of economics. A field within economics encompassing several alternatives to neoclassical economics, including Marxist economics. Also called radical political economy.
Liability	A liability is a present obligation of the enterprise arizing from past events, the settlement of which is expected to result in an outflow from the enterprise of resources embodying economic benefits.
Economy	The income, expenditures, and resources that affect the cost of running a business and household are called an economy.
Market value	Market value refers to the price of an asset agreed on between a willing buyer and a willing

133

seller; the price an asset could demand if it is sold on the open market.

Employee stock option	An employee stock option is a stock option for the company's own stock that is often offered to upper-level employees as part of the executive compenzation package, especially by American corporations. An employee stock option is identical to a call option on the company's stock, with some extra restrictions.
Innovation	Innovation refers to the first commercially successful introduction of a new product, the use of a new method of production, or the creation of a new form of business organization.
Senior executive	Senior executive means a chief executive officer, chief operating officer, chief financial officer and anyone in charge of a principal business unit or function.
Incentive	An incentive is any factor (financial or non-financial) that provides a motive for a particular course of action, or counts as a reason for preferring one choice to the alternatives.
Pension fund	Amounts of money put aside by corporations, nonprofit organizations, or unions to cover part of the financial needs of members when they retire is a pension fund.
Pension	A pension is a steady income given to a person (usually after retirement). Pensions are typically payments made in the form of a guaranteed annuity to a retired or disabled employee.
Fund	Independent accounting entity with a self-balancing set of accounts segregated for the purposes of carrying on specific activities is referred to as a fund.
Audit	An examination of the financial reports to ensure that they represent what they claim and conform with generally accepted accounting principles is referred to as audit.
Conglomerate	A conglomerate is a large company that consists of divisions of often seemingly unrelated businesses.
Arthur Andersen	Arthur Andersen was once one of the Big Five accounting firms, performing auditing, tax, and consulting services for large corporations. In 2002 the firm voluntarily surrendered its licenses to practice as Certified Public Accountants in the U.S. pending the result of prosecution by the U.S. Department of Justice over the firm's handling of the auditing of Enron.
Deception	According to the Federal Trade Commission, a misrepresentation, omission, or practice that is likely to mislead the consumer acting reasonably in the circumstances to the consumer's detriment is referred to as deception.
Trend	Trend refers to the long-term movement of an economic variable, such as its average rate of increase or decrease over enough years to encompass several business cycles.
Business analysis	Business analysis is a structured methodology that is focused on completely understanding the customer's needs, identifying how best to meet those needs, and then "reinventing" the stream of processes to meet those needs.
Layoff	A layoff is the termination of an employee or (more commonly) a group of employees for business reasons, such as the decision that certain positions are no longer necessary.
Competitor	Other organizations in the same industry or type of business that provide a good or service to the same set of customers is referred to as a competitor.
Alpha	Alpha is a risk-adjusted measure of the so-called "excess return" on an investment. It is a common measure of assessing active manager's performance as it is the return in excess of a benchmark index or "risk-free" investment.
Brokerage firm	A company that conducts various aspects of securities trading, analysis and advisory services

	is a brokerage firm.
Downturn	A decline in a stock market or economic cycle is a downturn.
Abstraction	Abstraction is a model building simplification process that refers to retaining only the essential facts, and the elimination of irrelevant and non-economic facts, to obtain an economic principle.
Rate of return	A rate of return is a comparison of the money earned (or lost) on an investment to the amount of money invested.
Required rate of return	Required rate of return refers to the rate of return that investors demand from an investment to compensate them for the amount of risk involved.
Revenue	Revenue is a U.S. business term for the amount of money that a company receives from its activities, mostly from sales of products and/or services to customers.

Portfolio theory	Portfolio theory refers to an economic theory that describes how rational investors allocate their wealth among different financial assets-that is, how they put their wealth into a 'portfolio.'
Portfolio	In finance, a portfolio is a collection of investments held by an institution or a private individual. Holding but not always a portfolio is part of an investment and risk-limiting strategy called diversification. By owning several assets, certain types of risk (in particular specific risk) can be reduced.
Investment	Investment refers to spending for the production and accumulation of capital and additions to inventories. In a financial sense, buying an asset with the expectation of making a return.
Bond	Bond refers to a debt instrument, issued by a borrower and promising a specified stream of payments to the purchaser, usually regular interest payments plus a final repayment of principal.
Equity investment	Equity investment generally refers to the buying and holding of shares of stock on a stock market by individuals and funds in anticipation of income from dividends and capital gain as the value of the stock rises.
Equity	Equity is the name given to the set of legal principles, in countries following the English common law tradition, which supplement strict rules of law where their application would operate harshly, so as to achieve what is sometimes referred to as "natural justice."
Long run	In economic models, the long run time frame assumes no fixed factors of production. Firms can enter or leave the marketplace, and the cost (and availability) of land, labor, raw materials, and capital goods can be assumed to vary.
Stock	In financial terminology, stock is the capital raized by a corporation, through the issuance and sale of shares.
Time horizon	A time horizon is a fixed point of time in the future at which point certain processes will be evaluated or assumed to end. It is necessary in an accounting, finance or risk management regime to assign such a fixed horizon time so that alternatives can be evaluated for performance over the same period of time.
Rate of return	A rate of return is a comparison of the money earned (or lost) on an investment to the amount of money invested.
Asset	An item of property, such as land, capital, money, a share in ownership, or a claim on others for future payment, such as a bond or a bank deposit is an asset.
Discounted cash flow	In finance, the discounted cash flow approach describes a method to value a project or an entire company. The DCF methods determine the present value of future cash flows by discounting them using the appropriate cost of capital.
Cash flow	In finance, cash flow refers to the amounts of cash being received and spent by a business during a defined period of time, sometimes tied to a specific project. Most of the time they are being used to determine gaps in the liquid position of a company.
Security	Security refers to a claim on the borrower future income that is sold by the borrower to the lender. A security is a type of transferable interest representing financial value.
Business opportunity	A business opportunity involves the sale or lease of any product, service, equipment, etc. that will enable the purchaser-licensee to begin a business
Profit	Profit refers to the return to the resource entrepreneurial ability; total revenue minus total cost.
Industry	A group of firms that produce identical or similar products is an industry. It is also used specifically to refer to an area of economic production focused on manufacturing which

involves large amounts of capital investment before any profit can be realized, also called "heavy industry".

Discount	The difference between the face value of a bond and its selling price, when a bond is sold for less than its face value it's referred to as a discount.
Interest	In finance and economics, interest is the price paid by a borrower for the use of a lender's money. In other words, interest is the amount of paid to "rent" money for a period of time.
Points	Loan origination fees that may be deductible as interest by a buyer of property. A seller of property who pays points reduces the selling price by the amount of the points paid for the buyer.
Interest rate	The rate of return on bonds, loans, or deposits. When one speaks of 'the' interest rate, it is usually in a model where there is only one.
Capital gain	Capital gain refers to the gain in value that the owner of an asset experiences when the price of the asset rises, including when the currency in which the asset is denominated appreciates.
Dividend	Amount of corporate profits paid out for each share of stock is referred to as dividend.
Capital	Capital generally refers to financial wealth, especially that used to start or maintain a business. In classical economics, capital is one of four factors of production, the others being land and labor and entrepreneurship.
Gain	In finance, gain is a profit or an increase in value of an investment such as a stock or bond. Gain is calculated by fair market value or the proceeds from the sale of the investment minus the sum of the purchase price and all costs associated with it.
Expected return	Expected return refers to the return on an asset expected over the next period.
Perceived risk	The anxieties felt because the consumer cannot anticipate the outcomes of a purchase but believes that there may be negative consequences is called a perceived risk.
Context	The effect of the background under which a message often takes on more and richer meaning is a context. Context is especially important in cross-cultural interactions because some cultures are said to be high context or low context.
Federal government	Federal government refers to the government of the United States, as distinct from the state and local governments.
Risk aversion	Risk aversion is the reluctance of a person to accept a bargain with an uncertain payoff rather than another bargain with a more certain but possibly lower expected payoff.
Random variable	Random variable refers to an economic or statistical variable that takes on multiple values, each with some probability that is specified by a probability distribution.
Variable	A variable is something measured by a number; it is used to analyze what happens to other things when the size of that number changes.
Distribution	Distribution in economics, the manner in which total output and income is distributed among individuals or factors.
Probability distribution	A specification of the probabilities for each possible value of a random variable is called probability distribution.
Expected value	A representative value from a probability distribution arrived at by multiplying each outcome by the associated probability and summing up the values is called the expected value.
Peak	Peak refers to the point in the business cycle when an economic expansion reaches its highest point before turning down. Contrasts with trough.

Go to **Cram101.com** for the Practice Tests for this Chapter.

Weighted average	The weighted average unit cost of the goods available for sale for both cost of goods sold and ending inventory.
Standard deviation	A measure of the spread or dispersion of a series of numbers around the expected value is the standard deviation. The standard deviation tells us how well the expected value represents a series of values.
Variance	Variance refers to a measure of how much an economic or statistical variable varies across values or observations. Its calculation is the same as that of the covariance, being the covariance of the variable with itself.
Financial market	In economics, a financial market is a mechanism which allows people to trade money for securities or commodities such as gold or other precious metals. In general, any commodity market might be considered to be a financial market, if the usual purpose of traders is not the immediate consumption of the commodity, but rather as a means of delaying or accelerating consumption over time.
Market	A market is, as defined in economics, a social arrangement that allows buyers and sellers to discover information and carry out a voluntary exchange of goods or services.
Shares	Shares refer to an equity security, representing a shareholder's ownership of a corporation. Shares are one of a finite number of equal portions in the capital of a company, entitling the owner to a proportion of distributed, non-reinvested profits known as dividends and to a portion of the value of the company in case of liquidation.
Public utility	A firm that produces an essential good or service, has obtained from a government the right to be the sole supplier of the good or service in the area, and is regulated by that government to prevent the abuse of its monopoly power is a public utility.
Utility	Utility refers to the want-satisfying power of a good or service; the satisfaction or pleasure a consumer obtains from the consumption of a good or service.
Stockholder	A stockholder is an individual or company (including a corporation) that legally owns one or more shares of stock in a joined stock company. The shareholders are the owners of a corporation. Companies listed at the stock market strive to enhance shareholder value.
Broker	In commerce, a broker is a party that mediates between a buyer and a seller. A broker who also acts as a seller or as a buyer becomes a principal party to the deal.
Firm	An organization that employs resources to produce a good or service for profit and owns and operates one or more plants is referred to as a firm.
Option	A contract that gives the purchaser the option to buy or sell the underlying financial instrument at a specified price, called the exercise price or strike price, within a specific period of time.
Regulation	Regulation refers to restrictions state and federal laws place on business with regard to the conduct of its activities.
Yield	The interest rate that equates a future value or an annuity to a given present value is a yield.
Inflation	An increase in the overall price level of an economy, usually as measured by the CPI or by the implicit price deflator is called inflation.
Labor	People's physical and mental talents and efforts that are used to help produce goods and services are called labor.
Monopoly	A monopoly is defined as a persistent market situation where there is only one provider of a kind of product or service.

Systematic risk	Movements in a stock portfolio's value that are attributable to macroeconomic forces affecting all firms in an economy, rather than factors specific to an individual firm are referred to as systematic risk.
Market risk	Market risk is the risk that the value of an investment will decrease due to moves in market factors.
Management	Management characterizes the process of leading and directing all or part of an organization, often a business, through the deployment and manipulation of resources. Early twentieth-century management writer Mary Parker Follett defined management as "the art of getting things done through people."
Strike	The withholding of labor services by an organized group of workers is referred to as a strike.
Fund	Independent accounting entity with a self-balancing set of accounts segregated for the purposes of carrying on specific activities is referred to as a fund.
Diversified portfolio	Diversified portfolio refers to a portfolio that includes a variety of assets whose prices are not likely all to change together. In international economics, this usually means holding assets denominated in different currencies.
Diversification	Investing in a collection of assets whose returns do not always move together, with the result that overall risk is lower than for individual assets is referred to as diversification.
Forming	The first stage of team development, where the team is formed and the objectives for the team are set is referred to as forming.
Positively correlated	Positively correlated refers to values or amounts of two items that move in the same direction. In accounting and finance, the amount of risk and the amount of return on an investment move in the same direction.
Modern portfolio theory	Modern portfolio theory proposes how rational investors will use diversification to optimize their portfolios, and how an asset should be priced given its risk relative to the market as a whole.
Beta coefficient	The Beta coefficient (sensitivity of the asset returns to market returns, relative volatility), is a key parameter in the Capital asset pricing model. It can also be defined as the risk of the stock to a diversified portfolio.
Scatter diagram	Plots the values of one variable against values of another variable for a specific time interval is a scatter diagram.
Regression line	A line fit to a set of data points using least-squares regression is referred to as a regression line.
Slope	The slope of a line in the plane containing the x and y axes is generally represented by the letter m, and is defined as the change in the y coordinate divided by the corresponding change in the x coordinate, between two distinct points on the line.
Securities market	The securities market is the market for securities, where companies and the government can raise long-term funds.
Stock market	An organized marketplace in which common stocks are traded. In the United States, the largest stock market is the New York Stock Exchange, on which are traded the stocks of the largest U.S. companies.
Supply	Supply is the aggregate amount of any material good that can be called into being at a certain price point; it comprises one half of the equation of supply and demand. In classical economic theory, a curve representing supply is one of the factors that produce price.

Go to **Cram101.com** for the Practice Tests for this Chapter.

145

Budget	Budget refers to an account, usually for a year, of the planned expenditures and the expected receipts of an entity. For a government, the receipts are tax revenues.
Contract	A contract is a "promise" or an "agreement" that is enforced or recognized by the law. In the civil law, a contract is considered to be part of the general law of obligations.
Production	The creation of finished goods and services using the factors of production: land, labor, capital, entrepreneurship, and knowledge.
Volatility	Volatility refers to the extent to which an economic variable, such as a price or an exchange rate, moves up and down over time.
Regression analysis	Regression analysis refers to the statistical technique of finding a straight line that approximates the information in a group of data points. Used throughout empirical economics, including both international trade and finance.
Manufacturing	Production of goods primarily by the application of labor and capital to raw materials and other intermediate inputs, in contrast to agriculture, mining, forestry, fishing, and services a manufacturing.
Technology	The body of knowledge and techniques that can be used to combine economic resources to produce goods and services is called technology.
Service	Service refers to a "non tangible product" that is not embodied in a physical good and that typically effects some change in another product, person, or institution. Contrasts with good.
Bell Labs	In the early 1940s, the photovoltaic cell was developed by Russell Ohl. In 1947, the transistor, probably the most important invention developed by Bell Labs, was invented by John Bardeen, William Bradford Shockley, and Walter Houser Brattain (all of whom subsequently won the Nobel Prize in Physics in 1956).
Lucent Technologies	Lucent Technologies is a company composed of what was formerly AT&T Technologies, which included Western Electric and Bell Labs. It was spun-off from AT&T on September 30, 1996. On April 2, 2006, they announced a merger with its French competitor, Alcatel. The combined company has revenues of approximately $25 billion U.S. based on 2005 calendar results.
Operation	A standardized method or technique that is performed repetitively, often on different materials resulting in different finished goods is called an operation.
Enterprise	Enterprise refers to another name for a business organization. Other similar terms are business firm, sometimes simply business, sometimes simply firm, as well as company, and entity.
Economics	The social science dealing with the use of scarce resources to obtain the maximum satisfaction of society's virtually unlimited economic wants is an economics.
Required rate of return	Required rate of return refers to the rate of return that investors demand from an investment to compensate them for the amount of risk involved.
Stock valuation	There are several methods used for stock valuation. They try to give an estimate of their fair value, by using fundamental economic criteria. This theoretical valuation has to be perfected with market criteria, as the final purpose is to determine potential market prices.
Valuation	In finance, valuation is the process of estimating the market value of a financial asset or liability. They can be done on assets (for example, investments in marketable securities such as stocks, options, business enterprises, or intangible assets such as patents and trademarks) or on liabilities (e.g., Bonds issued by a company).
Risk premium	In finance, the risk premium can be the expected rate of return above the risk-free interest rate.

Premium	Premium refers to the fee charged by an insurance company for an insurance policy. The rate of losses must be relatively predictable: In order to set the premium (prices) insurers must be able to estimate them accurately.
Treasury bills	Short-term obligations of the federal government are treasury bills. They are like zero coupon bonds in that they do not pay interest prior to maturity; instead they are sold at a discount of the par value to create a positive yield to maturity.
Allowance	Reduction in the selling price of goods extended to the buyer because the goods are defective or of lower quality than the buyer ordered and to encourage a buyer to keep merchandise that would otherwise be returned is the allowance.
Security market line	A line or equation that depicts the risk-related return of a security based on a risk-free rate plus a market premium related to the beta coefficient of the security is referred to as the security market line.
Market risk premium	Market risk premium refers to a premium over and above the risk-free rate. It is represented by the difference between the market return and the risk-free rate, and it may be multiplied by the beta coefficient to determine the additional risk-adjusted return on a security.
Expected rate of return	Expected rate of return refers to the increase in profit a firm anticipates it will obtain by purchasing capital ; expressed as a percentage of the total cost of the investment activity.
Holding	The holding is a court's determination of a matter of law based on the issue presented in the particular case. In other words: under this law, with these facts, this result.
Buyer	A buyer refers to a role in the buying center with formal authority and responsibility to select the supplier and negotiate the terms of the contract.
Market price	Market price is an economic concept with commonplace familiarity; it is the price that a good or service is offered at, or will fetch, in the marketplace; it is of interest mainly in the study of microeconomics.
Capital asset pricing model	The capital asset pricing model is used in finance to determine a theoretically appropriate required rate of return (and thus the price if expected cash flows can be estimated) of an asset, if that asset is to be added to an already well-diversified portfolio, given that asset's non-diversifiable risk.
Capital asset	In accounting, a capital asset is an asset that is recorded as property that creates more property, e.g. a factory that creates shoes, or a forest that yields a quantity of wood.
Inputs	The inputs used by a firm or an economy are the labor, raw materials, electricity and other resources it uses to produce its outputs.
Policy	Similar to a script in that a policy can be a less than completely rational decision-making method. Involves the use of a pre-existing set of decision steps for any problem that presents itself.
Shareholder	A shareholder is an individual or company (including a corporation) that legally owns one or more shares of stock in a joined stock company.
Argument	The discussion by counsel for the respective parties of their contentions on the law and the facts of the case being tried in order to aid the jury in arriving at a correct and just conclusion is called argument.
Business analysis	Business analysis is a structured methodology that is focused on completely understanding the customer's needs, identifying how best to meet those needs, and then "reinventing" the stream of processes to meet those needs.
Brokerage firm	A company that conducts various aspects of securities trading, analysis and advisory services is a brokerage firm.

Go to **Cram101.com** for the Practice Tests for this Chapter.

Analyst	Analyst refers to a person or tool with a primary function of information analysis, generally with a more limited, practical and short term set of goals than a researcher.
Present value	The value today of a stream of payments and/or receipts over time in the future and/or the past, converted to the present using an interest rate. If X t is the amount in period t and r the interest rate, then present value at time t=0 is V = ?T /t.
Actual investment	Actual investment refers to the amount that firms do invest; equal to planned investment plus unplanned investment. Unplanned investment may be positive or negative.
Economic environment	The economic environment represents the external conditions under which people are engaged in, and benefit from, economic activity. It includes aspects of economic status, paid employment, and finances.
Corporation	A legal entity chartered by a state or the Federal government that is distinct and separate from the individuals who own it is a corporation. This separation gives the corporation unique powers which other legal entities lack.
Intrinsic value	Intrinsic value refers to as applied to a warrant, this represents the market value of common stock minus the exercise price. The difference is then multiplied by the number of shares each warrant entitles the holder to purchase.
Acquisition	A company's purchase of the property and obligations of another company is an acquisition.
Recession	A significant decline in economic activity. In the U.S., recession is approximately defined as two successive quarters of falling GDP, as judged by NBER.
General Motors	General Motors is the world's largest automaker. Founded in 1908, today it employs about 327,000 people around the world. With global headquarters in Detroit, it manufactures its cars and trucks in 33 countries.
Microsoft	Microsoft is a multinational computer technology corporation with 2004 global annual sales of US$39.79 billion and 71,553 employees in 102 countries and regions as of July 2006. It develops, manufactures, licenses, and supports a wide range of software products for computing devices.
Starbucks	Although it has endured much criticism for its purported monopoly on the global coffee-bean market, Starbucks purchases only 3% of the coffee beans grown worldwide. In 2000 the company introduced a line of fair trade products and now offers three options for socially conscious coffee drinkers. According to Starbucks, they purchased 4.8 million pounds of Certified Fair Trade coffee in fiscal year 2004 and 11.5 million pounds in 2005.

150

Go to **Cram101.com** for the Practice Tests for this Chapter.

Inventory	Tangible property held for sale in the normal course of business or used in producing goods or services for sale is an inventory.
Expense	In accounting, an expense represents an event in which an asset is used up or a liability is incurred. In terms of the accounting equation, expenses reduce owners' equity.
Fund	Independent accounting entity with a self-balancing set of accounts segregated for the purposes of carrying on specific activities is referred to as a fund.
Firm	An organization that employs resources to produce a good or service for profit and owns and operates one or more plants is referred to as a firm.
Capital	Capital generally refers to financial wealth, especially that used to start or maintain a business. In classical economics, capital is one of four factors of production, the others being land and labor and entrepreneurship.
Capital budgeting	Capital budgeting is the planning process used to determine a firm's long term investments such as new machinery, replacement machinery, new plants, new products, and research and development projects.
Consideration	Consideration in contract law, a basic requirement for an enforceable agreement under traditional contract principles, defined in this text as legal value, bargained for and given in exchange for an act or promise. In corporation law, cash or property contributed to a corporation in exchange for shares, or a promise to contribute such cash or property.
Investment	Investment refers to spending for the production and accumulation of capital and additions to inventories. In a financial sense, buying an asset with the expectation of making a return.
Increase in demand	Increase in demand refers to an increase in the quantity demanded of a good or service at every price; a shift of the demand curve to the right.
Context	The effect of the background under which a message often takes on more and richer meaning is a context. Context is especially important in cross-cultural interactions because some cultures are said to be high context or low context.
Management	Management characterizes the process of leading and directing all or part of an organization, often a business, through the deployment and manipulation of resources. Early twentieth-century management writer Mary Parker Follett defined management as "the art of getting things done through people."
Personnel	A collective term for all of the employees of an organization. Personnel is also commonly used to refer to the personnel management function or the organizational unit responsible for administering personnel programs.
Cash flow	In finance, cash flow refers to the amounts of cash being received and spent by a business during a defined period of time, sometimes tied to a specific project. Most of the time they are being used to determine gaps in the liquid position of a company.
Return on investment	Return on investment refers to the return a businessperson gets on the money he and other owners invest in the firm; for example, a business that earned $100 on a $1,000 investment would have a ROI of 10 percent: 100 divided by 1000.
Time value of money	Time value of money is the concept that the value of money varies depending on the timing of the cash flows, given any interest rate greater than zero.
Cost of capital	Cost of capital refers to the percentage cost of funds used for acquiring resources for an organization, typically a weighted average of the firms cost of equity and cost of debt.
Value of money	Value of money refers to the quantity of goods and services for which a unit of money can be exchanged; the purchasing power of a unit of money; the reciprocal of the price level.

Go to **Cram101.com** for the Practice Tests for this Chapter.

Equity	Equity is the name given to the set of legal principles, in countries following the English common law tradition, which supplement strict rules of law where their application would operate harshly, so as to achieve what is sometimes referred to as "natural justice."
Supply	Supply is the aggregate amount of any material good that can be called into being at a certain price point; it comprises one half of the equation of supply and demand. In classical economic theory, a curve representing supply is one of the factors that produce price.
Stockholder	A stockholder is an individual or company (including a corporation) that legally owns one or more shares of stock in a joined stock company. The shareholders are the owners of a corporation. Companies listed at the stock market strive to enhance shareholder value.
Creditor	A person to whom a debt or legal obligation is owed, and who has the right to enforce payment of that debt or obligation is referred to as creditor.
Interest	In finance and economics, interest is the price paid by a borrower for the use of a lender's money. In other words, interest is the amount of paid to "rent" money for a period of time.
Weighted average	The weighted average unit cost of the goods available for sale for both cost of goods sold and ending inventory.
Weighted average cost of capital	Weighted average cost of capital refers to the computed cost of capital determined by multiplying the cost of each item in the optimal capital structure by its weighted representation in the overall capital structure and summing up the results.
Average cost	Average cost is equal to total cost divided by the number of goods produced (Quantity-Q). It is also equal to the sum of average variable costs (total variable costs divided by Q) plus average fixed costs (total fixed costs divided by Q).
Decision rule	Decision rule refers to a statement that tells a decision maker which alternative to choose based on the characteristics of the decision situation.
Payback period	The amount of time required for a project's after-tax cash inflows to accumulate to an amount that covers the initial investment is a payback period.
Payback	A value that indicates the time period required to recoup an initial investment is a payback. The payback does not include the time-value-of-money concept.
Cash outflow	Cash flowing out of the business from all sources over a period of time is cash outflow.
Recovery	Characterized by rizing output, falling unemployment, rizing profits, and increasing economic activity following a decline is a recovery.
Policy	Similar to a script in that a policy can be a less than completely rational decision-making method. Involves the use of a pre-existing set of decision steps for any problem that presents itself.
Cash inflow	Cash coming into the company as the result of a previous investment is a cash inflow.
Screening	Screening in economics refers to a strategy of combating adverse selection, one of the potential decision-making complications in cases of asymmetric information.
Present value	The value today of a stream of payments and/or receipts over time in the future and/or the past, converted to the present using an interest rate. If X t is the amount in period t and r the interest rate, then present value at time t=0 is V = ?T /t.
Net present value	Net present value is a standard method in finance of capital budgeting – the planning of long-term investments. Using this method a potential investment project should be undertaken if the present value of all cash inflows minus the present value of all cash outflows (which equals the net present value) is greater than zero.
Economics	The social science dealing with the use of scarce resources to obtain the maximum

satisfaction of society's virtually unlimited economic wants is an economics.

Interest rate	The rate of return on bonds, loans, or deposits. When one speaks of 'the' interest rate, it is usually in a model where there is only one.
Shareholder	A shareholder is an individual or company (including a corporation) that legally owns one or more shares of stock in a joined stock company.
Alpha	Alpha is a risk-adjusted measure of the so-called "excess return" on an investment. It is a common measure of assessing active manager's performance as it is the return in excess of a benchmark index or "risk-free" investment.
Diversification	Investing in a collection of assets whose returns do not always move together, with the result that overall risk is lower than for individual assets is referred to as diversification.
Manufacturing	Production of goods primarily by the application of labor and capital to raw materials and other intermediate inputs, in contrast to agriculture, mining, forestry, fishing, and services a manufacturing.
Technology	The body of knowledge and techniques that can be used to combine economic resources to produce goods and services is called technology.
Marketing	Promoting and selling products or services to customers, or prospective customers, is referred to as marketing.
Analyst	Analyst refers to a person or tool with a primary function of information analysis, generally with a more limited, practical and short term set of goals than a researcher.
Argument	The discussion by counsel for the respective parties of their contentions on the law and the facts of the case being tried in order to aid the jury in arriving at a correct and just conclusion is called argument.
Extension	Extension refers to an out-of-court settlement in which creditors agree to allow the firm more time to meet its financial obligations. A new repayment schedule will be developed, subject to the acceptance of creditors.
Rate of return	A rate of return is a comparison of the money earned (or lost) on an investment to the amount of money invested.
Internal rate of return	Internal rate of return refers to a discounted cash flow method for evaluating capital budgeting projects. The internal rate of return is a discount rate that makes the present value of the cash inflows equal to the present value of the cash outflows.
Asset	An item of property, such as land, capital, money, a share in ownership, or a claim on others for future payment, such as a bond or a bank deposit is an asset.
Dividend	Amount of corporate profits paid out for each share of stock is referred to as dividend.
Analogy	Analogy is either the cognitive process of transferring information from a particular subject to another particular subject (the target), or a linguistic expression corresponding to such a process. In a narrower sense, analogy is an inference or an argument from a particular to another particular, as opposed to deduction, induction, and abduction, where at least one of the premises or the conclusion is general.
Yield	The interest rate that equates a future value or an annuity to a given present value is a yield.
Bond	Bond refers to a debt instrument, issued by a borrower and promising a specified stream of payments to the purchaser, usually regular interest payments plus a final repayment of principal.

Interest payment	The payment to holders of bonds payable, calculated by multiplying the stated rate on the face of the bond by the par, or face, value of the bond. If bonds are issued at a discount or premium, the interest payment does not equal the interest expense.
Purchasing	Purchasing refers to the function in a firm that searches for quality material resources, finds the best suppliers, and negotiates the best price for goods and services.
Principal	In agency law, one under whose direction an agent acts and for whose benefit that agent acts is a principal.
Gain	In finance, gain is a profit or an increase in value of an investment such as a stock or bond. Gain is calculated by fair market value or the proceeds from the sale of the investment minus the sum of the purchase price and all costs associated with it.
Variable	A variable is something measured by a number; it is used to analyze what happens to other things when the size of that number changes.
Trial	An examination before a competent tribunal, according to the law of the land, of the facts or law put in issue in a cause, for the purpose of determining such issue is a trial. When the court hears and determines any issue of fact or law for the purpose of determining the rights of the parties, it may be considered a trial.
Discount rate	Discount rate refers to the rate, per year, at which future values are diminished to make them comparable to values in the present. Can be either subjective or objective .
Discount	The difference between the face value of a bond and its selling price, when a bond is sold for less than its face value it's referred to as a discount.
Slope	The slope of a line in the plane containing the x and y axes is generally represented by the letter m, and is defined as the change in the y coordinate divided by the corresponding change in the x coordinate, between two distinct points on the line.
Points	Loan origination fees that may be deductible as interest by a buyer of property. A seller of property who pays points reduces the selling price by the amount of the points paid for the buyer.
Reinvestment assumption	Reinvestment assumption refers to an assumption that is made concerning the rate of return that can be earned on the cash flows generated by capital budgeting projects. The NPV method assumes the rate of reinvestment to be the cost of capital, while the IRR method assumes the rate to be the actual internal rate of return.
Net present value method	Capital budgeting DCF method that calculates the expected monetary gain or loss from a project by discounting all expected future cash inflows and outflows to the present point in time, using the required rate of return a net present value method.
Aid	Assistance provided by countries and by international institutions such as the World Bank to developing countries in the form of monetary grants, loans at low interest rates, in kind, or a combination of these is called aid. Aid can also refer to assistance of any type rendered to benefit some group or individual.
Frequency	Frequency refers to the speed of the up and down movements of a fluctuating economic variable; that is, the number of times per unit of time that the variable completes a cycle of up and down movement.
Microsoft	Microsoft is a multinational computer technology corporation with 2004 global annual sales of US$39.79 billion and 71,553 employees in 102 countries and regions as of July 2006. It develops, manufactures, licenses, and supports a wide range of software products for computing devices.
Annuity	A contract to make regular payments to a person for life or for a fixed period is an annuity.

Present value of an annuity	The sum of the present value of a series of consecutive equal payments is called present value of an annuity.
Profitability index	The present value of a project's future cash flows, divided by the initial investment is referred to as the profitability index.
Option	A contract that gives the purchaser the option to buy or sell the underlying financial instrument at a specified price, called the exercise price or strike price, within a specific period of time.
Entrepreneur	The owner/operator. The person who organizes, manages, and assumes the risks of a firm, taking a new idea or a new product and turning it into a successful business is an entrepreneur.
Short run	Short run refers to a period of time that permits an increase or decrease in current production volume with existing capacity, but one that is too short to permit enlargement of that capacity itself (eg, the building of new plants, training of additional workers, etc.).
Disparity	Disparity refers to the regional and economic differences in a country, province, state, or continent
Time horizon	A time horizon is a fixed point of time in the future at which point certain processes will be evaluated or assumed to end. It is necessary in an accounting, finance or risk management regime to assign such a fixed horizon time so that alternatives can be evaluated for performance over the same period of time.
Drawback	Drawback refers to rebate of import duties when the imported good is re-exported or used as input to the production of an exported good.
Perpetuity	A perpetuity is an annuity in which the periodic payments begin on a fixed date and continue indefinitely. Fixed coupon payments on permanently invested (irredeemable) sums of money are prime examples of perpetuities. Scholarships paid perpetually from an endowment fit the definition of perpetuity.
Capital budget	A long-term budget that shows planned acquisition and disposal of capital assets, such as land, building, and equipment is a capital budget. Also a separate budget used by state governments for items such as new construction, major renovations, and acquisition of physical property.
Budget	Budget refers to an account, usually for a year, of the planned expenditures and the expected receipts of an entity. For a government, the receipts are tax revenues.
Rationing	Rationing is the controlled distribution of resources and scarce goods or services: it restricts how much people are allowed to buy or consume.
Capital rationing	Capital rationing occurs when a corporation has more dollars of capital budgeting projects with positive net present values than it has money to invest in them. Therefore, some projects that should be accepted are excluded because financial capital is rationed.
Financial manager	Managers who make recommendations to top executives regarding strategies for improving the financial strength of a firm are referred to as a financial manager.
Discounted cash flow	In finance, the discounted cash flow approach describes a method to value a project or an entire company. The DCF methods determine the present value of future cash flows by discounting them using the appropriate cost of capital.
Market	A market is, as defined in economics, a social arrangement that allows buyers and sellers to discover information and carry out a voluntary exchange of goods or services.
Service	Service refers to a "non tangible product" that is not embodied in a physical good and that typically effects some change in another product, person, or institution. Contrasts with

good.

Useful life

The length of service of a productive facility or piece of equipment is its useful life. The period of time during which an asset will have economic value and be usable.

Operation

A standardized method or technique that is performed repetitively, often on different materials resulting in different finished goods is called an operation.

Closing

The finalization of a real estate sales transaction that passes title to the property from the seller to the buyer is referred to as a closing. Closing is a sales term which refers to the process of making a sale. It refers to reaching the final step, which may be an exchange of money or acquiring a signature.

Industry

A group of firms that produce identical or similar products is an industry. It is also used specifically to refer to an area of economic production focused on manufacturing which involves large amounts of capital investment before any profit can be realized, also called "heavy industry".

Contract

A contract is a "promise" or an "agreement" that is enforced or recognized by the law. In the civil law, a contract is considered to be part of the general law of obligations.

Production

The creation of finished goods and services using the factors of production: land, labor, capital, entrepreneurship, and knowledge.

Quality improvement

Quality is inversely proportional to variability thus quality Improvement is the reduction of variability in products and processes.

Warranty

An obligation of a company to replace defective goods or correct any deficiencies in performance or quality of a product is called a warranty.

Labor

People's physical and mental talents and efforts that are used to help produce goods and services are called labor.

163

Capital budgeting	Capital budgeting is the planning process used to determine a firm's long term investments such as new machinery, replacement machinery, new plants, new products, and research and development projects.
Cash flow	In finance, cash flow refers to the amounts of cash being received and spent by a business during a defined period of time, sometimes tied to a specific project. Most of the time they are being used to determine gaps in the liquid position of a company.
Capital	Capital generally refers to financial wealth, especially that used to start or maintain a business. In classical economics, capital is one of four factors of production, the others being land and labor and entrepreneurship.
Investment	Investment refers to spending for the production and accumulation of capital and additions to inventories. In a financial sense, buying an asset with the expectation of making a return.
Security	Security refers to a claim on the borrower future income that is sold by the borrower to the lender. A security is a type of transferable interest representing financial value.
Inputs	The inputs used by a firm or an economy are the labor, raw materials, electricity and other resources it uses to produce its outputs.
Creep	Creep is a problem in project management where the initial objectives of the project are jeopardized by a gradual increase in overall objectives as the project progresses.
Sales forecast	Sales forecast refers to the maximum total sales of a product that a firm expects to sell during a specified time period under specified environmental conditions and its own marketing efforts.
Cash inflow	Cash coming into the company as the result of a previous investment is a cash inflow.
Expense	In accounting, an expense represents an event in which an asset is used up or a liability is incurred. In terms of the accounting equation, expenses reduce owners' equity.
Asset	An item of property, such as land, capital, money, a share in ownership, or a claim on others for future payment, such as a bond or a bank deposit is an asset.
Revenue	Revenue is a U.S. business term for the amount of money that a company receives from its activities, mostly from sales of products and/or services to customers.
Cost of sales	Cost of sales refers to the total costs of goods made or purchased and sold.
Working capital	The dollar difference between total current assets and total current liabilities is called working capital.
Physical asset	A physical asset is an item of economic value that has a tangible or material existence. A physical asset usually refers to cash, equipment, inventory and properties owned by a business.
Depreciation	Depreciation is an accounting and finance term for the method of attributing the cost of an asset across the useful life of the asset. Depreciation is a reduction in the value of a currency in floating exchange rate.
Fund	Independent accounting entity with a self-balancing set of accounts segregated for the purposes of carrying on specific activities is referred to as a fund.
Salvage value	In accounting, the salvage value of an asset is its remaining value after depreciation. The estimated value of an asset at the end of its useful life.
Sunk cost	Sunk cost refers to a cost that has been incurred and cannot be recovered to any significant degree.
Opportunity cost	The cost of something in terms of opportunity foregone. The opportunity cost to a country of

Go to **Cram101.com** for the Practice Tests for this Chapter.

producing a unit more of a good, such as for export or to replace an import, is the quantity of some other good that could have been produced instead.

Market value	Market value refers to the price of an asset agreed on between a willing buyer and a willing seller; the price an asset could demand if it is sold on the open market.
Market	A market is, as defined in economics, a social arrangement that allows buyers and sellers to discover information and carry out a voluntary exchange of goods or services.
Personnel	A collective term for all of the employees of an organization. Personnel is also commonly used to refer to the personnel management function or the organizational unit responsible for administering personnel programs.
Profit	Profit refers to the return to the resource entrepreneurial ability; total revenue minus total cost.
Cash outflow	Cash flowing out of the business from all sources over a period of time is cash outflow.
Accounting	A system that collects and processes financial information about an organization and reports that information to decision makers is referred to as accounting.
Net income	Net income is equal to the income that a firm has after subtracting costs and expenses from the total revenue. Expenses will typically include tax expense.
Payables	Obligations to make future economic sacrifices, usually cash payments, are referred to as payables. Same as current liabilities.
Acquisition	A company's purchase of the property and obligations of another company is an acquisition.
Interest expense	The cost a business incurs to borrow money. With respect to bonds payable, the interest expense is calculated by multiplying the market rate of interest by the carrying value of the bonds on the date of the payment.
Interest	In finance and economics, interest is the price paid by a borrower for the use of a lender's money. In other words, interest is the amount of paid to "rent" money for a period of time.
Evaluation	The consumer's appraisal of the product or brand on important attributes is called evaluation.
Accounting profit	Total revenue minus total explicit cost is an accounting profit.
Management	Management characterizes the process of leading and directing all or part of an organization, often a business, through the deployment and manipulation of resources. Early twentieth-century management writer Mary Parker Follett defined management as "the art of getting things done through people."
Advertising	Advertising refers to paid, nonpersonal communication through various media by organizations and individuals who are in some way identified in the advertising message.
Production	The creation of finished goods and services using the factors of production: land, labor, capital, entrepreneurship, and knowledge.
Unit cost	Unit cost refers to cost computed by dividing some amount of total costs by the related number of units. Also called average cost.
Direct cost	A direct cost is a cost that can be identified specifically with a particular sponsored project, an instructional activity, or any other institutional activity, or that can be directly assigned to such activities relatively easily with a high degree of accuracy.
Inventory	Tangible property held for sale in the normal course of business or used in producing goods or services for sale is an inventory.

Go to **Cram101.com** for the Practice Tests for this Chapter.

Turnover	Turnover in a financial context refers to the rate at which a provider of goods cycles through its average inventory. Turnover in a human resources context refers to the characteristic of a given company or industry, relative to rate at which an employer gains and loses staff.
Tax credit	Allows a firm to reduce the taxes paid to the home government by the amount of taxes paid to the foreign government is referred to as tax credit.
Credit	Credit refers to a recording as positive in the balance of payments, any transaction that gives rise to a payment into the country, such as an export, the sale of an asset, or borrowing from abroad.
Marginal tax rate	The percentage of an additional dollar of earnings that goes to taxes is referred to as the marginal tax rate.
Deductible	The dollar sum of costs that an insured individual must pay before the insurer begins to pay is called deductible.
Capital gain	Capital gain refers to the gain in value that the owner of an asset experiences when the price of the asset rises, including when the currency in which the asset is denominated appreciates.
Property	Assets defined in the broadest legal sense. Property includes the unrealized receivables of a cash basis taxpayer, but not services rendered.
Gain	In finance, gain is a profit or an increase in value of an investment such as a stock or bond. Gain is calculated by fair market value or the proceeds from the sale of the investment minus the sum of the purchase price and all costs associated with it.
Corporation	A legal entity chartered by a state or the Federal government that is distinct and separate from the individuals who own it is a corporation. This separation gives the corporation unique powers which other legal entities lack.
Yield	The interest rate that equates a future value or an annuity to a given present value is a yield.
Gross margin	Gross margin is an ambiguous phrase that expresses the relationship between gross profit and sales revenue as Gross Margin = Revenue - costs of good sold.
Margin	A deposit by a buyer in stocks with a seller or a stockbroker, as security to cover fluctuations in the market in reference to stocks that the buyer has purchased but for which he has not paid is a margin. Commodities are also traded on margin.
Product line	A group of products that are physically similar or are intended for a similar market are called the product line.
Allowance	Reduction in the selling price of goods extended to the buyer because the goods are defective or of lower quality than the buyer ordered and to encourage a buyer to keep merchandise that would otherwise be returned is the allowance.
Cost of goods sold	In accounting, the cost of goods sold describes the direct expenses incurred in producing a particular good for sale, including the actual cost of materials that comprise the good, and direct labor expense in putting the good in salable condition.
Capital requirement	The capital requirement is a bank regulation, which sets a framework on how banks and depository institutions must handle their capital. The categorization of assets and capital is highly standardized so that it can be risk weighted.
Cost of capital	Cost of capital refers to the percentage cost of funds used for acquiring resources for an organization, typically a weighted average of the firms cost of equity and cost of debt.

Go to **Cram101.com** for the Practice Tests for this Chapter.

Terminal value	In finance, the terminal value of a security is the present value at a future point in time of all future cash flows. It is most often used in multi-stage discounted cash flow analysis, and allows for the limitation of cash flow projections to a several-year period.
Present value	The value today of a stream of payments and/or receipts over time in the future and/or the past, converted to the present using an interest rate. If X t is the amount in period t and r the interest rate, then present value at time t=0 is V = ?T /t.
Perpetuity	A perpetuity is an annuity in which the periodic payments begin on a fixed date and continue indefinitely. Fixed coupon payments on permanently invested (irredeemable) sums of money are prime examples of perpetuities. Scholarships paid perpetually from an endowment fit the definition of perpetuity.
Argument	The discussion by counsel for the respective parties of their contentions on the law and the facts of the case being tried in order to aid the jury in arriving at a correct and just conclusion is called argument.
Manufacturing	Production of goods primarily by the application of labor and capital to raw materials and other intermediate inputs, in contrast to agriculture, mining, forestry, fishing, and services a manufacturing.
Complaint	The pleading in a civil case in which the plaintiff states his claim and requests relief is called complaint. In the common law, it is a formal legal document that sets out the basic facts and legal reasons that the filing party (the plaintiffs) believes are sufficient to support a claim against another person, persons, entity or entities (the defendants) that entitles the plaintiff(s) to a remedy (either money damages or injunctive relief).
Financial statement	Financial statement refers to a summary of all the transactions that have occurred over a particular period.
Operation	A standardized method or technique that is performed repetitively, often on different materials resulting in different finished goods is called an operation.
Accelerated method	Depreciation methods that recognize more depreciation expense in the early years of an asset's life and less in later years are referred to asan accelerated method.
Deferred tax	Deferred tax is an accounting term, meaning future tax liability or asset, resulting from temporary differences between book (accounting) value of assets and liabilities, and their tax value.
Accelerated depreciation	Methods that result in higher depreciation expense in the early years of an asset's life, and lower expense in the later years are referred to as accelerated depreciation.
Short run	Short run refers to a period of time that permits an increase or decrease in current production volume with existing capacity, but one that is too short to permit enlargement of that capacity itself (eg, the building of new plants, training of additional workers, etc.).
Recovery	Characterized by rizing output, falling unemployment, rizing profits, and increasing economic activity following a decline is a recovery.
Modified accelerated cost recovery system	A method in which the cost of tangible property is recovered over a prescribed period of time is the modified accelerated cost recovery system. Enacted by the Economic Recovery Tax Act of 1981 and substantially modified by the Tax Reform Act of 1986, the approach disregards salvage value.
Accelerated Cost Recovery System	Accelerated cost recovery system refers to an accounting depreciation method where the cost of tangible property is weighted more toward the early years of an asset's life.
Service	Service refers to a "non tangible product" that is not embodied in a physical good and that

Go to **Cram101.com** for the Practice Tests for this Chapter.

typically effects some change in another product, person, or institution. Contrasts with good.

Estate
An estate is the totality of the legal rights, interests, entitlements and obligations attaching to property. In the context of wills and probate, it refers to the totality of the property which the deceased owned or in which some interest was held.

Warranty
An obligation of a company to replace defective goods or correct any deficiencies in performance or quality of a product is called a warranty.

Customer satisfaction
Customer satisfaction is a business term which is used to capture the idea of measuring how satisfied an enterprise's customers are with the organization's efforts in a marketplace.

Book value
The book value of an asset or group of assets is sometimes the price at which they were originally acquired, in many cases equal to purchase price.

Labor
People's physical and mental talents and efforts that are used to help produce goods and services are called labor.

Purchasing
Purchasing refers to the function in a firm that searches for quality material resources, finds the best suppliers, and negotiates the best price for goods and services.

Depreciation tax shield
Depreciation tax shield refers to the reduction in a firm's income-tax expense due to the depreciation expense associated with a depreciable asset.

Analyst
Analyst refers to a person or tool with a primary function of information analysis, generally with a more limited, practical and short term set of goals than a researcher.

Variable
A variable is something measured by a number; it is used to analyze what happens to other things when the size of that number changes.

Business analysis
Business analysis is a structured methodology that is focused on completely understanding the customer's needs, identifying how best to meet those needs, and then "reinventing" the stream of processes to meet those needs.

Diversification
Investing in a collection of assets whose returns do not always move together, with the result that overall risk is lower than for individual assets is referred to as diversification.

Firm
An organization that employs resources to produce a good or service for profit and owns and operates one or more plants is referred to as a firm.

Marketing
Promoting and selling products or services to customers, or prospective customers, is referred to as marketing.

Option
A contract that gives the purchaser the option to buy or sell the underlying financial instrument at a specified price, called the exercise price or strike price, within a specific period of time.

Bid
A bid price is a price offered by a buyer when he/she buys a good. In the context of stock trading on a stock exchange, the bid price is the highest price a buyer of a stock is willing to pay for a share of that given stock.

Vendor
A person who sells property to a vendee is a vendor. The words vendor and vendee are more commonly applied to the seller and purchaser of real estate, and the words seller and buyer are more commonly applied to the seller and purchaser of personal property.

Board of directors
The group of individuals elected by the stockholders of a corporation to oversee its operations is a board of directors.

Enterprise
Enterprise refers to another name for a business organization. Other similar terms are business firm, sometimes simply business, sometimes simply firm, as well as company, and

entity.

Customer service	The ability of logistics management to satisfy users in terms of time, dependability, communication, and convenience is called the customer service.
Cabinet	The heads of the executive departments of a jurisdiction who report to and advise its chief executive; examples would include the president's cabinet, the governor's cabinet, and the mayor's cabinet.
Consultant	A professional that provides expert advice in a particular field or area in which customers occassionaly require this type of knowledge is a consultant.
Long run	In economic models, the long run time frame assumes no fixed factors of production. Firms can enter or leave the marketplace, and the cost (and availability) of land, labor, raw materials, and capital goods can be assumed to vary.
Contribution	In business organization law, the cash or property contributed to a business by its owners is referred to as contribution.
Effective tax rate	The effective tax rate is the amount of income tax an individual or firm pays divided by the individual or firm's total taxable income. This ratio is usually expressed as a percentage.
Depreciate	A nation's currency is said to depreciate when exchange rates change so that a unit of its currency can buy fewer units of foreign currency.
Industry	A group of firms that produce identical or similar products is an industry. It is also used specifically to refer to an area of economic production focused on manufacturing which involves large amounts of capital investment before any profit can be realized, also called "heavy industry".
Operating expense	In throughput accounting, the cost accounting aspect of Theory of Constraints (TOC), operating expense is the money spent turning inventory into throughput. In TOC, operating expense is limited to costs that vary strictly with the quantity produced, like raw materials and purchased components.
Cash flow forecast	Forecast that predicts the cash inflows and outflows in future periods is a cash flow forecast.It is a company's projected cash receipts and disbursements over a set time horizon.
Incremental cost	Additional total cost incurred for an activity is called incremental cost. A form of costing that classifies costs into their fixed and variable elements in order to calculate the extra cost of making and selling an additional batch of units.
Household	An economic unit that provides the economy with resources and uses the income received to purchase goods and services that satisfy economic wants is called household.
Accounts receivable	Accounts receivable is one of a series of accounting transactions dealing with the billing of customers which owe money to a person, company or organization for goods and services that have been provided to the customer. This is typically done in a one person organization by writing an invoice and mailing or delivering it to each customer.
Accounts payable	A written record of all vendors to whom the business firm owes money is referred to as accounts payable.
Insurance	Insurance refers to a system by which individuals can reduce their exposure to risk of large losses by spreading the risks among a large number of persons.
Operating cash flows	Operating cash flows refers to the cash inflows and cash outflows from the general operating activities of the business; one of the three sections in the statement of cash flows.
Supervisor	A Supervisor is an employee of an organization with some of the powers and responsibilities of management, occupying a role between true manager and a regular employee. A Supervisor

	position is typically the first step towards being promoted into a management role.
Fringe benefits	The rewards other than wages that employees receive from their employers and that include pensions, medical and dental insurance, paid vacations, and sick leaves are referred to as fringe benefits.
Fringe benefit	Benefits such as sick-leave pay, vacation pay, pension plans, and health plans that represent additional compenzation to employees beyond base wages is a fringe benefit.
Wage	The payment for the service of a unit of labor, per unit time. In trade theory, it is the only payment to labor, usually unskilled labor. In empirical work, wage data may exclude other compenzation, which must be added to get the total cost of employment.
Contract	A contract is a "promise" or an "agreement" that is enforced or recognized by the law. In the civil law, a contract is considered to be part of the general law of obligations.
Distribution channel	A distribution channel is a chain of intermediaries, each passing a product down the chain to the next organization, before it finally reaches the consumer or end-user.
Distribution	Distribution in economics, the manner in which total output and income is distributed among individuals or factors.
Channel	Channel, in communications (sometimes called communications channel), refers to the medium used to convey information from a sender (or transmitter) to a receiver.
Direct labor	The earnings of employees who work directly on the products being manufactured are direct labor.
Wholesale	According to the United Nations Statistics Division Wholesale is the resale of new and used goods to retailers, to industrial, commercial, institutional or professional users, or to other wholesalers, or involves acting as an agent or broker in buying merchandise for, or selling merchandise, to such persons or companies.
Accrual	An accrual is an accounting event in which the transaction is recognized when the action takes place, instead of when cash is disbursed or received.
Writing off	Writing off refers to the allocation of the cost of an asset over several accounting periods. Also, to expense a cost, that is, put it on the income statement as an expense.
Leasehold	Leasehold is a form of property tenure where one party buys the right to occupy land or a building for a given length of time. A lease is a legal estate leasehold estate that can be bought and sold on the open market and differs from a tenancy where a property is let on a periodic basis such as weekly or monthly.
Tenant	The party to whom the leasehold is transferred is a tenant. A leasehold estate is an ownership interest in land in which a lessee or a tenant holds real property by some form of title from a lessor or landlord.
Current account	Current account refers to a country's international transactions arising from current flows, as opposed to changes in stocks which are part of the capital account. Includes trade in goods and services plus inflows and outflows of transfers. A current account is a deposit account in the UK and countries with a UK banking heritage.
Discount rate	Discount rate refers to the rate, per year, at which future values are diminished to make them comparable to values in the present. Can be either subjective or objective .
Discount	The difference between the face value of a bond and its selling price, when a bond is sold for less than its face value it's referred to as a discount.
Rate of return	A rate of return is a comparison of the money earned (or lost) on an investment to the amount of money invested.

Go to **Cram101.com** for the Practice Tests for this Chapter.

Required rate of return	Required rate of return refers to the rate of return that investors demand from an investment to compensate them for the amount of risk involved.
Economy	The income, expenditures, and resources that affect the cost of running a business and household are called an economy.
Planning horizon	The length of time it takes to conceive, develop, and complete a project and to recover the cost of the project on a discounted cash flow basis is referred to as planning horizon.

Cash flow	In finance, cash flow refers to the amounts of cash being received and spent by a business during a defined period of time, sometimes tied to a specific project. Most of the time they are being used to determine gaps in the liquid position of a company.
Variable	A variable is something measured by a number; it is used to analyze what happens to other things when the size of that number changes.
Random variable	Random variable refers to an economic or statistical variable that takes on multiple values, each with some probability that is specified by a probability distribution.
Distribution	Distribution in economics, the manner in which total output and income is distributed among individuals or factors.
Probability distribution	A specification of the probabilities for each possible value of a random variable is called probability distribution.
Expected value	A representative value from a probability distribution arrived at by multiplying each outcome by the associated probability and summing up the values is called the expected value.
Variance	Variance refers to a measure of how much an economic or statistical variable varies across values or observations. Its calculation is the same as that of the covariance, being the covariance of the variable with itself.
Standard deviation	A measure of the spread or dispersion of a series of numbers around the expected value is the standard deviation. The standard deviation tells us how well the expected value represents a series of values.
Capital budgeting	Capital budgeting is the planning process used to determine a firm's long term investments such as new machinery, replacement machinery, new plants, new products, and research and development projects.
Capital	Capital generally refers to financial wealth, especially that used to start or maintain a business. In classical economics, capital is one of four factors of production, the others being land and labor and entrepreneurship.
Portfolio theory	Portfolio theory refers to an economic theory that describes how rational investors allocate their wealth among different financial assets-that is, how they put their wealth into a 'portfolio.'
Risk aversion	Risk aversion is the reluctance of a person to accept a bargain with an uncertain payoff rather than another bargain with a more certain but possibly lower expected payoff.
Portfolio	In finance, a portfolio is a collection of investments held by an institution or a private individual. Holding but not always a portfolio is part of an investment and risk-limiting strategy called diversification. By owning several assets, certain types of risk (in particular specific risk) can be reduced.
Investment	Investment refers to spending for the production and accumulation of capital and additions to inventories. In a financial sense, buying an asset with the expectation of making a return.
Firm	An organization that employs resources to produce a good or service for profit and owns and operates one or more plants is referred to as a firm.
Expected return	Expected return refers to the return on an asset expected over the next period.
Stock	In financial terminology, stock is the capital raized by a corporation, through the issuance and sale of shares.
Bond	Bond refers to a debt instrument, issued by a borrower and promising a specified stream of payments to the purchaser, usually regular interest payments plus a final repayment of principal.

Go to **Cram101.com** for the Practice Tests for this Chapter.

Long run	In economic models, the long run time frame assumes no fixed factors of production. Firms can enter or leave the marketplace, and the cost (and availability) of land, labor, raw materials, and capital goods can be assumed to vary.
Management	Management characterizes the process of leading and directing all or part of an organization, often a business, through the deployment and manipulation of resources. Early twentieth-century management writer Mary Parker Follett defined management as "the art of getting things done through people."
Scenario analysis	Scenario analysis is a process of analyzing possible future events by considering alternative possible outcomes. The analysis is designed to allow improved decision-making by allowing more complete consideration of outcomes and their implications.
Cash inflow	Cash coming into the company as the result of a previous investment is a cash inflow.
Sensitivity analysis	A what-if technique that managers use to examine how a result will change if the original predicted data are not achieved or if an underlying assumption changes is sensitivity analysis.
Yield	The interest rate that equates a future value or an annuity to a given present value is a yield.
Context	The effect of the background under which a message often takes on more and richer meaning is a context. Context is especially important in cross-cultural interactions because some cultures are said to be high context or low context.
Option	A contract that gives the purchaser the option to buy or sell the underlying financial instrument at a specified price, called the exercise price or strike price, within a specific period of time.
Histogram	A representation of data in a bar chart format is called histogram.
Drawback	Drawback refers to rebate of import duties when the imported good is re-exported or used as input to the production of an exported good.
Positively correlated	Positively correlated refers to values or amounts of two items that move in the same direction. In accounting and finance, the amount of risk and the amount of return on an investment move in the same direction.
Correlation	A correlation is the measure of the extent to which two economic or statistical variables move together, normalized so that its values range from -1 to +1. It is defined as the covariance of the two variables divided by the square root of the product of their variances.
Decision rule	Decision rule refers to a statement that tells a decision maker which alternative to choose based on the characteristics of the decision situation.
Practical approach	The approach to decision-making that combines the steps of the rational approach with the conditions in the behavioral approach to create a more realistic process for making decisions in organizations is referred to as practical approach.
Decision tree	In decision theory, a decision tree is a graph of decisions and their possible consequences, (including resource costs and risks) used to create a plan to reach a goal.
Technology	The body of knowledge and techniques that can be used to combine economic resources to produce goods and services is called technology.
Market	A market is, as defined in economics, a social arrangement that allows buyers and sellers to discover information and carry out a voluntary exchange of goods or services.
Manufacturing	Production of goods primarily by the application of labor and capital to raw materials and other intermediate inputs, in contrast to agriculture, mining, forestry, fishing, and

	services a manufacturing.
Consumer demand	Consumer demand or consumption is also known as personal consumption expenditure. It is the largest part of aggregate demand or effective demand at the macroeconomic level.There are two variants of consumption in the aggregate demand model, including induced consumption and autonomous consumption.
Cost of capital	Cost of capital refers to the percentage cost of funds used for acquiring resources for an organization, typically a weighted average of the firms cost of equity and cost of debt.
Present value	The value today of a stream of payments and/or receipts over time in the future and/or the past, converted to the present using an interest rate. If X t is the amount in period t and r the interest rate, then present value at time t=0 is V = ?T /t.
Credit	Credit refers to a recording as positive in the balance of payments, any transaction that gives rise to a payment into the country, such as an export, the sale of an asset, or borrowing from abroad.
Interest rate	The rate of return on bonds, loans, or deposits. When one speaks of 'the' interest rate, it is usually in a model where there is only one.
Standing	Standing refers to the legal requirement that anyone seeking to challenge a particular action in court must demonstrate that such action substantially affects his legitimate interests before he will be entitled to bring suit.
Interest	In finance and economics, interest is the price paid by a borrower for the use of a lender's money. In other words, interest is the amount of paid to "rent" money for a period of time.
Increase in demand	Increase in demand refers to an increase in the quantity demanded of a good or service at every price; a shift of the demand curve to the right.
Profit	Profit refers to the return to the resource entrepreneurial ability; total revenue minus total cost.
Fixed price	Fixed price is a phrase used to mean that no bargaining is allowed over the price of a good or, less commonly, a service.
Call option	Call option refers to an option contract that provides the right to buy a security at a specified price within a certain time period.
Market price	Market price is an economic concept with commonplace familiarity; it is the price that a good or service is offered at, or will fetch, in the marketplace; it is of interest mainly in the study of microeconomics.
Holder	A person in possession of a document of title or an instrument payable or indorsed to him, his order, or to bearer is a holder.
Realization	Realization is the sale of assets when an entity is being liquidated.
Abandonment	Abandonment in law, is the relinquishment of an interest, claim, privilege or possession. This broad meaning has a number of applications in different branches of law.
Contribution	In business organization law, the cash or property contributed to a business by its owners is referred to as contribution.
Preference	The act of a debtor in paying or securing one or more of his creditors in a manner more favorable to them than to other creditors or to the exclusion of such other creditors is a preference. In the absence of statute, a preference is perfectly good, but to be legal it must be bona fide, and not a mere subterfuge of the debtor to secure a future benefit to himself or to prevent the application of his property to his debts.
Industry	A group of firms that produce identical or similar products is an industry. It is also used

	specifically to refer to an area of economic production focused on manufacturing which involves large amounts of capital investment before any profit can be realized, also called "heavy industry".
Bankruptcy	Bankruptcy is a legally declared inability or impairment of ability of an individual or organization to pay their creditors.
Enron	Enron Corportaion's global reputation was undermined by persistent rumours of bribery and political pressure to secure contracts in Central America, South America, Africa, and the Philippines. Especially controversial was its $3 billion contract with the Maharashtra State Electricity Board in India, where it is alleged that Enron officials used political connections within the Clinton and Bush administrations to exert pressure on the board.
Scope	Scope of a project is the sum total of all projects products and their requirements or features.
Deregulation	The lessening or complete removal of government regulations on an industry, especially concerning the price that firms are allowed to charge and leaving price to be determined by market forces a deregulation.
Wholesale	According to the United Nations Statistics Division Wholesale is the resale of new and used goods to retailers, to industrial, commercial, institutional or professional users, or to other wholesalers, or involves acting as an agent or broker in buying merchandise for, or selling merchandise, to such persons or companies.
Utility	Utility refers to the want-satisfying power of a good or service; the satisfaction or pleasure a consumer obtains from the consumption of a good or service.
Volatility	Volatility refers to the extent to which an economic variable, such as a price or an exchange rate, moves up and down over time.
Peak	Peak refers to the point in the business cycle when an economic expansion reaches its highest point before turning down. Contrasts with trough.
Operation	A standardized method or technique that is performed repetitively, often on different materials resulting in different finished goods is called an operation.
Airbus	In 2003, for the first time in its 33-year history, Airbus delivered more jet-powered airliners than Boeing. Boeing states that the Boeing 777 has outsold its Airbus counterparts, which include the A340 family as well as the A330-300. The smaller A330-200 competes with the 767, outselling its Boeing counterpart.
Commodity	Could refer to any good, but in trade a commodity is usually a raw material or primary product that enters into international trade, such as metals or basic agricultural products.
Contract	A contract is a "promise" or an "agreement" that is enforced or recognized by the law. In the civil law, a contract is considered to be part of the general law of obligations.
Financial analysis	Financial analysis is the analysis of the accounts and the economic prospects of a firm.
Property	Assets defined in the broadest legal sense. Property includes the unrealized receivables of a cash basis taxpayer, but not services rendered.
Grant	Grant refers to an intergovernmental transfer of funds . Since the New Deal, state and local governments have become increasingly dependent upon federal grants for an almost infinite variety of programs.
Buyer	A buyer refers to a role in the buying center with formal authority and responsibility to select the supplier and negotiate the terms of the contract.

Go to **Cram101.com** for the Practice Tests for this Chapter.

187

Discount rate	Discount rate refers to the rate, per year, at which future values are diminished to make them comparable to values in the present. Can be either subjective or objective .
Discount	The difference between the face value of a bond and its selling price, when a bond is sold for less than its face value it's referred to as a discount.
Fund	Independent accounting entity with a self-balancing set of accounts segregated for the purposes of carrying on specific activities is referred to as a fund.
Enterprise	Enterprise refers to another name for a business organization. Other similar terms are business firm, sometimes simply business, sometimes simply firm, as well as company, and entity.
Premium	Premium refers to the fee charged by an insurance company for an insurance policy. The rate of losses must be relatively predictable: In order to set the premium (prices) insurers must be able to estimate them accurately.
Risk premium	In finance, the risk premium can be the expected rate of return above the risk-free interest rate.
Rate of return	A rate of return is a comparison of the money earned (or lost) on an investment to the amount of money invested.
Points	Loan origination fees that may be deductible as interest by a buyer of property. A seller of property who pays points reduces the selling price by the amount of the points paid for the buyer.
Capital asset pricing model	The capital asset pricing model is used in finance to determine a theoretically appropriate required rate of return (and thus the price if expected cash flows can be estimated) of an asset, if that asset is to be added to an already well-diversified portfolio, given that asset's non-diversifiable risk.
Capital asset	In accounting, a capital asset is an asset that is recorded as property that creates more property, e.g. a factory that creates shoes, or a forest that yields a quantity of wood.
Asset	An item of property, such as land, capital, money, a share in ownership, or a claim on others for future payment, such as a bond or a bank deposit is an asset.
Diversification	Investing in a collection of assets whose returns do not always move together, with the result that overall risk is lower than for individual assets is referred to as diversification.
Shareholder	A shareholder is an individual or company (including a corporation) that legally owns one or more shares of stock in a joined stock company.
Stockholder	A stockholder is an individual or company (including a corporation) that legally owns one or more shares of stock in a joined stock company. The shareholders are the owners of a corporation. Companies listed at the stock market strive to enhance shareholder value.
Systematic risk	Movements in a stock portfolio's value that are attributable to macroeconomic forces affecting all firms in an economy, rather than factors specific to an individual firm are referred to as systematic risk.
Required rate of return	Required rate of return refers to the rate of return that investors demand from an investment to compensate them for the amount of risk involved.
Market share	That fraction of an industry's output accounted for by an individual firm or group of firms is called market share.
Competitor	Other organizations in the same industry or type of business that provide a good or service to the same set of customers is referred to as a competitor.

Treasury bills	Short-term obligations of the federal government are treasury bills. They are like zero coupon bonds in that they do not pay interest prior to maturity; instead they are sold at a discount of the par value to create a positive yield to maturity.
Market leader	The market leader is dominant in its industry. It has substantial market share and often extensive distribution arrangements with retailers. It typically is the industry leader in developing innovative new business models and new products (although not always).
Consideration	Consideration in contract law, a basic requirement for an enforceable agreement under traditional contract principles, defined in this text as legal value, bargained for and given in exchange for an act or promise. In corporation law, cash or property contributed to a corporation in exchange for shares, or a promise to contribute such cash or property.
Accounting	A system that collects and processes financial information about an organization and reports that information to decision makers is referred to as accounting.
Proxy	Proxy refers to a person who is authorized to vote the shares of another person. Also, the written authorization empowering a person to vote the shares of another person.
Stock market	An organized marketplace in which common stocks are traded. In the United States, the largest stock market is the New York Stock Exchange, on which are traded the stocks of the largest U.S. companies.
Service	Service refers to a "non tangible product" that is not embodied in a physical good and that typically effects some change in another product, person, or institution. Contrasts with good.
Shares	Shares refer to an equity security, representing a shareholder's ownership of a corporation. Shares are one of a finite number of equal portions in the capital of a company, entitling the owner to a proportion of distributed, non-reinvested profits known as dividends and to a portion of the value of the company in case of liquidation.
Public utility	A firm that produces an essential good or service, has obtained from a government the right to be the sole supplier of the good or service in the area, and is regulated by that government to prevent the abuse of its monopoly power is a public utility.
Regulation	Regulation refers to restrictions state and federal laws place on business with regard to the conduct of its activities.
Monopoly	A monopoly is defined as a persistent market situation where there is only one provider of a kind of product or service.
Cash flow forecast	Forecast that predicts the cash inflows and outflows in future periods is a cash flow forecast. It is a company's projected cash receipts and disbursements over a set time horizon.
Installations	Support goods, consisting of buildings and fixed equipment are called installations.
Committee	A long-lasting, sometimes permanent team in the organization structure created to deal with tasks that recur regularly is the committee.
Adoption	In corporation law, a corporation's acceptance of a pre-incorporation contract by action of its board of directors, by which the corporation becomes liable on the contract, is referred to as adoption.
Estate	An estate is the totality of the legal rights, interests, entitlements and obligations attaching to property. In the context of wills and probate, it refers to the totality of the property which the deceased owned or in which some interest was held.
Production	The creation of finished goods and services using the factors of production: land, labor, capital, entrepreneurship, and knowledge.

Economy	The income, expenditures, and resources that affect the cost of running a business and household are called an economy.
Target market	One or more specific groups of potential consumers toward which an organization directs its marketing program are a target market.
Downturn	A decline in a stock market or economic cycle is a downturn.
Marketing	Promoting and selling products or services to customers, or prospective customers, is referred to as marketing.
Consultant	A professional that provides expert advice in a particular field or area in which customers occassionaly require this type of knowledge is a consultant.
Operating cash flows	Operating cash flows refers to the cash inflows and cash outflows from the general operating activities of the business; one of the three sections in the statement of cash flows.

Go to **Cram101.com** for the Practice Tests for this Chapter.
And, **NEVER** highlight a book again!

Cost of capital	Cost of capital refers to the percentage cost of funds used for acquiring resources for an organization, typically a weighted average of the firms cost of equity and cost of debt.
Capital	Capital generally refers to financial wealth, especially that used to start or maintain a business. In classical economics, capital is one of four factors of production, the others being land and labor and entrepreneurship.
Fund	Independent accounting entity with a self-balancing set of accounts segregated for the purposes of carrying on specific activities is referred to as a fund.
Capital budgeting	Capital budgeting is the planning process used to determine a firm's long term investments such as new machinery, replacement machinery, new plants, new products, and research and development projects.
Investment	Investment refers to spending for the production and accumulation of capital and additions to inventories. In a financial sense, buying an asset with the expectation of making a return.
Firm	An organization that employs resources to produce a good or service for profit and owns and operates one or more plants is referred to as a firm.
Management	Management characterizes the process of leading and directing all or part of an organization, often a business, through the deployment and manipulation of resources. Early twentieth-century management writer Mary Parker Follett defined management as "the art of getting things done through people."
Stock	In financial terminology, stock is the capital raized by a corporation, through the issuance and sale of shares.
Expected return	Expected return refers to the return on an asset expected over the next period.
Financial statement	Financial statement refers to a summary of all the transactions that have occurred over a particular period.
Balance sheet	A statement of the assets, liabilities, and net worth of a firm or individual at some given time often at the end of its "fiscal year," is referred to as a balance sheet.
Balance	In banking and accountancy, the outstanding balance is the amount of money owned, (or due), that remains in a deposit account (or a loan account) at a given date, after all past remittances, payments and withdrawal have been accounted for. It can be positive (then, in the balance sheet of a firm, it is an asset) or negative (a liability).
Common equity	The common stock or ownership capital of the firm is common equity. Common equity may be supplied through retained earnings or the sale of new common stock.
Equity	Equity is the name given to the set of legal principles, in countries following the English common law tradition, which supplement strict rules of law where their application would operate harshly, so as to achieve what is sometimes referred to as "natural justice."
Bond	Bond refers to a debt instrument, issued by a borrower and promising a specified stream of payments to the purchaser, usually regular interest payments plus a final repayment of principal.
Preferred stock	Stock that has specified rights over common stock is a preferred stock.
Common stock	Common stock refers to the basic, normal, voting stock issued by a corporation; called residual equity because it ranks after preferred stock for dividend and liquidation distributions.
Interest	In finance and economics, interest is the price paid by a borrower for the use of a lender's money. In other words, interest is the amount of paid to "rent" money for a period of time.
Capital	Capital Structure refers to the way a corporation finances itself through some combination of

194

Go to **Cram101.com** for the Practice Tests for this Chapter.

structure	equity sales, equity options, bonds, and loans. Optimal capital structure refers to the particular combination that minimizes the cost of capital while maximizing the stock price.
Enterprise	Enterprise refers to another name for a business organization. Other similar terms are business firm, sometimes simply business, sometimes simply firm, as well as company, and entity.
Entrepreneur	The owner/operator. The person who organizes, manages, and assumes the risks of a firm, taking a new idea or a new product and turning it into a successful business is an entrepreneur.
Security	Security refers to a claim on the borrower future income that is sold by the borrower to the lender. A security is a type of transferable interest representing financial value.
Retained earnings	Cumulative earnings of a company that are not distributed to the owners and are reinvested in the business are called retained earnings.
Distortion	Distortion refers to any departure from the ideal of perfect competition that interferes with economic agents maximizing social welfare when they maximize their own.
Purchasing	Purchasing refers to the function in a firm that searches for quality material resources, finds the best suppliers, and negotiates the best price for goods and services.
Equity investment	Equity investment generally refers to the buying and holding of shares of stock on a stock market by individuals and funds in anticipation of income from dividends and capital gain as the value of the stock rises.
Debt security	Type of security acquired by loaning assets is called a debt security.
Cost of debt	The cost of debt is the cost of borrowing money (usually denoted by Kd). It is derived by dividing debt's interest payments on the total market value of the debts.
Weighted average	The weighted average unit cost of the goods available for sale for both cost of goods sold and ending inventory.
Weighted average cost of capital	Weighted average cost of capital refers to the computed cost of capital determined by multiplying the cost of each item in the optimal capital structure by its weighted representation in the overall capital structure and summing up the results.
Average cost	Average cost is equal to total cost divided by the number of goods produced (Quantity-Q). It is also equal to the sum of average variable costs (total variable costs divided by Q) plus average fixed costs (total fixed costs divided by Q).
Market value	Market value refers to the price of an asset agreed on between a willing buyer and a willing seller; the price an asset could demand if it is sold on the open market.
Market	A market is, as defined in economics, a social arrangement that allows buyers and sellers to discover information and carry out a voluntary exchange of goods or services.
Capital account	The capital account is one of two primary components of the balance of payments. It tracks the movement of funds for investments and loans into and out of a country.
Book value	The book value of an asset or group of assets is sometimes the price at which they were originally acquired, in many cases equal to purchase price.
Market price	Market price is an economic concept with commonplace familiarity; it is the price that a good or service is offered at, or will fetch, in the marketplace; it is of interest mainly in the study of microeconomics.
Interest rate	The rate of return on bonds, loans, or deposits. When one speaks of 'the' interest rate, it is usually in a model where there is only one.

Go to **Cram101.com** for the Practice Tests for this Chapter.

Corporation	A legal entity chartered by a state or the Federal government that is distinct and separate from the individuals who own it is a corporation. This separation gives the corporation unique powers which other legal entities lack.
Shares	Shares refer to an equity security, representing a shareholder's ownership of a corporation. Shares are one of a finite number of equal portions in the capital of a company, entitling the owner to a proportion of distributed, non-reinvested profits known as dividends and to a portion of the value of the company in case of liquidation.
Context	The effect of the background under which a message often takes on more and richer meaning is a context. Context is especially important in cross-cultural interactions because some cultures are said to be high context or low context.
Capital market	A financial market in which long-term debt and equity instruments are traded is referred to as a capital market. The capital market includes the stock market and the bond market.
Coupon rate	In bonds, notes or other fixed income securities, the stated percentage rate of interest, usually paid twice a year is the coupon rate.
Face value	The nominal or par value of an instrument as expressed on its face is referred to as the face value.
Coupon	In finance, a coupon is "attached" to a bond, either physically (as with old bonds) or electronically. Each coupon represents a predetermined payment promized to the bond-holder in return for his or her loan of money to the bond-issuer. .
Dividend	Amount of corporate profits paid out for each share of stock is referred to as dividend.
Yield	The interest rate that equates a future value or an annuity to a given present value is a yield.
Financial market	In economics, a financial market is a mechanism which allows people to trade money for securities or commodities such as gold or other precious metals. In general, any commodity market might be considered to be a financial market, if the usual purpose of traders is not the immediate consumption of the commodity, but rather as a means of delaying or accelerating consumption over time.
Transaction cost	A transaction cost is a cost incurred in making an economic exchange. For example, most people, when buying or selling a stock, must pay a commission to their broker; that commission is a transaction cost of doing the stock deal.
Interest payment	The payment to holders of bonds payable, calculated by multiplying the stated rate on the face of the bond by the par, or face, value of the bond. If bonds are issued at a discount or premium, the interest payment does not equal the interest expense.
Deductible	The dollar sum of costs that an insured individual must pay before the insurer begins to pay is called deductible.
Marginal tax rate	The percentage of an additional dollar of earnings that goes to taxes is referred to as the marginal tax rate.
Flotation cost	Flotation cost refers to the distribution cost of selling securities to the public. The cost includes the underwriter's spread and any associated fees.
Expense	In accounting, an expense represents an event in which an asset is used up or a liability is incurred. In terms of the accounting equation, expenses reduce owners' equity.
Cash flow	In finance, cash flow refers to the amounts of cash being received and spent by a business during a defined period of time, sometimes tied to a specific project. Most of the time they are being used to determine gaps in the liquid position of a company.

Present value	The value today of a stream of payments and/or receipts over time in the future and/or the past, converted to the present using an interest rate. If X t is the amount in period t and r the interest rate, then present value at time t=0 is V = ?T /t.
Perpetuity	A perpetuity is an annuity in which the periodic payments begin on a fixed date and continue indefinitely. Fixed coupon payments on permanently invested (irredeemable) sums of money are prime examples of perpetuities. Scholarships paid perpetually from an endowment fit the definition of perpetuity.
A share	In finance the term A share has two distinct meanings, both relating to securities. The first is a designation for a 'class' of common or preferred stock. A share of common or preferred stock typically has enhanced voting rights or other benefits compared to the other forms of shares that may have been created. The equity structure, or how many types of shares are offered, is determined by the corporate charter.
Par value	The central value of a pegged exchange rate, around which the actual rate is permitted to fluctuate within set bounds is a par value.
Cost of equity	In finance, the cost of equity is the minimum rate of return a firm must offer shareholders to compensate for waiting for their returns, and for bearing some risk.
Operation	A standardized method or technique that is performed repetitively, often on different materials resulting in different finished goods is called an operation.
Shareholder	A shareholder is an individual or company (including a corporation) that legally owns one or more shares of stock in a joined stock company.
Rate of return	A rate of return is a comparison of the money earned (or lost) on an investment to the amount of money invested.
Expected rate of return	Expected rate of return refers to the increase in profit a firm anticipates it will obtain by purchasing capital ; expressed as a percentage of the total cost of the investment activity.
Security market line	A line or equation that depicts the risk-related return of a security based on a risk-free rate plus a market premium related to the beta coefficient of the security is referred to as the security market line.
Required rate of return	Required rate of return refers to the rate of return that investors demand from an investment to compensate them for the amount of risk involved.
Market risk	Market risk is the risk that the value of an investment will decrease due to moves in market factors.
Beta coefficient	The Beta coefficient (sensitivity of the asset returns to market returns, relative volatility), is a key parameter in the Capital asset pricing model. It can also be defined as the risk of the stock to a diversified portfolio.
Treasury bills	Short-term obligations of the federal government are treasury bills. They are like zero coupon bonds in that they do not pay interest prior to maturity; instead they are sold at a discount of the par value to create a positive yield to maturity.
Buyer	A buyer refers to a role in the buying center with formal authority and responsibility to select the supplier and negotiate the terms of the contract.
Equity capital	Equity capital refers to money raized from within the firm or through the sale of ownership in the firm.
Risk premium	In finance, the risk premium can be the expected rate of return above the risk-free interest rate.
Premium	Premium refers to the fee charged by an insurance company for an insurance policy. The rate

Go to **Cram101.com** for the Practice Tests for this Chapter.

of losses must be relatively predictable: In order to set the premium (prices) insurers must be able to estimate them accurately.

Points	Loan origination fees that may be deductible as interest by a buyer of property. A seller of property who pays points reduces the selling price by the amount of the points paid for the buyer.
Marginal cost of capital	Marginal cost of capital refers to the cost of the last dollar of funds raized. It is assumed that each dollar is financed in proportion to the firm's optimum capital structure.
Marginal cost	Marginal cost refers to the increase in cost that accompanies a unit increase in output; the partial derivative of the cost function with respect to output.
At par	At equality refers to at par. Two currencies are said to be 'at par' if they are trading one-for-one.
Business plan	A detailed written statement that describes the nature of the business, the target market, the advantages the business will have in relation to competition, and the resources and qualifications of the owner is referred to as a business plan.
Consideration	Consideration in contract law, a basic requirement for an enforceable agreement under traditional contract principles, defined in this text as legal value, bargained for and given in exchange for an act or promise. In corporation law, cash or property contributed to a corporation in exchange for shares, or a promise to contribute such cash or property.
Return on equity	Net profit after taxes per dollar of equity capital is referred to as return on equity.
Mistake	In contract law a mistake is incorrect understanding by one or more parties to a contract and may be used as grounds to invalidate the agreement. Common law has identified three different types of mistake in contract: unilateral mistake, mutual mistake, and common mistake.
Matching	Matching refers to an accounting concept that establishes when expenses are recognized. Expenses are matched with the revenues they helped to generate and are recognized when those revenues are recognized.
Economic value added	After-tax operating income minus the weighted average cost of capital multiplied by total assets minus current liabilities is called economic value added.
Market value added	Market value added is the difference between the current market value of a firm and the capital contributed by investors. If market value added is positive, the firm has added value. If it is negative the firm has destroyed value.
Ratio analysis	Ratio analysis refers to an analytical tool designed to identify significant relationships; measures the proportional relationship between two financial statement amounts.
Value added	The value of output minus the value of all intermediate inputs, representing therefore the contribution of, and payments to, primary factors of production a value added.
Net income	Net income is equal to the income that a firm has after subtracting costs and expenses from the total revenue. Expenses will typically include tax expense.
Performance measurement	The process by which someone evaluates an employee's work behaviors by measurement and comparison with previously established standards, documents the results, and communicates the results to the employee is called performance measurement.
Revenue	Revenue is a U.S. business term for the amount of money that a company receives from its activities, mostly from sales of products and/or services to customers.
Operating income	Total revenues from operation minus cost of goods sold and operating costs are called operating income.
Analyst	Analyst refers to a person or tool with a primary function of information analysis, generally

with a more limited, practical and short term set of goals than a researcher.

Accounting	A system that collects and processes financial information about an organization and reports that information to decision makers is referred to as accounting.
Annual report	An annual report is prepared by corporate management that presents financial information including financial statements, footnotes, and the management discussion and analysis.
Budget	Budget refers to an account, usually for a year, of the planned expenditures and the expected receipts of an entity. For a government, the receipts are tax revenues.
Business analysis	Business analysis is a structured methodology that is focused on completely understanding the customer's needs, identifying how best to meet those needs, and then "reinventing" the stream of processes to meet those needs.
Variable	A variable is something measured by a number; it is used to analyze what happens to other things when the size of that number changes.
Return on investment	Return on investment refers to the return a businessperson gets on the money he and other owners invest in the firm; for example, a business that earned $100 on a $1,000 investment would have a ROI of 10 percent: 100 divided by 1000.
Brief	Brief refers to a statement of a party's case or legal arguments, usually prepared by an attorney. Also used to make legal arguments before appellate courts.
Marketing	Promoting and selling products or services to customers, or prospective customers, is referred to as marketing.
Objection	In the trial of a case the formal remonstrance made by counsel to something that has been said or done, in order to obtain the court's ruling thereon is an objection.
Acquisition	A company's purchase of the property and obligations of another company is an acquisition.
Industry	A group of firms that produce identical or similar products is an industry. It is also used specifically to refer to an area of economic production focused on manufacturing which involves large amounts of capital investment before any profit can be realized, also called "heavy industry".
Secondary market	Secondary market refers to the market for securities that have already been issued. It is a market in which investors trade back and forth with each other.
Insurance	Insurance refers to a system by which individuals can reduce their exposure to risk of large losses by spreading the risks among a large number of persons.
Investment banker	Investment banker refers to a financial organization that specializes in selling primary offerings of securities. Investment bankers can also perform other financial functions, such as advising clients, negotiating mergers and takeovers, and selling secondary offerings.

Capital structure	Capital Structure refers to the way a corporation finances itself through some combination of equity sales, equity options, bonds, and loans. Optimal capital structure refers to the particular combination that minimizes the cost of capital while maximizing the stock price.
Management	Management characterizes the process of leading and directing all or part of an organization, often a business, through the deployment and manipulation of resources. Early twentieth-century management writer Mary Parker Follett defined management as "the art of getting things done through people."
Capital	Capital generally refers to financial wealth, especially that used to start or maintain a business. In classical economics, capital is one of four factors of production, the others being land and labor and entrepreneurship.
Stock	In financial terminology, stock is the capital raized by a corporation, through the issuance and sale of shares.
Preferred stock	Stock that has specified rights over common stock is a preferred stock.
Equity	Equity is the name given to the set of legal principles, in countries following the English common law tradition, which supplement strict rules of law where their application would operate harshly, so as to achieve what is sometimes referred to as "natural justice."
Firm	An organization that employs resources to produce a good or service for profit and owns and operates one or more plants is referred to as a firm.
Interest payment	The payment to holders of bonds payable, calculated by multiplying the stated rate on the face of the bond by the par, or face, value of the bond. If bonds are issued at a discount or premium, the interest payment does not equal the interest expense.
Stock dividend	Stock dividend refers to pro rata distributions of stock or stock rights on common stock. They are usually issued in proportion to shares owned.
Common stock	Common stock refers to the basic, normal, voting stock issued by a corporation; called residual equity because it ranks after preferred stock for dividend and liquidation distributions.
Dividend	Amount of corporate profits paid out for each share of stock is referred to as dividend.
Interest	In finance and economics, interest is the price paid by a borrower for the use of a lender's money. In other words, interest is the amount paid to "rent" money for a period of time.
Financial leverage	A measure of the amount of debt used in the capital structure of the firm is the financial leverage.
Leverage	Leverage is using given resources in such a way that the potential positive or negative outcome is magnified. In finance, this generally refers to borrowing.
Enterprise	Enterprise refers to another name for a business organization. Other similar terms are business firm, sometimes simply business, sometimes simply firm, as well as company, and entity.
Equity capital	Equity capital refers to money raized from within the firm or through the sale of ownership in the firm.
Restructuring	Restructuring is the corporate management term for the act of partially dismantling and reorganizing a company for the purpose of making it more efficient and therefore more profitable.
Shares	Shares refer to an equity security, representing a shareholder's ownership of a corporation. Shares are one of a finite number of equal portions in the capital of a company, entitling the owner to a proportion of distributed, non-reinvested profits known as dividends and to a

portion of the value of the company in case of liquidation.

Earnings before interest and taxes	Income from operations before subtracting interest expense and income taxes is an earnings before interest and taxes.
Operating income	Total revenues from operation minus cost of goods sold and operating costs are called operating income.
Income statement	Income statement refers to a financial statement that presents the revenues and expenses and resulting net income or net loss of a company for a specific period of time.
Interest expense	The cost a business incurs to borrow money. With respect to bonds payable, the interest expense is calculated by multiplying the market rate of interest by the carrying value of the bonds on the date of the payment.
Expense	In accounting, an expense represents an event in which an asset is used up or a liability is incurred. In terms of the accounting equation, expenses reduce owners' equity.
Earnings per share	Earnings per share refers to annual profit of the corporation divided by the number of shares outstanding.
Return on equity	Net profit after taxes per dollar of equity capital is referred to as return on equity.
Market price	Market price is an economic concept with commonplace familiarity; it is the price that a good or service is offered at, or will fetch, in the marketplace; it is of interest mainly in the study of microeconomics.
Market	A market is, as defined in economics, a social arrangement that allows buyers and sellers to discover information and carry out a voluntary exchange of goods or services.
Investment	Investment refers to spending for the production and accumulation of capital and additions to inventories. In a financial sense, buying an asset with the expectation of making a return.
Business risk	The risk related to the inability of the firm to hold its competitive position and maintain stability and growth in earnings is business risk.
Revenue	Revenue is a U.S. business term for the amount of money that a company receives from its activities, mostly from sales of products and/or services to customers.
Business operations	Business operations are those activities involved in the running of a business for the purpose of producing value for the stakeholders. The outcome of business operations is the harvesting of value from assets owned by a business.
Financial risk	The risk related to the inability of the firm to meet its debt obligations as they come due is called financial risk.
Operation	A standardized method or technique that is performed repetitively, often on different materials resulting in different finished goods is called an operation.
Industry	A group of firms that produce identical or similar products is an industry. It is also used specifically to refer to an area of economic production focused on manufacturing which involves large amounts of capital investment before any profit can be realized, also called "heavy industry".
Regulation	Regulation refers to restrictions state and federal laws place on business with regard to the conduct of its activities.
Debt financing	Obtaining financing by borrowing money is debt financing.
Operating leverage	Effects that fixed costs have on changes in operating income as changes occur in units sold and hence in contribution margin are called operating leverage.

Cost structure	The relative proportion of an organization's fixed, variable, and mixed costs is referred to as cost structure.
Variable cost	The portion of a firm or industry's cost that changes with output, in contrast to fixed cost is referred to as variable cost.
Variable	A variable is something measured by a number; it is used to analyze what happens to other things when the size of that number changes.
Corporation	A legal entity chartered by a state or the Federal government that is distinct and separate from the individuals who own it is a corporation. This separation gives the corporation unique powers which other legal entities lack.
Book value	The book value of an asset or group of assets is sometimes the price at which they were originally acquired, in many cases equal to purchase price.
Debt capital	Debt capital refers to funds raized through various forms of borrowing to finance a company that must be repaid.
Holding	The holding is a court's determination of a matter of law based on the issue presented in the particular case. In other words: under this law, with these facts, this result.
Bid	A bid price is a price offered by a buyer when he/she buys a good. In the context of stock trading on a stock exchange, the bid price is the highest price a buyer of a stock is willing to pay for a share of that given stock.
Return on Assets	The Return on Assets percentage shows how profitable a company's assets are in generating revenue.
Cost of debt	The cost of debt is the cost of borrowing money (usually denoted by Kd). It is derived by dividing debt's interest payments on the total market value of the debts.
Asset	An item of property, such as land, capital, money, a share in ownership, or a claim on others for future payment, such as a bond or a bank deposit is an asset.
Interest rate	The rate of return on bonds, loans, or deposits. When one speaks of 'the' interest rate, it is usually in a model where there is only one.
Operating results	Operating results refers to measures that are important to monitoring and tracking the effectiveness of a company's operations.
Downturn	A decline in a stock market or economic cycle is a downturn.
Treasurer	In many governments, a treasurer is the person responsible for running the treasury. Treasurers are also employed by organizations to look after funds.
Trial	An examination before a competent tribunal, according to the law of the land, of the facts or law put in issue in a cause, for the purpose of determining such issue is a trial. When the court hears and determines any issue of fact or law for the purpose of determining the rights of the parties, it may be considered a trial.
Yield	The interest rate that equates a future value or an annuity to a given present value is a yield.
Financial statement	Financial statement refers to a summary of all the transactions that have occurred over a particular period.
Face value	The nominal or par value of an instrument as expressed on its face is referred to as the face value.
Optimum	Optimum refers to the best. Usually refers to a most preferred choice by consumers subject to a budget constraint or a profit maximizing choice by firms or industry subject to a

211

	technological constraint.
Profit	Profit refers to the return to the resource entrepreneurial ability; total revenue minus total cost.
Cost of capital	Cost of capital refers to the percentage cost of funds used for acquiring resources for an organization, typically a weighted average of the firms cost of equity and cost of debt.
America Online	In 2000 America Online and Time Warner announced plans to merge, and the deal was approved by the Federal Trade Commission on January 11, 2001. This merger was primarily a product of the Internet mania of the late-1990s, known as the Internet bubble. The deal is known as one of the worst corporate mergers in history, destroying over $200 billion in shareholder value.
Market value	Market value refers to the price of an asset agreed on between a willing buyer and a willing seller; the price an asset could demand if it is sold on the open market.
Time Warner	Time Warner is the world's largest media company with major Internet, publishing, film, telecommunications and television divisions.
Slump	A decline in performance, in a firm is a slump in sales or profits, or in a country is a slump in output or employment.
Advertising	Advertising refers to paid, nonpersonal communication through various media by organizations and individuals who are in some way identified in the advertising message.
Fair market value	Fair market value refers to the amount at which property would change hands between a willing buyer and a willing seller, neither being under any compulsion to buy or to sell, and both having reasonable knowledge of the relevant facts.
Goodwill	Goodwill is an important accounting concept that describes the value of a business entity not directly attributable to its tangible assets and liabilities.
Property	Assets defined in the broadest legal sense. Property includes the unrealized receivables of a cash basis taxpayer, but not services rendered.
Balance sheet	A statement of the assets, liabilities, and net worth of a firm or individual at some given time often at the end of its "fiscal year," is referred to as a balance sheet.
Balance	In banking and accountancy, the outstanding balance is the amount of money owned, (or due), that remains in a deposit account (or a loan account) at a given date, after all past remittances, payments and withdrawal have been accounted for. It can be positive (then, in the balance sheet of a firm, it is an asset) or negative (a liability).
Accounting	A system that collects and processes financial information about an organization and reports that information to decision makers is referred to as accounting.
Analyst	Analyst refers to a person or tool with a primary function of information analysis, generally with a more limited, practical and short term set of goals than a researcher.
Book value per share	Total shareholders' equity divided by the number of outstanding common shares is referred to as book value per share.
Degree of financial leverage	Degree of financial leverage refers to a measure of the impact of debt on the earnings capability of the firm. The percentage change in earnings per share is divided by the percentage change in earnings before interest and taxes at a given level of operation.
Manufacturing	Production of goods primarily by the application of labor and capital to raw materials and other intermediate inputs, in contrast to agriculture, mining, forestry, fishing, and services a manufacturing.
Exchange	The trade of things of value between buyer and seller so that each is better off after the trade is called the exchange.

Go to **Cram101.com** for the Practice Tests for this Chapter.

Peak	Peak refers to the point in the business cycle when an economic expansion reaches its highest point before turning down. Contrasts with trough.
Operating profit	Operating profit is a measure of a company's earning power from ongoing operations, equal to earnings before the deduction of interest payments and income taxes.
Option	A contract that gives the purchaser the option to buy or sell the underlying financial instrument at a specified price, called the exercise price or strike price, within a specific period of time.
Fixed cost	The cost that a firm bears if it does not produce at all and that is independent of its output. The presence of a fixed cost tends to imply increasing returns to scale. Contrasts with variable cost.
Depreciation	Depreciation is an accounting and finance term for the method of attributing the cost of an asset across the useful life of the asset. Depreciation is a reduction in the value of a currency in floating exchange rate.
Utility	Utility refers to the want-satisfying power of a good or service; the satisfaction or pleasure a consumer obtains from the consumption of a good or service.
Total cost	The sum of fixed cost and variable cost is referred to as total cost.
Contribution margin	A company's contribution margin can be expressed as the percentage of each sale that remains after the variable costs are subtracted. In simplest terms, the contribution margin is total revenue minus total variable cost.
Contribution	In business organization law, the cash or property contributed to a business by its owners is referred to as contribution.
Margin	A deposit by a buyer in stocks with a seller or a stockbroker, as security to cover fluctuations in the market in reference to stocks that the buyer has purchased but for which he has not paid is a margin. Commodities are also traded on margin.
Total variable Cost	The total of all costs that vary with output in the short run is called total variable cost.
Breakeven point	Breakeven point refers to quantity of output sold at which total revenues equal total costs, that is where the economic profit is zero.
Points	Loan origination fees that may be deductible as interest by a buyer of property. A seller of property who pays points reduces the selling price by the amount of the points paid for the buyer.
Degree of operating leverage	Contribution margin divided by operating income at any given level of sales is a degree of operating leverage.
Brief	Brief refers to a statement of a party's case or legal arguments, usually prepared by an attorney. Also used to make legal arguments before appellate courts.
Stockholder	A stockholder is an individual or company (including a corporation) that legally owns one or more shares of stock in a joined stock company. The shareholders are the owners of a corporation. Companies listed at the stock market strive to enhance shareholder value.
Technology	The body of knowledge and techniques that can be used to combine economic resources to produce goods and services is called technology.
Production	The creation of finished goods and services using the factors of production: land, labor, capital, entrepreneurship, and knowledge.
Volatility	Volatility refers to the extent to which an economic variable, such as a price or an exchange

Go to **Cram101.com** for the Practice Tests for this Chapter.
And, **NEVER** highlight a book again!

rate, moves up and down over time.

Capital structure theory	A theory that addresses the relative importance of debt and equity in the overall financing of the firm is called capital structure theory.
Inherent Risk	Inherent risk is the auditor's assessment that there are material misstatements in the financial statements before considering the effectiveness of internal controls. If the auditor concludes that there is a high likelihood of misstamtement, ignoring internal controls, the auditor would conclude that the inherent risk is high.
Equity securities	Equity securities refer to representation of ownership rights to the corporation.
Security	Security refers to a claim on the borrower future income that is sold by the borrower to the lender. A security is a type of transferable interest representing financial value.
Flotation cost	Flotation cost refers to the distribution cost of selling securities to the public. The cost includes the underwriter's spread and any associated fees.
Bond	Bond refers to a debt instrument, issued by a borrower and promising a specified stream of payments to the purchaser, usually regular interest payments plus a final repayment of principal.
Transaction cost	A transaction cost is a cost incurred in making an economic exchange. For example, most people, when buying or selling a stock, must pay a commission to their broker; that commission is a transaction cost of doing the stock deal.
Weighted average	The weighted average unit cost of the goods available for sale for both cost of goods sold and ending inventory.
Business strategy	Business strategy, which refers to the aggregated operational strategies of single business firm or that of an SBU in a diversified corporation refers to the way in which a firm competes in its chosen arenas.
Credit	Credit refers to a recording as positive in the balance of payments, any transaction that gives rise to a payment into the country, such as an export, the sale of an asset, or borrowing from abroad.
Unit cost	Unit cost refers to cost computed by dividing some amount of total costs by the related number of units. Also called average cost.
Bondholder	The individual or entity that purchases a bond, thus loaning money to the company that issued the bond is the bondholder.
Principal	In agency law, one under whose direction an agent acts and for whose benefit that agent acts is a principal.
Present value	The value today of a stream of payments and/or receipts over time in the future and/or the past, converted to the present using an interest rate. If X_t is the amount in period t and r the interest rate, then present value at time $t=0$ is $V = ?T/t$.
Perpetuity	A perpetuity is an annuity in which the periodic payments begin on a fixed date and continue indefinitely. Fixed coupon payments on permanently invested (irredeemable) sums of money are prime examples of perpetuities. Scholarships paid perpetually from an endowment fit the definition of perpetuity.
Average cost	Average cost is equal to total cost divided by the number of goods produced (Quantity-Q). It is also equal to the sum of average variable costs (total variable costs divided by Q) plus average fixed costs (total fixed costs divided by Q).

Capital market	A financial market in which long-term debt and equity instruments are traded is referred to as a capital market. The capital market includes the stock market and the bond market.
Bankruptcy	Bankruptcy is a legally declared inability or impairment of ability of an individual or organization to pay their creditors.
Liquidation	Liquidation refers to a process whereby the assets of a business are converted to money. The conversion may be coerced by a legal process to pay off the debt of the business, or to satisfy any other business obligation that the business has not voluntarily satisfied.
Holder	A person in possession of a document of title or an instrument payable or indorsed to him, his order, or to bearer is a holder.
Arbitrage	An arbitrage is a combination of nearly simultaneous transactions designed to profit from an existing discrepancy among prices, exchange rates, and/or interest rates on different markets without assuming risk.
Equity financing	Financing that consists of funds that are invested in exchange for ownership in the company is called equity financing.
Deductible	The dollar sum of costs that an insured individual must pay before the insurer begins to pay is called deductible.
Distribution	Distribution in economics, the manner in which total output and income is distributed among individuals or factors.
Fund	Independent accounting entity with a self-balancing set of accounts segregated for the purposes of carrying on specific activities is referred to as a fund.
Discount rate	Discount rate refers to the rate, per year, at which future values are diminished to make them comparable to values in the present. Can be either subjective or objective .
Discount	The difference between the face value of a bond and its selling price, when a bond is sold for less than its face value it's referred to as a discount.
Contract	A contract is a "promise" or an "agreement" that is enforced or recognized by the law. In the civil law, a contract is considered to be part of the general law of obligations.
Shareholder	A shareholder is an individual or company (including a corporation) that legally owns one or more shares of stock in a joined stock company.
Cost of equity	In finance, the cost of equity is the minimum rate of return a firm must offer shareholders to compensate for waiting for their returns, and for bearing some risk.
Mergers and acquisitions	The phrase mergers and acquisitions refers to the aspect of corporate finance strategy and management dealing with the merging and acquiring of different companies as well as other assets. Usually mergers occur in a friendly setting where executives from the respective companies participate in a due diligence process to ensure a successful combination of all parts.
Acquisition	A company's purchase of the property and obligations of another company is an acquisition.
Merger	Merger refers to the combination of two firms into a single firm.
Stock market	An organized marketplace in which common stocks are traded. In the United States, the largest stock market is the New York Stock Exchange, on which are traded the stocks of the largest U.S. companies.
Premium	Premium refers to the fee charged by an insurance company for an insurance policy. The rate of losses must be relatively predictable: In order to set the premium (prices) insurers must be able to estimate them accurately.

Argument	The discussion by counsel for the respective parties of their contentions on the law and the facts of the case being tried in order to aid the jury in arriving at a correct and just conclusion is called argument.
Fixed interest rate	Interest rate that does not change over the life of the loan is called the fixed interest rate. A rate that does not fluctuate with general market conditions.
Fixed interest	A fixed interest rate loan is a loan where the interest rate doesn't fluctuate over the life of the loan. This allows the borrower to accurately predict their future payments. When the prevailing interest rate is very low, a fixed rate loan will be slightly higher than variable rate loans because the lender is taking a risk they he could get a higher interest rate by loaning money later.
Marketing	Promoting and selling products or services to customers, or prospective customers, is referred to as marketing.
Debt to equity ratio	The debt to equity ratio is a financial ratio debt divided by shareholders' equity. The two components are often taken from the firm's balance sheet, but they might also be caluated as market values if both the companiy's debt and equity are publicly traded. It is used to calculate a company's "financial leverage" and indicates what proportion of equity and debt the company is using to finance its assets.
Draft	A signed, written order by which one party instructs another party to pay a specified sum to a third party, at sight or at a specific date is a draft.
Labor intensive	Describing an industry or sector of the economy that relies relatively heavily on inputs of labor, usually relative to capital but sometimes to human capital or skilled labor, compared to other industries or sectors is labor intensive.
Labor	People's physical and mental talents and efforts that are used to help produce goods and services are called labor.
Management team	A management team is directly responsible for managing the day-to-day operations (and profitability) of a company.
Investment banker	Investment banker refers to a financial organization that specializes in selling primary offerings of securities. Investment bankers can also perform other financial functions, such as advising clients, negotiating mergers and takeovers, and selling secondary offerings.
Financial plan	The financial plan section of a business plan consists of three financial statements (the income statement, the cash flow projection, and the balance sheet) and a brief analysis of these three statements.
Aid	Assistance provided by countries and by international institutions such as the World Bank to developing countries in the form of monetary grants, loans at low interest rates, in kind, or a combination of these is called aid. Aid can also refer to assistance of any type rendered to benefit some group or individual.
Marginal tax rate	The percentage of an additional dollar of earnings that goes to taxes is referred to as the marginal tax rate.
Quality improvement	Quality is inversely proportional to variability thus quality Improvement is the reduction of variability in products and processes.
Coupon rate	In bonds, notes or other fixed income securities, the stated percentage rate of interest, usually paid twice a year is the coupon rate.
Coupon	In finance, a coupon is "attached" to a bond, either physically (as with old bonds) or electronically. Each coupon represents a predetermined payment promized to the bond-holder in return for his or her loan of money to the bond-issuer. .

Transactions cost	Any cost associated with bringing buyers and sellers together is referred to as transactions cost.
Financial market	In economics, a financial market is a mechanism which allows people to trade money for securities or commodities such as gold or other precious metals. In general, any commodity market might be considered to be a financial market, if the usual purpose of traders is not the immediate consumption of the commodity, but rather as a means of delaying or accelerating consumption over time.
General Motors	General Motors is the world's largest automaker. Founded in 1908, today it employs about 327,000 people around the world. With global headquarters in Detroit, it manufactures its cars and trucks in 33 countries.
Debt ratio	Debt ratio refers to the calculation of the total liabilities divided by the total liabilities plus capital. This results in the measurment of the debt level of the business (leverage).
General Mills	In 2001, the General Mills purchased Pillsbury, although it was officially described as a "merger." While many of the Pillsbury-branded products are still manufactured by General Mills, some products had to be sold off to allow the merger since the new company would have held a very strong monopoly position.
Microsoft	Microsoft is a multinational computer technology corporation with 2004 global annual sales of US$39.79 billion and 71,553 employees in 102 countries and regions as of July 2006. It develops, manufactures, licenses, and supports a wide range of software products for computing devices.
Starbucks	Although it has endured much criticism for its purported monopoly on the global coffee-bean market, Starbucks purchases only 3% of the coffee beans grown worldwide. In 2000 the company introduced a line of fair trade products and now offers three options for socially conscious coffee drinkers. According to Starbucks, they purchased 4.8 million pounds of Certified Fair Trade coffee in fiscal year 2004 and 11.5 million pounds in 2005.
Oracle	In 2004, sales at Oracle grew at a rate of 14.5% to $6.2 billion, giving it 41.3% and the top share of the relational-database market. Their main competitors in the database arena are IBM DB2 and Microsoft SQL Server, and to a lesser extent Sybase, Teradata, Informix, and MySQL. In the applications arena, their main competitor is SAP.
Liability	A liability is a present obligation of the enterprise arizing from past events, the settlement of which is expected to result in an outflow from the enterprise of resources embodying economic benefits.

Go to **Cram101.com** for the Practice Tests for this Chapter.

Dividend	Amount of corporate profits paid out for each share of stock is referred to as dividend.
Stock	In financial terminology, stock is the capital raized by a corporation, through the issuance and sale of shares.
Market	A market is, as defined in economics, a social arrangement that allows buyers and sellers to discover information and carry out a voluntary exchange of goods or services.
Shares	Shares refer to an equity security, representing a shareholder's ownership of a corporation. Shares are one of a finite number of equal portions in the capital of a company, entitling the owner to a proportion of distributed, non-reinvested profits known as dividends and to a portion of the value of the company in case of liquidation.
Stockholder	A stockholder is an individual or company (including a corporation) that legally owns one or more shares of stock in a joined stock company. The shareholders are the owners of a corporation. Companies listed at the stock market strive to enhance shareholder value.
Cash flow	In finance, cash flow refers to the amounts of cash being received and spent by a business during a defined period of time, sometimes tied to a specific project. Most of the time they are being used to determine gaps in the liquid position of a company.
Equity	Equity is the name given to the set of legal principles, in countries following the English common law tradition, which supplement strict rules of law where their application would operate harshly, so as to achieve what is sometimes referred to as "natural justice."
Expected return	Expected return refers to the return on an asset expected over the next period.
Return on equity	Net profit after taxes per dollar of equity capital is referred to as return on equity.
Present value	The value today of a stream of payments and/or receipts over time in the future and/or the past, converted to the present using an interest rate. If X t is the amount in period t and r the interest rate, then present value at time t=0 is V = ?T /t.
Time horizon	A time horizon is a fixed point of time in the future at which point certain processes will be evaluated or assumed to end. It is necessary in an accounting, finance or risk management regime to assign such a fixed horizon time so that alternatives can be evaluated for performance over the same period of time.
Firm	An organization that employs resources to produce a good or service for profit and owns and operates one or more plants is referred to as a firm.
Board of directors	The group of individuals elected by the stockholders of a corporation to oversee its operations is a board of directors.
Authority	Authority in agency law, refers to an agent's ability to affect his principal's legal relations with third parties. Also used to refer to an actor's legal power or ability to do something. In addition, sometimes used to refer to a statute, case, or other legal source that justifies a particular result.
Valuation	In finance, valuation is the process of estimating the market value of a financial asset or liability. They can be done on assets (for example, investments in marketable securities such as stocks, options, business enterprises, or intangible assets such as patents and trademarks) or on liabilities (e.g., Bonds issued by a company).
Management	Management characterizes the process of leading and directing all or part of an organization, often a business, through the deployment and manipulation of resources. Early twentieth-century management writer Mary Parker Follett defined management as "the art of getting things done through people."
Option	A contract that gives the purchaser the option to buy or sell the underlying financial instrument at a specified price, called the exercise price or strike price, within a specific

Go to **Cram101.com** for the Practice Tests for this Chapter.

period of time.

Financial assets	Financial assets refer to monetary claims or obligations by one party against another party. Examples are bonds, mortgages, bank loans, and equities.
Profit	Profit refers to the return to the resource entrepreneurial ability; total revenue minus total cost.
Asset	An item of property, such as land, capital, money, a share in ownership, or a claim on others for future payment, such as a bond or a bank deposit is an asset.
Appreciation	Appreciation refers to a rise in the value of a country's currency on the exchange market, relative either to a particular other currency or to a weighted average of other currencies. The currency is said to appreciate. Opposite of 'depreciation.' Appreciation can also refer to the increase in value of any asset.
Preference	The act of a debtor in paying or securing one or more of his creditors in a manner more favorable to them than to other creditors or to the exclusion of such other creditors is a preference. In the absence of statute, a preference is perfectly good, but to be legal it must be bona fide, and not a mere subterfuge of the debtor to secure a future benefit to himself or to prevent the application of his property to his debts.
Bid	A bid price is a price offered by a buyer when he/she buys a good. In the context of stock trading on a stock exchange, the bid price is the highest price a buyer of a stock is willing to pay for a share of that given stock.
Argument	The discussion by counsel for the respective parties of their contentions on the law and the facts of the case being tried in order to aid the jury in arriving at a correct and just conclusion is called argument.
Investment	Investment refers to spending for the production and accumulation of capital and additions to inventories. In a financial sense, buying an asset with the expectation of making a return.
Security	Security refers to a claim on the borrower future income that is sold by the borrower to the lender. A security is a type of transferable interest representing financial value.
Holding	The holding is a court's determination of a matter of law based on the issue presented in the particular case. In other words: under this law, with these facts, this result.
Corporation	A legal entity chartered by a state or the Federal government that is distinct and separate from the individuals who own it is a corporation. This separation gives the corporation unique powers which other legal entities lack.
Principal	In agency law, one under whose direction an agent acts and for whose benefit that agent acts is a principal.
Economic theory	Economic theory refers to a statement of a cause-effect relationship; when accepted by all economists, an economic principle.
Capital market	A financial market in which long-term debt and equity instruments are traded is referred to as a capital market. The capital market includes the stock market and the bond market.
Capital	Capital generally refers to financial wealth, especially that used to start or maintain a business. In classical economics, capital is one of four factors of production, the others being land and labor and entrepreneurship.
Financial market	In economics, a financial market is a mechanism which allows people to trade money for securities or commodities such as gold or other precious metals. In general, any commodity market might be considered to be a financial market, if the usual purpose of traders is not the immediate consumption of the commodity, but rather as a means of delaying or accelerating consumption over time.

Go to **Cram101.com** for the Practice Tests for this Chapter.

227

Transaction cost	A transaction cost is a cost incurred in making an economic exchange. For example, most people, when buying or selling a stock, must pay a commission to their broker; that commission is a transaction cost of doing the stock deal.
Market price	Market price is an economic concept with commonplace familiarity; it is the price that a good or service is offered at, or will fetch, in the marketplace; it is of interest mainly in the study of microeconomics.
Capital gain	Capital gain refers to the gain in value that the owner of an asset experiences when the price of the asset rises, including when the currency in which the asset is denominated appreciates.
Gain	In finance, gain is a profit or an increase in value of an investment such as a stock or bond. Gain is calculated by fair market value or the proceeds from the sale of the investment minus the sum of the purchase price and all costs associated with it.
Retained earnings	Cumulative earnings of a company that are not distributed to the owners and are reinvested in the business are called retained earnings.
Flotation cost	Flotation cost refers to the distribution cost of selling securities to the public. The cost includes the underwriter's spread and any associated fees.
Trust	An arrangement in which shareholders of independent firms agree to give up their stock in exchange for trust certificates that entitle them to a share of the trust's common profits.
Time value of money	Time value of money is the concept that the value of money varies depending on the timing of the cash flows, given any interest rate greater than zero.
Value of money	Value of money refers to the quantity of goods and services for which a unit of money can be exchanged; the purchasing power of a unit of money; the reciprocal of the price level.
Incentive	An incentive is any factor (financial or non-financial) that provides a motive for a particular course of action, or counts as a reason for preferring one choice to the alternatives.
Economy	The income, expenditures, and resources that affect the cost of running a business and household are called an economy.
Tax reform	Tax reform is the process of changing the way taxes are collected or managed by the government. Some seek to reduce the level of taxation of all people by the government. Some seek to make the tax system more/less progressive in its effect. Some may be trying to make the tax system more understandable, or more accountable.
Tax Reform Act of 1986	Tax legislation that eliminated many of the abuses in the tax code and, at the same time, lowered the overall tax rates is a Tax Reform Act of 1986.
Social Security	Social security primarily refers to a field of social welfare concerned with social protection, or protection against socially recognized conditions, including poverty, old age, disability, unemployment, families with children and others.
Pension	A pension is a steady income given to a person (usually after retirement). Pensions are typically payments made in the form of a guaranteed annuity to a retired or disabled employee.
Policy	Similar to a script in that a policy can be a less than completely rational decision-making method. Involves the use of a pre-existing set of decision steps for any problem that presents itself.
Public utility	A firm that produces an essential good or service, has obtained from a government the right to be the sole supplier of the good or service in the area, and is regulated by that government to prevent the abuse of its monopoly power is a public utility.

Utility	Utility refers to the want-satisfying power of a good or service; the satisfaction or pleasure a consumer obtains from the consumption of a good or service.
Clientele effect	Clientele effect refers to the effect of investor preferences for dividends or capital gains. Investors tend to purchase securities that meet their needs.
Dividend yield	Dividends per share divided by market price per share are called a dividend yield. Dividend yield indicates the percentage return that a stockholder will receive on dividends alone.
Yield	The interest rate that equates a future value or an annuity to a given present value is a yield.
Residual	Residual payments can refer to an ongoing stream of payments in respect of the completion of past achievements.
Fund	Independent accounting entity with a self-balancing set of accounts segregated for the purposes of carrying on specific activities is referred to as a fund.
Appeal	Appeal refers to the act of asking an appellate court to overturn a decision after the trial court's final judgment has been entered.
Shareholder	A shareholder is an individual or company (including a corporation) that legally owns one or more shares of stock in a joined stock company.
Long run	In economic models, the long run time frame assumes no fixed factors of production. Firms can enter or leave the marketplace, and the cost (and availability) of land, labor, raw materials, and capital goods can be assumed to vary.
Downturn	A decline in a stock market or economic cycle is a downturn.
Cash dividend	A pro rata distribution of cash to stockholders of corporate stock is called a cash dividend.
Expectations theory	The proposition that the interest rate on a long-term bond will equal the average of the short-term interest rates that people expect to occur over the life of the long-term bond is referred to as expectations theory.
Microsoft	Microsoft is a multinational computer technology corporation with 2004 global annual sales of US$39.79 billion and 71,553 employees in 102 countries and regions as of July 2006. It develops, manufactures, licenses, and supports a wide range of software products for computing devices.
Speculation	The purchase or sale of an asset in hopes that its price will rise or fall respectively, in order to make a profit is called speculation.
A share	In finance the term A share has two distinct meanings, both relating to securities. The first is a designation for a 'class' of common or preferred stock. A share of common or preferred stock typically has enhanced voting rights or other benefits compared to the other forms of shares that may have been created. The equity structure, or how many types of shares are offered, is determined by the corporate charter.
Analyst	Analyst refers to a person or tool with a primary function of information analysis, generally with a more limited, practical and short term set of goals than a researcher.
Technology	The body of knowledge and techniques that can be used to combine economic resources to produce goods and services is called technology.
Mutual fund	A mutual fund is a form of collective investment that pools money from many investors and invests the money in stocks, bonds, short-term money market instruments, and/or other securities. In a mutual fund, the fund manager trades the fund's underlying securities, realizing capital gains or loss, and collects the dividend or interest income.
Double taxation	The taxation of both corporate net income and the dividends paid from this net income when

Go to **Cram101.com** for the Practice Tests for this Chapter.
And, **NEVER** highlight a book again!

they become the personal income of households a double taxation.

Administration	Administration refers to the management and direction of the affairs of governments and institutions; a collective term for all policymaking officials of a government; the execution and implementation of public policy.
Antitrust	Government intervention to alter market structure or prevent abuse of market power is called antitrust.
Monopoly	A monopoly is defined as a persistent market situation where there is only one provider of a kind of product or service.
Consideration	Consideration in contract law, a basic requirement for an enforceable agreement under traditional contract principles, defined in this text as legal value, bargained for and given in exchange for an act or promise. In corporation law, cash or property contributed to a corporation in exchange for shares, or a promise to contribute such cash or property.
Business Week	Business Week is a business magazine published by McGraw-Hill. It was first published in 1929 under the direction of Malcolm Muir, who was serving as president of the McGraw-Hill Publishing company at the time. It is considered to be the standard both in industry and among students.
Reuters	Reuters is best known as a news service that provides reports from around the world to newspapers and broadcasters. Its main focus is on supplying the financial markets with information and trading products.
Contributed capital	Contributed capital is the value of funds or other consideration contributed to a company in return for an ownership interest. For instance, contributed capital increases when a person invests money in a company and received a stock certificate recognizing their right to share in the profits and losses of a company and increases or decreases in the equity value of the company.
Bankruptcy	Bankruptcy is a legally declared inability or impairment of ability of an individual or organization to pay their creditors.
Liability	A liability is a present obligation of the enterprise arizing from past events, the settlement of which is expected to result in an outflow from the enterprise of resources embodying economic benefits.
Stock dividend	Stock dividend refers to pro rata distributions of stock or stock rights on common stock. They are usually issued in proportion to shares owned.
Common stock	Common stock refers to the basic, normal, voting stock issued by a corporation; called residual equity because it ranks after preferred stock for dividend and liquidation distributions.
Indenture	A bond contract that specifies the legal provisions of a bond issue is called an indenture.
Covenant	A covenant is a signed written agreement between two or more parties. Also referred to as a contract.
Preferred stock	Stock that has specified rights over common stock is a preferred stock.
Stock market	An organized marketplace in which common stocks are traded. In the United States, the largest stock market is the New York Stock Exchange, on which are traded the stocks of the largest U.S. companies.
Industry	A group of firms that produce identical or similar products is an industry. It is also used specifically to refer to an area of economic production focused on manufacturing which involves large amounts of capital investment before any profit can be realized, also called "heavy industry".

Go to **Cram101.com** for the Practice Tests for this Chapter.

Competitive market	A market in which no buyer or seller has market power is called a competitive market.
Payout ratio	A measure of the percentage of earnings distributed in the form of cash dividends to common stockholders is referred to as the payout ratio. More specifically, the firm's cash dividend divided by the firm's earnings in the same reporting period.
Accrual accounting	Method of accounting that records the effects of accounting events in the period in which such events occur regardless of when cash is exchanged is accrual accounting.
Accounting	A system that collects and processes financial information about an organization and reports that information to decision makers is referred to as accounting.
Net income	Net income is equal to the income that a firm has after subtracting costs and expenses from the total revenue. Expenses will typically include tax expense.
Accrual	An accrual is an accounting event in which the transaction is recognized when the action takes place, instead of when cash is disbursed or received.
Declaration date	The date on which the board of directors officially approves a dividend is called declaration date.
Date of record	Date of record refers to the date that establishes who will receive the dividend payment: Shareholders who actually own the stock on the record date will be paid the dividend even if the stock is sold before the dividend is paid.
Buyer	A buyer refers to a role in the buying center with formal authority and responsibility to select the supplier and negotiate the terms of the contract.
Brokerage firm	A company that conducts various aspects of securities trading, analysis and advisory services is a brokerage firm.
Open market	In economics, the open market is the term used to refer to the environment in which bonds are bought and sold.
Equity capital	Equity capital refers to money raized from within the firm or through the sale of ownership in the firm.
Stock split	Stock split refers to a corporate action that increases the shares in a public company. The price of the shares are adjusted such that the before and after market capitalization of the company remains the same and dilution does not occur.
Outstanding shares	Total number of shares of stock that are owned by stockholders on any particular date is referred to as outstanding shares.
Real value	Real value is the value of anything expressed in money of the day with the effects of inflation removed.
Holder	A person in possession of a document of title or an instrument payable or indorsed to him, his order, or to bearer is a holder.
Par value	The central value of a pegged exchange rate, around which the actual rate is permitted to fluctuate within set bounds is a par value.
Common equity	The common stock or ownership capital of the firm is common equity. Common equity may be supplied through retained earnings or the sale of new common stock.
Book value	The book value of an asset or group of assets is sometimes the price at which they were originally acquired, in many cases equal to purchase price.
Book value per share	Total shareholders' equity divided by the number of outstanding common shares is referred to as book value per share.

Go to **Cram101.com** for the Practice Tests for this Chapter.
And, **NEVER** highlight a book again!

Market value	Market value refers to the price of an asset agreed on between a willing buyer and a willing seller; the price an asset could demand if it is sold on the open market.
Wall Street Journal	Dow Jones & Company was founded in 1882 by reporters Charles Dow, Edward Jones and Charles Bergstresser. Jones converted the small Customers' Afternoon Letter into The Wall Street Journal, first published in 1889, and began delivery of the Dow Jones News Service via telegraph. The Journal featured the Jones 'Average', the first of several indexes of stock and bond prices on the New York Stock Exchange.
Journal	Book of original entry, in which transactions are recorded in a general ledger system, is referred to as a journal.
Dividend reinvestment plans	Plans that provide the investor with an opportunity to buy additional shares of stock with the cash dividends paid by the company are called dividend reinvestment plans.
Purchasing	Purchasing refers to the function in a firm that searches for quality material resources, finds the best suppliers, and negotiates the best price for goods and services.
Pro rata	Proportionate is referred to as pro rata. A method of equally and proportionately allocating money, profits or liabilities by percentage.
Premium	Premium refers to the fee charged by an insurance company for an insurance policy. The rate of losses must be relatively predictable: In order to set the premium (prices) insurers must be able to estimate them accurately.
Distribution	Distribution in economics, the manner in which total output and income is distributed among individuals or factors.
Restructuring	Restructuring is the corporate management term for the act of partially dismantling and reorganizing a company for the purpose of making it more efficient and therefore more profitable.
Business analysis	Business analysis is a structured methodology that is focused on completely understanding the customer's needs, identifying how best to meet those needs, and then "reinventing" the stream of processes to meet those needs.
Treasurer	In many governments, a treasurer is the person responsible for running the treasury. Treasurers are also employed by organizations to look after funds.
Management team	A management team is directly responsible for managing the day-to-day operations (and profitability) of a company.
Expense	In accounting, an expense represents an event in which an asset is used up or a liability is incurred. In terms of the accounting equation, expenses reduce owners' equity.
Dividend payout ratio	A measure of the percentage of earnings paid out in dividends; found by dividing cash dividends by the net income available to each class of stock is the dividend payout ratio.
Capital structure	Capital Structure refers to the way a corporation finances itself through some combination of equity sales, equity options, bonds, and loans. Optimal capital structure refers to the particular combination that minimizes the cost of capital while maximizing the stock price.
Enterprise	Enterprise refers to another name for a business organization. Other similar terms are business firm, sometimes simply business, sometimes simply firm, as well as company, and entity.
Par value stock	Par value stock refers to capital stock that has been assigned a value per share in the corporate charter. .
Value stock	In financial terminology, a stock that appears attractive using the fundamental criteria of

Go to **Cram101.com** for the Practice Tests for this Chapter.

stock valuation because of valuable assets, particularly cash and real estate, owned by its company. A stock may be named a value stock if its earnings per share, cash per share or book value is high relative to the stock price

239

Working capital management	Working capital management refers to the financing and management of the current assets of the firm. The financial manager determines the mix between temporary and permanent 'current assets' and the nature of the financing arrangement.
Working capital	The dollar difference between total current assets and total current liabilities is called working capital.
Controlling	A management function that involves determining whether or not an organization is progressing toward its goals and objectives, and taking corrective action if it is not is called controlling.
Management	Management characterizes the process of leading and directing all or part of an organization, often a business, through the deployment and manipulation of resources. Early twentieth-century management writer Mary Parker Follett defined management as "the art of getting things done through people."
Capital	Capital generally refers to financial wealth, especially that used to start or maintain a business. In classical economics, capital is one of four factors of production, the others being land and labor and entrepreneurship.
Balance	In banking and accountancy, the outstanding balance is the amount of money owned, (or due), that remains in a deposit account (or a loan account) at a given date, after all past remittances, payments and withdrawal have been accounted for. It can be positive (then, in the balance sheet of a firm, it is an asset) or negative (a liability).
Gain	In finance, gain is a profit or an increase in value of an investment such as a stock or bond. Gain is calculated by fair market value or the proceeds from the sale of the investment minus the sum of the purchase price and all costs associated with it.
Liability	A liability is a present obligation of the enterprise arizing from past events, the settlement of which is expected to result in an outflow from the enterprise of resources embodying economic benefits.
Asset	An item of property, such as land, capital, money, a share in ownership, or a claim on others for future payment, such as a bond or a bank deposit is an asset.
Inventory	Tangible property held for sale in the normal course of business or used in producing goods or services for sale is an inventory.
Payables	Obligations to make future economic sacrifices, usually cash payments, are referred to as payables. Same as current liabilities.
Accrual	An accrual is an accounting event in which the transaction is recognized when the action takes place, instead of when cash is disbursed or received.
Balance sheet	A statement of the assets, liabilities, and net worth of a firm or individual at some given time often at the end of its "fiscal year," is referred to as a balance sheet.
Equity	Equity is the name given to the set of legal principles, in countries following the English common law tradition, which supplement strict rules of law where their application would operate harshly, so as to achieve what is sometimes referred to as "natural justice."
Operation	A standardized method or technique that is performed repetitively, often on different materials resulting in different finished goods is called an operation.
Firm	An organization that employs resources to produce a good or service for profit and owns and operates one or more plants is referred to as a firm.
Operating activities	Cash flow activities that include the cash effects of transactions that create revenues and expenses and thus enter into the determination of net income is an operating activities.

Go to **Cram101.com** for the Practice Tests for this Chapter.

Accounts receivable	Accounts receivable is one of a series of accounting transactions dealing with the billing of customers which owe money to a person, company or organization for goods and services that have been provided to the customer. This is typically done in a one person organization by writing an invoice and mailing or delivering it to each customer.
Current account	Current account refers to a country's international transactions arising from current flows, as opposed to changes in stocks which are part of the capital account. Includes trade in goods and services plus inflows and outflows of transfers. A current account is a deposit account in the UK and countries with a UK banking heritage.
Fund	Independent accounting entity with a self-balancing set of accounts segregated for the purposes of carrying on specific activities is referred to as a fund.
Investment	Investment refers to spending for the production and accumulation of capital and additions to inventories. In a financial sense, buying an asset with the expectation of making a return.
Mistake	In contract law a mistake is incorrect understanding by one or more parties to a contract and may be used as grounds to invalidate the agreement. Common law has identified three different types of mistake in contract: unilateral mistake, mutual mistake, and common mistake.
Long run	In economic models, the long run time frame assumes no fixed factors of production. Firms can enter or leave the marketplace, and the cost (and availability) of land, labor, raw materials, and capital goods can be assumed to vary.
Entrepreneur	The owner/operator. The person who organizes, manages, and assumes the risks of a firm, taking a new idea or a new product and turning it into a successful business is an entrepreneur.
Lease	A contract for the possession and use of land or other property, including goods, on one side, and a recompense of rent or other income on the other is the lease.
Invoice	The itemized bill for a transaction, stating the nature of the transaction and its cost. In international trade, the invoice price is often the preferred basis for levying an ad valorem tariff.
Purchase order	A form on which items or services needed by a business firm are specified and then communicated to the vendor is a purchase order.
Matching	Matching refers to an accounting concept that establishes when expenses are recognized. Expenses are matched with the revenues they helped to generate and are recognized when those revenues are recognized.
Income statement	Income statement refers to a financial statement that presents the revenues and expenses and resulting net income or net loss of a company for a specific period of time.
Bail	Bail refers to an amount of money the defendant pays to the court upon release from custody as security that he or she will return for trial.
Capital account	The capital account is one of two primary components of the balance of payments. It tracks the movement of funds for investments and loans into and out of a country.
Credit	Credit refers to a recording as positive in the balance of payments, any transaction that gives rise to a payment into the country, such as an export, the sale of an asset, or borrowing from abroad.
Current liability	Current liability refers to a debt that can reasonably be expected to be paid from existing current assets or through the creation of other current liabilities, within one year or the operating cycle, whichever is longer.
Current asset	A current asset is an asset on the balance sheet which is expected to be sold or otherwise used up in the near future, usually within one year.

Grant	Grant refers to an intergovernmental transfer of funds . Since the New Deal, state and local governments have become increasingly dependent upon federal grants for an almost infinite variety of programs.
Vendor	A person who sells property to a vendee is a vendor. The words vendor and vendee are more commonly applied to the seller and purchaser of real estate, and the words seller and buyer are more commonly applied to the seller and purchaser of personal property.
Policy	Similar to a script in that a policy can be a less than completely rational decision-making method. Involves the use of a pre-existing set of decision steps for any problem that presents itself.
Conversion	Conversion refers to any distinct act of dominion wrongfully exerted over another's personal property in denial of or inconsistent with his rights therein. That tort committed by a person who deals with chattels not belonging to him in a manner that is inconsistent with the ownership of the lawful owner.
Cash conversion cycle	Cash conversion cycle, also known as asset conversion cycle, net operating cycle, working capital cycle or just cash cycle, is a figure used in the financial analysis of a business. The higher the number, the longer a firm's money is tied up in operations of the business and unavailable for other activities such as investing.
Labor	People's physical and mental talents and efforts that are used to help produce goods and services are called labor.
Operating cycle	Operating cycle refers to the time it takes for a company to purchase goods or services from suppliers, sell those goods and services to customers, and collect cash from customers.
Realization	Realization is the sale of assets when an entity is being liquidated.
Acquisition	A company's purchase of the property and obligations of another company is an acquisition.
Production	The creation of finished goods and services using the factors of production: land, labor, capital, entrepreneurship, and knowledge.
Peak	Peak refers to the point in the business cycle when an economic expansion reaches its highest point before turning down. Contrasts with trough.
Variable	A variable is something measured by a number; it is used to analyze what happens to other things when the size of that number changes.
Merchant	Under the Uniform Commercial Code, one who regularly deals in goods of the kind sold in the contract at issue, or holds himself out as having special knowledge or skill relevant to such goods, or who makes the sale through an agent who regularly deals in such goods or claims such knowledge or skill is referred to as merchant.
Pledge	In law a pledge (also pawn) is a bailment of personal property as a security for some debt or engagement.
Security	Security refers to a claim on the borrower future income that is sold by the borrower to the lender. A security is a type of transferable interest representing financial value.
Lender	Suppliers and financial institutions that lend money to companies is referred to as a lender.
Matching principle	The matching principle indictates that when it is reasonable to do so, expenses should be matched with revenues. When expenses are matched with revenues, they are not recognized until the associated revenue is also recognized.
Matching concept	Matching concept refers to process of matching expenses with the revenues they produce; three ways to match expenses with revenues include matching expenses directly to revenues, matching expenses to the period in which they are incurred, and matching expenses systematically with

revenues.

Maturity date	The date on which the final payment on a bond is due from the bond issuer to the investor is a maturity date.
Maturity	Maturity refers to the final payment date of a loan or other financial instrument, after which point no further interest or principal need be paid.
Interest	In finance and economics, interest is the price paid by a borrower for the use of a lender's money. In other words, interest is the amount of paid to "rent" money for a period of time.
Default	In finance, default occurs when a debtor has not met its legal obligations according to the debt contract, e.g. it has not made a scheduled payment, or violated a covenant (condition) of the debt contract.
Bankruptcy	Bankruptcy is a legally declared inability or impairment of ability of an individual or organization to pay their creditors.
Capital asset	In accounting, a capital asset is an asset that is recorded as property that creates more property, e.g. a factory that creates shoes, or a forest that yields a quantity of wood.
Context	The effect of the background under which a message often takes on more and richer meaning is a context. Context is especially important in cross-cultural interactions because some cultures are said to be high context or low context.
Option	A contract that gives the purchaser the option to buy or sell the underlying financial instrument at a specified price, called the exercise price or strike price, within a specific period of time.
Flotation cost	Flotation cost refers to the distribution cost of selling securities to the public. The cost includes the underwriter's spread and any associated fees.
Transaction cost	A transaction cost is a cost incurred in making an economic exchange. For example, most people, when buying or selling a stock, must pay a commission to their broker; that commission is a transaction cost of doing the stock deal.
Short rate	The balance advertisers have to pay if they estimated that they would run more ads in a year than they did and entered a contract to pay at a favorable rate is a short rate. The short rate is figured at the end of the year or sooner if advertisers fall behind schedule. It is calculated at a higher rate for the fewer insertions.
Market	A market is, as defined in economics, a social arrangement that allows buyers and sellers to discover information and carry out a voluntary exchange of goods or services.
Preferred stock	Stock that has specified rights over common stock is a preferred stock.
Stock	In financial terminology, stock is the capital raized by a corporation, through the issuance and sale of shares.
Tight money	A term to indicate time periods in which financing may be difficult to find and interest rates may be quite high by normal standards is called tight money.
Equity financing	Financing that consists of funds that are invested in exchange for ownership in the company is called equity financing.
Debt financing	Obtaining financing by borrowing money is debt financing.
Fixed asset	Fixed asset, also known as property, plant, and equipment (PP&E), is a term used in accountancy for assets and property which cannot easily be converted into cash. This can be compared with current assets such as cash or bank accounts, which are described as liquid assets. In most cases, only tangible assets are referred to as fixed.

Marketable securities	Marketable securities refer to securities that are readily traded in the secondary securities market.
Accounts payable	A written record of all vendors to whom the business firm owes money is referred to as accounts payable.
Commercial paper	Commercial paper is a money market security issued by large banks and corporations. It is generally not used to finance long-term investments but rather for purchases of inventory or to manage working capital. It is commonly bought by money funds (the issuing amounts are often too high for individual investors), and is generally regarded as a very safe investment.
Secured loan	Secured loan refers to a loan backed by something valuable, such as property.
Service	Service refers to a "non tangible product" that is not embodied in a physical good and that typically effects some change in another product, person, or institution. Contrasts with good.
Insurance	Insurance refers to a system by which individuals can reduce their exposure to risk of large losses by spreading the risks among a large number of persons.
Liquidated	Damages made certain by the prior agreement of the parties are called liquidated.
Trade credit	Trade credit refers to an amount that is loaned to an exporter to be repaid when the exports are paid for by the foreign importer.
Buyer	A buyer refers to a role in the buying center with formal authority and responsibility to select the supplier and negotiate the terms of the contract.
Contract	A contract is a "promise" or an "agreement" that is enforced or recognized by the law. In the civil law, a contract is considered to be part of the general law of obligations.
Discount	The difference between the face value of a bond and its selling price, when a bond is sold for less than its face value it's referred to as a discount.
Interest rate	The rate of return on bonds, loans, or deposits. When one speaks of 'the' interest rate, it is usually in a model where there is only one.
Effective interest rate	Yield rate of bonds, which is usually equal to the market rate of interest on the day the bonds are sold is the effective interest rate.
Accommodation	Accommodation is a term used to describe a delivery of nonconforming goods meant as a partial performance of a contract for the sale of goods, where a full performance is not possible.
Privilege	Generally, a legal right to engage in conduct that would otherwise result in legal liability is a privilege. Privileges are commonly classified as absolute or conditional. Occasionally, privilege is also used to denote a legal right to refrain from particular behavior.
Credit report	Information about a person's credit history that can be secured from a credit bureau is referred to as credit report.
Applicant	In many tribunal and administrative law suits, the person who initiates the claim is called the applicant.
Commercial bank	A firm that engages in the business of banking is a commercial bank.
Promissory note	Commercial paper or instrument in which the maker promises to pay a specific sum of money to another person, to his order, or to bearer is referred to as a promissory note.
Press release	A written public news announcement normally distributed to major news services is referred to as press release.
Corporation	A legal entity chartered by a state or the Federal government that is distinct and separate

from the individuals who own it is a corporation. This separation gives the corporation unique powers which other legal entities lack.

Collateral	Property that is pledged to the lender to guarantee payment in the event that the borrower is unable to make debt payments is called collateral.
Line of credit	Line of credit refers to a given amount of unsecured short-term funds a bank will lend to a business, provided the funds are readily available.
Creditworthiness	Creditworthiness indicates whether a borrower has in the past made loan payments when due.
Revolving credit agreement	A line of credit that is guaranteed by the bank is called a revolving credit agreement.
Prime rate	The rate that a bank charges its most creditworthy customers is referred to as the prime rate.
Compensating balance	A required minimum amount of funds that a firm receiving a loan must keep in a checking account at the lending bank is called compensating balance.
Interest payment	The payment to holders of bonds payable, calculated by multiplying the stated rate on the face of the bond by the par, or face, value of the bond. If bonds are issued at a discount or premium, the interest payment does not equal the interest expense.
Compensating balances	Compensating balances refer to a bank requirement that business customers maintain a minimum average balance. The required amount is usually computed as a percentage of customer loans outstanding or as a percentage of the future loans to which the bank has committed itself.
Interest expense	The cost a business incurs to borrow money. With respect to bonds payable, the interest expense is calculated by multiplying the market rate of interest by the carrying value of the bonds on the date of the payment.
Expense	In accounting, an expense represents an event in which an asset is used up or a liability is incurred. In terms of the accounting equation, expenses reduce owners' equity.
Corporate bond	A Corporate bond is a bond issued by a corporation, as the name suggests. The term is usually applied to longer term debt instruments, generally with a maturity date falling at least 12 months after their issue date (the term "commercial paper" being sometimes used for instruments with a shorter maturity).
Bond	Bond refers to a debt instrument, issued by a borrower and promising a specified stream of payments to the purchaser, usually regular interest payments plus a final repayment of principal.
Unsecured debt	Unsecured debt is a financial term that refers to any type of debt that is not collateralized by any specified assets in the event of default.
Money market mutual fund	Money market mutual fund refers to a fund operated by a financial institution that sells shares in the fund and holds liquid assets such as U.S. Treasury bills and short-term commercial bills.
Money market	The money market, in macroeconomics and international finance, refers to the equilibration of demand for a country's domestic money to its money supply; market for short-term financial instruments.
Pension fund	Amounts of money put aside by corporations, nonprofit organizations, or unions to cover part of the financial needs of members when they retire is a pension fund.
Mutual fund	A mutual fund is a form of collective investment that pools money from many investors and invests the money in stocks, bonds, short-term money market instruments, and/or other

securities. In a mutual fund, the fund manager trades the fund's underlying securities, realizing capital gains or loss, and collects the dividend or interest income.

Pension	A pension is a steady income given to a person (usually after retirement). Pensions are typically payments made in the form of a guaranteed annuity to a retired or disabled employee.
Dealer	People who link buyers with sellers by buying and selling securities at stated prices are referred to as a dealer.
Debt security	Type of security acquired by loaning assets is called a debt security.
Financial institution	A financial institution acts as an agent that provides financial services for its clients. Financial institutions generally fall under financial regulation from a government authority.
Industry	A group of firms that produce identical or similar products is an industry. It is also used specifically to refer to an area of economic production focused on manufacturing which involves large amounts of capital investment before any profit can be realized, also called "heavy industry".
Factoring	In mathematics, factorization or factoring is the decomposition of an object into a product of other objects, or factors, which when multiplied together give the original.
Cash value	The cash value of an insurance policy is the amount available to the policy holder in cash upon cancellation of the policy. This term is normally used with a whole life policy in which a portion of the premiums go toward an investment. The cash value is the value of this investment at any particular time.
Face value	The nominal or par value of an instrument as expressed on its face is referred to as the face value.
Cooperative	A business owned and controlled by the people who use it, producers, consumers, or workers with similar needs who pool their resources for mutual gain is called cooperative.
Administration	Administration refers to the management and direction of the affairs of governments and institutions; a collective term for all policymaking officials of a government; the execution and implementation of public policy.
Possession	Possession refers to respecting real property, exclusive dominion and control such as owners of like property usually exercise over it. Manual control of personal property either as owner or as one having a qualified right in it.
Profit	Profit refers to the return to the resource entrepreneurial ability; total revenue minus total cost.
Standing	Standing refers to the legal requirement that anyone seeking to challenge a particular action in court must demonstrate that such action substantially affects his legitimate interests before he will be entitled to bring suit.
Bad debt	In accounting and finance, bad debt is the portion of receivables that can no longer be collected, typically from accounts receivable or loans. Bad debt in accounting is considered an expense.
Inventory financing	The process of using inventory such as raw materials as collateral for a loan is inventory financing. Lenders may require additional collateral and may require an appraisal by a national appraisal firm acceptable to the lender. Depending on the type of inventory, the lender's advance rate can range from 35% to 80% of the orderly liquidation value of the inventory.
Lien	In its most extensive meaning, it is a charge on property for the payment or discharge of a debt or duty is referred to as lien.

Trust receipt	An instrument acknowledging that the borrower holds the inventory and proceeds for sale in trust for the lender is a trust receipt.
Chattel	Chattel refers to an article of tangible property other than land. It is distinguished from real property, or real estate. In the civil law systems personal property is often called movable property or movables - any property that can be moved from one location or another.
Trust	An arrangement in which shareholders of independent firms agree to give up their stock in exchange for trust certificates that entitle them to a share of the trust's common profits.
Compliance	A type of influence process where a receiver accepts the position advocated by a source to obtain favorable outcomes or to avoid punishment is the compliance.
Warehouse	Warehouse refers to a location, often decentralized, that a firm uses to store, consolidate, age, or mix stock; house product-recall programs; or ease tax burdens.
Administrative cost	An administrative cost is all executive, organizational, and clerical costs associated with the general management of an organization rather than with manufacturing, marketing, or selling
Property	Assets defined in the broadest legal sense. Property includes the unrealized receivables of a cash basis taxpayer, but not services rendered.
Holding	The holding is a court's determination of a matter of law based on the issue presented in the particular case. In other words: under this law, with these facts, this result.
Transactions demand	Transactions demand is the demand for financial assets, e.g., securities, money or foreign currency. It is used for purposes of business transactions and personal consumption.
Authority	Authority in agency law, refers to an agent's ability to affect his principal's legal relations with third parties. Also used to refer to an actor's legal power or ability to do something. In addition, sometimes used to refer to a statute, case, or other legal source that justifies a particular result.
Utility	Utility refers to the want-satisfying power of a good or service; the satisfaction or pleasure a consumer obtains from the consumption of a good or service.
Raw material	Raw material refers to a good that has not been transformed by production; a primary product.
Overtime	Overtime is the amount of time someone works beyond normal working hours.
Demand deposit	Demand deposit refers to a bank deposit that can be withdrawn 'on demand.' The term usually refers only to checking accounts, even though depositors in many other kinds of accounts may be able to write checks and regard their deposits as readily available.
Liquidity	Liquidity refers to the capacity to turn assets into cash, or the amount of assets in a portfolio that have that capacity.
Treasury bills	Short-term obligations of the federal government are treasury bills. They are like zero coupon bonds in that they do not pay interest prior to maturity; instead they are sold at a discount of the par value to create a positive yield to maturity.
Cash equivalent	A short-term investment with original maturities of three months or less that is readily convertible to cash and whose value is unlikely to change is a cash equivalent.
Payee	A person to whom a payment is made or is made payable is called the payee. It is an individual who is receiving tax-free damage payments under a structured settlement and proposes to make a transfer of payment rights under that settlement.
Federal Reserve	The Federal Reserve System was created via the Federal Reserve Act of December 23rd, 1913. All national banks were required to join the system and other banks could join. The Reserve Banks opened for business on November 16th, 1914. Federal Reserve Notes were created as part

Go to **Cram101.com** for the Practice Tests for this Chapter.
And, **NEVER** highlight a book again!

of the legislation, to provide an elastic supply of currency.

Clearing system	Clearing system refers to an arrangement among financial institutions for carrying out the transactions among them, including canceling out offsetting credits and debits on the same account.
Cash outflow	Cash flowing out of the business from all sources over a period of time is cash outflow.
Acceleration	Acceleration refers to the shortening of the time for the performance of a contract or the payment of a note by the operation of some provision in the contract or note itself.
Management system	A management system is the framework of processes and procedures used to ensure that an organization can fulfill all tasks required to achieve its objectives.
Revenue	Revenue is a U.S. business term for the amount of money that a company receives from its activities, mostly from sales of products and/or services to customers.
Fiduciary	Fiduciary refers to one who holds goods in trust for another or one who holds a position of trust and confidence.
Broker	In commerce, a broker is a party that mediates between a buyer and a seller. A broker who also acts as a seller or as a buyer becomes a principal party to the deal.
Stockbroker	A registered representative who works as a market intermediary to buy and sell securities for clients is a stockbroker.
Economies of scale	In economics, returns to scale and economies of scale are related terms that describe what happens as the scale of production increases. They are different terms and not to be used interchangeably.
Economy	The income, expenditures, and resources that affect the cost of running a business and household are called an economy.
Preference	The act of a debtor in paying or securing one or more of his creditors in a manner more favorable to them than to other creditors or to the exclusion of such other creditors is a preference. In the absence of statute, a preference is perfectly good, but to be legal it must be bona fide, and not a mere subterfuge of the debtor to secure a future benefit to himself or to prevent the application of his property to his debts.
Financial management	The job of managing a firm's resources so it can meet its goals and objectives is called financial management.
Credit sale	A credit sale occurs when a customer does not pay cash at the time of the sale but instead agrees to pay later. The sale occurs now, with payment from the customer to follow at a later time.
Specialist	A specialist is a trader who makes a market in one or several stocks and holds the limit order book for those stocks.
Current ratio	The current ratio is a comparison of a firm's current assets to its current liabilities. The current ratio is an indication of a firm's market liquidity and ability to meet short-term debt obligations.
Net worth	Net worth is the total assets minus total liabilities of an individual or company
Cash basis	Cash basis is a bookkeeping method that recognizes revenue and expenses at the time of cash receipt or payment. It is the opposite of Accrual Basis.
Frequency	Frequency refers to the speed of the up and down movements of a fluctuating economic variable; that is, the number of times per unit of time that the variable completes a cycle of up and down movement.

Go to **Cram101.com** for the Practice Tests for this Chapter.

257

Consumer market	All the individuals or households that want goods and services for personal consumption or use are a consumer market.
Marketing	Promoting and selling products or services to customers, or prospective customers, is referred to as marketing.
General manager	A manager who is responsible for several departments that perform different functions is called general manager.
Personnel	A collective term for all of the employees of an organization. Personnel is also commonly used to refer to the personnel management function or the organizational unit responsible for administering personnel programs.
Subsidiary	A company that is controlled by another company or corporation is a subsidiary.
Public company	A public company is a company owned by the public rather than by a relatively few individuals. There are two different meanings for this term: (1) A company that is owned by stockholders who are members of the general public and trade shares publicly, often through a listing on a stock exchange. Ownership is open to anyone that has the money and inclination to buy shares in the company. It is differentiated from privately held companies where the shares are held by a small group of individuals, who are often members of one or a small group of families or otherwise related individuals, or other companies. The variant of this type of company in the United Kingdom and Ireland is known as a public limited compan, and (2) A government-owned corporation. This meaning of a "public company" comes from the fact that government debt is sometimes referred to as "public debt" although there are no "public bonds", government finance is sometimes called "public finance", among similar uses. This is the less-common meaning.
Average collection period	The average amount of time that a receivable is outstanding, calculated by dividing 365 days by the receivables turnover ratio is an average collection period.
Shares	Shares refer to an equity security, representing a shareholder's ownership of a corporation. Shares are one of a finite number of equal portions in the capital of a company, entitling the owner to a proportion of distributed, non-reinvested profits known as dividends and to a portion of the value of the company in case of liquidation.
Complexity	The technical sophistication of the product and hence the amount of understanding required to use it is referred to as complexity. It is the opposite of simplicity.
Manufacturing	Production of goods primarily by the application of labor and capital to raw materials and other intermediate inputs, in contrast to agriculture, mining, forestry, fishing, and services a manufacturing.
Inventory management	The planning, coordinating, and controlling activities related to the flow of inventory into, through, and out of an organization is referred to as inventory management.
Idle time	Wages paid for unproductive time caused by lack of orders, machine breakdowns, material shortages, poor scheduling, and the like are called idle time.
Point of Sale	Point of sale can mean a retail shop, a checkout counter in a shop, or a variable location where a transaction occurs.
Levy	Levy refers to imposing and collecting a tax or tariff.
Shrinkage	Breakage and theft of merchandise by customers and employees is referred to as shrinkage.
Shelf life	Shelf life is the length of time that corresponds to a tolerable loss in quality of a processed food and other perishable items.
Carrying cost	The cost to hold an asset, usually inventory is called a carrying cost. For inventory, a

	carrying cost includes such items as interest, warehousing costs, insurance, and material-handling expenses.
Carrying costs	Carrying costs refers to costs that arise while holding an inventory of goods for sale.
Ordering costs	Costs of preparing, issuing, and paying purchase orders, plus receiving and inspecting the items included in the orders are ordering costs.
Control system	A control system is a device or set of devices that manage the behavior of other devices. Some devices or systems are not controllable.A control system is an interconnection of components connected or related in such a manner as to command, direct, or regulate itself or another system.
Economic order quantity	Decision model that calculates the optimal quantity of inventory to order under a set of assumptions is called economic order quantity.
Total cost	The sum of fixed cost and variable cost is referred to as total cost.
Galbraith	Galbraith was a prolific author, producing four dozen books and over a thousand articles on various subjects. His most famous works were perhaps a popular trilogy of books on economics, "American Capitalism" (1952), "The Affluent Society (1958)", and "The New Industrial State" (1967).
Safety stock	Safety stock is additional inventory planned to buffer against the variability in supply and demand plans, that could otherwise result in inventory shortages.
Points	Loan origination fees that may be deductible as interest by a buyer of property. A seller of property who pays points reduces the selling price by the amount of the points paid for the buyer.
Usage rate	Usage rate refers to quantity consumed or patronage-store visits during a specific period; varies significantly among different customer groups.
Supply	Supply is the aggregate amount of any material good that can be called into being at a certain price point; it comprises one half of the equation of supply and demand. In classical economic theory, a curve representing supply is one of the factors that produce price.
Warrant	A warrant is a security that entitles the holder to buy or sell a certain additional quantity of an underlying security at an agreed-upon price, at the holder's discretion.
Just In Time	Just In Time is an inventory strategy implemented to improve the return on investment of a business by reducing in-process inventory and its associated costs. The process is driven by a series of signals, or Kanban that tell production processes to make the next part.
Publicity	Publicity refers to any information about an individual, product, or organization that's distributed to the public through the media and that's not paid for or controlled by the seller.
Production line	A production line is a set of sequential operations established in a factory whereby materials are put through a refining process to produce an end-product that is suitable for onward consumption; or components are assembled to make a finished article.
Toyota	Toyota is a Japanese multinational corporation that manufactures automobiles, trucks and buses. Toyota is the world's second largest automaker by sales. Toyota also provides financial services through its subsidiary, Toyota Financial Services, and participates in other lines of business.
Technology	The body of knowledge and techniques that can be used to combine economic resources to produce goods and services is called technology.
Fixture	Fixture refers to a thing that was originally personal property and that has been actually or

Go to **Cram101.com** for the Practice Tests for this Chapter.

constructively affixed to the soil itself or to some structure legally a part of the land.

Inputs	The inputs used by a firm or an economy are the labor, raw materials, electricity and other resources it uses to produce its outputs.
Negotiation	Negotiation is the process whereby interested parties resolve disputes, agree upon courses of action, bargain for individual or collective advantage, and/or attempt to craft outcomes which serve their mutual interests.
Supervisor	A Supervisor is an employee of an organization with some of the powers and responsibilities of management, occupying a role between true manager and a regular employee. A Supervisor position is typically the first step towards being promoted into a management role.
Accounting	A system that collects and processes financial information about an organization and reports that information to decision makers is referred to as accounting.
Analyst	Analyst refers to a person or tool with a primary function of information analysis, generally with a more limited, practical and short term set of goals than a researcher.
Hearing	A hearing is a proceeding before a court or other decision-making body or officer. A hearing is generally distinguished from a trial in that it is usually shorter and often less formal.
Thinly capitalized	When debt owed by a corporation to the shareholders becomes too large in relation to the corporation's capital structure, the IRS may contend that the corporation is thinly capitalized.
Slump	A decline in performance, in a firm is a slump in sales or profits, or in a country is a slump in output or employment.
Trend	Trend refers to the long-term movement of an economic variable, such as its average rate of increase or decrease over enough years to encompass several business cycles.
Turnover	Turnover in a financial context refers to the rate at which a provider of goods cycles through its average inventory. Turnover in a human resources context refers to the characteristic of a given company or industry, relative to rate at which an employer gains and loses staff.
Cash flow	In finance, cash flow refers to the amounts of cash being received and spent by a business during a defined period of time, sometimes tied to a specific project. Most of the time they are being used to determine gaps in the liquid position of a company.
Unsecured loan	A loan that's not backed by any specific assets is an unsecured loan. The risk of repossession does not exist. This doesn't mean that the lender cannot take legal action in order to recover his money. However, such a legal process would be significantly longer and more expensive than with secured loans.
Gross margin	Gross margin is an ambiguous phrase that expresses the relationship between gross profit and sales revenue as Gross Margin = Revenue - costs of good sold.
Margin	A deposit by a buyer in stocks with a seller or a stockbroker, as security to cover fluctuations in the market in reference to stocks that the buyer has purchased but for which he has not paid is a margin. Commodities are also traded on margin.
Raw materials inventory	Raw materials inventory refers to inventory consisting of the basic inputs to the organization's production process.
Contribution margin	A company's contribution margin can be expressed as the percentage of each sale that remains after the variable costs are subtracted. In simplest terms, the contribution margin is total revenue minus total variable cost.
Contribution	In business organization law, the cash or property contributed to a business by its owners is

Go to **Cram101.com** for the Practice Tests for this Chapter.

referred to as contribution.

Fixed cost   The cost that a firm bears if it does not produce at all and that is independent of its output. The presence of a fixed cost tends to imply increasing returns to scale. Contrasts with variable cost.

Go to **Cram101.com** for the Practice Tests for this Chapter.

Cash flow	In finance, cash flow refers to the amounts of cash being received and spent by a business during a defined period of time, sometimes tied to a specific project. Most of the time they are being used to determine gaps in the liquid position of a company.
Futures	Futures refer to contracts for the sale and future delivery of stocks or commodities, wherein either party may waive delivery, and receive or pay, as the case may be, the difference in market price at the time set for delivery.
Firm	An organization that employs resources to produce a good or service for profit and owns and operates one or more plants is referred to as a firm.
Management	Management characterizes the process of leading and directing all or part of an organization, often a business, through the deployment and manipulation of resources. Early twentieth-century management writer Mary Parker Follett defined management as "the art of getting things done through people."
Business unit	The lowest level of the company which contains the set of functions that carry a product through its life span from concept through manufacture, distribution, sales and service is a business unit.
Business plan	A detailed written statement that describes the nature of the business, the target market, the advantages the business will have in relation to competition, and the resources and qualifications of the owner is referred to as a business plan.
Financial statement	Financial statement refers to a summary of all the transactions that have occurred over a particular period.
Operation	A standardized method or technique that is performed repetitively, often on different materials resulting in different finished goods is called an operation.
Comprehensive	A comprehensive refers to a layout accurate in size, color, scheme, and other necessary details to show how a final ad will look. For presentation only, never for reproduction.
Technology	The body of knowledge and techniques that can be used to combine economic resources to produce goods and services is called technology.
Revenue	Revenue is a U.S. business term for the amount of money that a company receives from its activities, mostly from sales of products and/or services to customers.
Capital	Capital generally refers to financial wealth, especially that used to start or maintain a business. In classical economics, capital is one of four factors of production, the others being land and labor and entrepreneurship.
Market	A market is, as defined in economics, a social arrangement that allows buyers and sellers to discover information and carry out a voluntary exchange of goods or services.
Charter	Charter refers to an instrument or authority from the sovereign power bestowing the right or power to do business under the corporate form of organization. Also, the organic law of a city or town, and representing a portion of the statute law of the state.
Competitor	Other organizations in the same industry or type of business that provide a good or service to the same set of customers is referred to as a competitor.
Personnel	A collective term for all of the employees of an organization. Personnel is also commonly used to refer to the personnel management function or the organizational unit responsible for administering personnel programs.
Staffing	Staffing refers to a management function that includes hiring, motivating, and retaining the best people available to accomplish the company's objectives.
Financial plan	The financial plan section of a business plan consists of three financial statements (the

Go to **Cram101.com** for the Practice Tests for this Chapter.

Go to **Cram101.com** for the Practice Tests for this Chapter.
And, **NEVER** highlight a book again!

income statement, the cash flow projection, and the balance sheet) and a brief analysis of these three statements.

Management team	A management team is directly responsible for managing the day-to-day operations (and profitability) of a company.
Expense	In accounting, an expense represents an event in which an asset is used up or a liability is incurred. In terms of the accounting equation, expenses reduce owners' equity.
Financial market	In economics, a financial market is a mechanism which allows people to trade money for securities or commodities such as gold or other precious metals. In general, any commodity market might be considered to be a financial market, if the usual purpose of traders is not the immediate consumption of the commodity, but rather as a means of delaying or accelerating consumption over time.
Treasurer	In many governments, a treasurer is the person responsible for running the treasury. Treasurers are also employed by organizations to look after funds.
Enterprise	Enterprise refers to another name for a business organization. Other similar terms are business firm, sometimes simply business, sometimes simply firm, as well as company, and entity.
Equity	Equity is the name given to the set of legal principles, in countries following the English common law tradition, which supplement strict rules of law where their application would operate harshly, so as to achieve what is sometimes referred to as "natural justice."
Security	Security refers to a claim on the borrower future income that is sold by the borrower to the lender. A security is a type of transferable interest representing financial value.
Analyst	Analyst refers to a person or tool with a primary function of information analysis, generally with a more limited, practical and short term set of goals than a researcher.
Parent company	Parent company refers to the entity that has a controlling influence over another company. It may have its own operations, or it may have been set up solely for the purpose of owning the Subject Company.
Credibility	The extent to which a source is perceived as having knowledge, skill, or experience relevant to a communication topic and can be trusted to give an unbiased opinion or present objective information on the issue is called credibility.
Profit	Profit refers to the return to the resource entrepreneurial ability; total revenue minus total cost.
Board of directors	The group of individuals elected by the stockholders of a corporation to oversee its operations is a board of directors.
Operational planning	The process of setting work standards and schedules necessary to implement the tactical objectives is operational planning.
Strategic planning	The process of determining the major goals of the organization and the policies and strategies for obtaining and using resources to achieve those goals is called strategic planning.
Planning horizon	The length of time it takes to conceive, develop, and complete a project and to recover the cost of the project on a discounted cash flow basis is referred to as planning horizon.
Operating budget	An operating budget is the annual budget of an activity stated in terms of Budget Classification Code, functional/subfunctional categories and cost accounts. It contains estimates of the total value of resources required for the performance of the operation including reimbursable work or services for others.

Budget	Budget refers to an account, usually for a year, of the planned expenditures and the expected receipts of an entity. For a government, the receipts are tax revenues.
Working capital management	Working capital management refers to the financing and management of the current assets of the firm. The financial manager determines the mix between temporary and permanent 'current assets' and the nature of the financing arrangement.
Working capital	The dollar difference between total current assets and total current liabilities is called working capital.
Strategic plan	The formal document that presents the ways and means by which a strategic goal will be achieved is a strategic plan. A long-term flexible plan that does not regulate activities but rather outlines the means to achieve certain results, and provides the means to alter the course of action should the desired ends change.
Market share	That fraction of an industry's output accounted for by an individual firm or group of firms is called market share.
Industry	A group of firms that produce identical or similar products is an industry. It is also used specifically to refer to an area of economic production focused on manufacturing which involves large amounts of capital investment before any profit can be realized, also called "heavy industry".
Product development	In business and engineering, new product development is the complete process of bringing a new product to market. There are two parallel aspects to this process : one involves product engineering ; the other marketing analysis. Marketers see new product development as the first stage in product life cycle management, engineers as part of Product Lifecycle Management.
Quota	A government-imposed restriction on quantity, or sometimes on total value, used to restrict the import of something to a specific quantity is called a quota.
Labor	People's physical and mental talents and efforts that are used to help produce goods and services are called labor.
Policy	Similar to a script in that a policy can be a less than completely rational decision-making method. Involves the use of a pre-existing set of decision steps for any problem that presents itself.
Small business	Small business refers to a business that is independently owned and operated, is not dominant in its field of operation, and meets certain standards of size in terms of employees or annual receipts.
Entrepreneur	The owner/operator. The person who organizes, manages, and assumes the risks of a firm, taking a new idea or a new product and turning it into a successful business is an entrepreneur.
Pro forma financial statements	Pro forma financial statements refer to a series of projected financial statements. Of major importance are the pro forma income statement, the pro forma balance sheet, and the cash budget.
Sales forecast	Sales forecast refers to the maximum total sales of a product that a firm expects to sell during a specified time period under specified environmental conditions and its own marketing efforts.
Liability	A liability is a present obligation of the enterprise arizing from past events, the settlement of which is expected to result in an outflow from the enterprise of resources embodying economic benefits.
Points	Loan origination fees that may be deductible as interest by a buyer of property. A seller of

property who pays points reduces the selling price by the amount of the points paid for the buyer.

Asset	An item of property, such as land, capital, money, a share in ownership, or a claim on others for future payment, such as a bond or a bank deposit is an asset.
Investment	Investment refers to spending for the production and accumulation of capital and additions to inventories. In a financial sense, buying an asset with the expectation of making a return.
Interest rate	The rate of return on bonds, loans, or deposits. When one speaks of 'the' interest rate, it is usually in a model where there is only one.
Inventory	Tangible property held for sale in the normal course of business or used in producing goods or services for sale is an inventory.
Turnover	Turnover in a financial context refers to the rate at which a provider of goods cycles through its average inventory. Turnover in a human resources context refers to the characteristic of a given company or industry, relative to rate at which an employer gains and loses staff.
Interest	In finance and economics, interest is the price paid by a borrower for the use of a lender's money. In other words, interest is the amount of paid to "rent" money for a period of time.
Benchmarking	The continuous process of comparing the levels of performance in producing products and services and executing activities against the best levels of performance is benchmarking.
Income statement	Income statement refers to a financial statement that presents the revenues and expenses and resulting net income or net loss of a company for a specific period of time.
Balance sheet	A statement of the assets, liabilities, and net worth of a firm or individual at some given time often at the end of its "fiscal year," is referred to as a balance sheet.
Balance	In banking and accountancy, the outstanding balance is the amount of money owned, (or due), that remains in a deposit account (or a loan account) at a given date, after all past remittances, payments and withdrawal have been accounted for. It can be positive (then, in the balance sheet of a firm, it is an asset) or negative (a liability).
Statement of cash flow	Reports inflows and outflows of cash during the accounting period in the categories of operating, investing, and financing is a statement of cash flow.
Total revenue	Total revenue refers to the total number of dollars received by a firm from the sale of a product; equal to the total expenditures for the product produced by the firm; equal to the quantity sold multiplied by the price at which it is sold.
Credit	Credit refers to a recording as positive in the balance of payments, any transaction that gives rise to a payment into the country, such as an export, the sale of an asset, or borrowing from abroad.
Interest expense	The cost a business incurs to borrow money. With respect to bonds payable, the interest expense is calculated by multiplying the market rate of interest by the carrying value of the bonds on the date of the payment.
Dividend	Amount of corporate profits paid out for each share of stock is referred to as dividend.
Stock	In financial terminology, stock is the capital raized by a corporation, through the issuance and sale of shares.
Current liability	Current liability refers to a debt that can reasonably be expected to be paid from existing current assets or through the creation of other current liabilities, within one year or the operating cycle, whichever is longer.
Percentage of	A budget method in which the advertising and/or promotions budget is set based on a

sales method	percentage of sales of the product is referred to as percentage of sales method.
Manufacturing	Production of goods primarily by the application of labor and capital to raw materials and other intermediate inputs, in contrast to agriculture, mining, forestry, fishing, and services a manufacturing.
Administration	Administration refers to the management and direction of the affairs of governments and institutions; a collective term for all policymaking officials of a government; the execution and implementation of public policy.
Marketing	Promoting and selling products or services to customers, or prospective customers, is referred to as marketing.
Yield	The interest rate that equates a future value or an annuity to a given present value is a yield.
Retained earnings	Cumulative earnings of a company that are not distributed to the owners and are reinvested in the business are called retained earnings.
Fixed asset	Fixed asset, also known as property, plant, and equipment (PP&E), is a term used in accountancy for assets and property which cannot easily be converted into cash. This can be compared with current assets such as cash or bank accounts, which are described as liquid assets. In most cases, only tangible assets are referred to as fixed.
Return on sales	Return on sales refers to the percent of net income generated by each dollar of sales; computed by dividing net income before taxes by sales revenue.
Payout ratio	A measure of the percentage of earnings distributed in the form of cash dividends to common stockholders is referred to as the payout ratio. More specifically, the firm's cash dividend divided by the firm's earnings in the same reporting period.
Fund	Independent accounting entity with a self-balancing set of accounts segregated for the purposes of carrying on specific activities is referred to as a fund.
Sustainable growth	A maximum amount of growth a firm can sustain without increasing financial leverage is called sustainable growth.
Financial ratio	A financial ratio is a ratio of two numbers of reported levels or flows of a company. It may be two financial flows categories divided by each other (profit margin, profit/revenue). It may be a level divided by a financial flow (price/earnings). It may be a flow divided by a level (return on equity or earnings/equity). The numerator or denominator may itself be a ratio (PEG ratio).
Dividend payout ratio	A measure of the percentage of earnings paid out in dividends; found by dividing cash dividends by the net income available to each class of stock is the dividend payout ratio.
Equity multiplier	The amount of assets per dollar of equity capital is referred to as equity multiplier.
Leverage	Leverage is using given resources in such a way that the potential positive or negative outcome is magnified. In finance, this generally refers to borrowing.
Accounting	A system that collects and processes financial information about an organization and reports that information to decision makers is referred to as accounting.
Capital budgeting	Capital budgeting is the planning process used to determine a firm's long term investments such as new machinery, replacement machinery, new plants, new products, and research and development projects.
Accumulated depreciation	Accumulated depreciation refers to the total depreciation that has been reported as depreciation expense for the entire life of a long-term tangible asset. It is a contra-asset

275

	account.
Depreciation	Depreciation is an accounting and finance term for the method of attributing the cost of an asset across the useful life of the asset. Depreciation is a reduction in the value of a currency in floating exchange rate.
Total cost	The sum of fixed cost and variable cost is referred to as total cost.
Capital expenditures	Major investments in long-term assets such as land, buildings, equipment, or research and development are referred to as capital expenditures.
Capital expenditure	A substantial expenditure that is used by a company to acquire or upgrade physical assets such as equipment, property, industrial buildings, including those which improve the quality and life of an asset is referred to as a capital expenditure.
Cash flow statement	A cash flow statement is a financial report that shows incoming and outgoing money during a particular period (often monthly or quarterly). The statement shows how changes in balance sheet and income accounts affected cash and cash equivalents and breaks the analysis down according to operating, investing, and financing activities.
Corporation	A legal entity chartered by a state or the Federal government that is distinct and separate from the individuals who own it is a corporation. This separation gives the corporation unique powers which other legal entities lack.
Inventory turnover ratio	Inventory turnover ratio refers to a ratio that measures the number of times on average the inventory sold during the period; computed by dividing cost of goods sold by the average inventory during the period.
Payables	Obligations to make future economic sacrifices, usually cash payments, are referred to as payables. Same as current liabilities.
Accrual	An accrual is an accounting event in which the transaction is recognized when the action takes place, instead of when cash is disbursed or received.
Wage	The payment for the service of a unit of labor, per unit time. In trade theory, it is the only payment to labor, usually unskilled labor. In empirical work, wage data may exclude other compenzation, which must be added to get the total cost of employment.
Cost ratio	An equality, the cost ratio shows the number of units of two products that can be produced with the same resources..
Inflation	An increase in the overall price level of an economy, usually as measured by the CPI or by the implicit price deflator is called inflation.
Economy	The income, expenditures, and resources that affect the cost of running a business and household are called an economy.
Vendor	A person who sells property to a vendee is a vendor. The words vendor and vendee are more commonly applied to the seller and purchaser of real estate, and the words seller and buyer are more commonly applied to the seller and purchaser of personal property.
Cost of goods sold	In accounting, the cost of goods sold describes the direct expenses incurred in producing a particular good for sale, including the actual cost of materials that comprise the good, and direct labor expense in putting the good in salable condition.
Accounts receivable	Accounts receivable is one of a series of accounting transactions dealing with the billing of customers which owe money to a person, company or organization for goods and services that have been provided to the customer. This is typically done in a one person organization by writing an invoice and mailing or delivering it to each customer.
Accounts payable	A written record of all vendors to whom the business firm owes money is referred to as

Go to **Cram101.com** for the Practice Tests for this Chapter.

	accounts payable.
Production	The creation of finished goods and services using the factors of production: land, labor, capital, entrepreneurship, and knowledge.
Product cost	Product cost refers to sum of the costs assigned to a product for a specific purpose. A concept used in applying the cost plus approach to product pricing in which only the costs of manufacturing the product are included in the cost amount to which the markup is added.
Closing date	Date when all advertising material must be submitted to a publication is referred to as the closing date.
Closing	The finalization of a real estate sales transaction that passes title to the property from the seller to the buyer is referred to as a closing. Closing is a sales term which refers to the process of making a sale. It refers to reaching the final step, which may be an exchange of money or acquiring a signature.
Current asset	A current asset is an asset on the balance sheet which is expected to be sold or otherwise used up in the near future, usually within one year.
Financing activities	Cash flow activities that include obtaining cash from issuing debt and repaying the amounts borrowed and obtaining cash from stockholders and paying dividends is referred to as financing activities.
Investing activities	Investing activities refers to cash flow activities that include purchasing and disposing of investments and productive long-lived assets using cash and lending money and collecting on those loans.
Operating activities	Cash flow activities that include the cash effects of transactions that create revenues and expenses and thus enter into the determination of net income is an operating activities.
Advertising	Advertising refers to paid, nonpersonal communication through various media by organizations and individuals who are in some way identified in the advertising message.
Supply	Supply is the aggregate amount of any material good that can be called into being at a certain price point; it comprises one half of the equation of supply and demand. In classical economic theory, a curve representing supply is one of the factors that produce price.
Cost accounting	Cost accounting measures and reports financial and nonfinancial information relating to the cost of acquiring or consuming resources in an organization. It provides information for both management accounting and financial accounting.
Senior management	Senior management is generally a team of individuals at the highest level of organizational management who have the day-to-day responsibilities of managing a corporation.
Cash budget	A projection of anticipated cash flows, usually over a one to two year period is called a cash budget.
Service	Service refers to a "non tangible product" that is not embodied in a physical good and that typically effects some change in another product, person, or institution. Contrasts with good.
Utility	Utility refers to the want-satisfying power of a good or service; the satisfaction or pleasure a consumer obtains from the consumption of a good or service.
Bad debt	In accounting and finance, bad debt is the portion of receivables that can no longer be collected, typically from accounts receivable or loans. Bad debt in accounting is considered an expense.
Discount	The difference between the face value of a bond and its selling price, when a bond is sold for less than its face value it's referred to as a discount.

Go to **Cram101.com** for the Practice Tests for this Chapter.
And, **NEVER** highlight a book again!

Interest payment	The payment to holders of bonds payable, calculated by multiplying the stated rate on the face of the bond by the par, or face, value of the bond. If bonds are issued at a discount or premium, the interest payment does not equal the interest expense.
Invoice	The itemized bill for a transaction, stating the nature of the transaction and its cost. In international trade, the invoice price is often the preferred basis for levying an ad valorem tariff.
Context	The effect of the background under which a message often takes on more and richer meaning is a context. Context is especially important in cross-cultural interactions because some cultures are said to be high context or low context.
Operating department	Operating department refers to department that directly adds value to a product or service. Also called a production department in manufacturing companies.
General manager	A manager who is responsible for several departments that perform different functions is called general manager.
Complaint	The pleading in a civil case in which the plaintiff states his claim and requests relief is called complaint. In the common law, it is a formal legal document that sets out the basic facts and legal reasons that the filing party (the plaintiffs) believes are sufficient to support a claim against another person, persons, entity or entities (the defendants) that entitles the plaintiff(s) to a remedy (either money damages or injunctive relief).
Inputs	The inputs used by a firm or an economy are the labor, raw materials, electricity and other resources it uses to produce its outputs.
Process planning	Choosing the best means for turning resources into useful goods and services is process planning.
Compromise	Compromise occurs when the interaction is moderately important to meeting goals and the goals are neither completely compatible nor completely incompatible.
Financial management	The job of managing a firm's resources so it can meet its goals and objectives is called financial management.
Scenario analysis	Scenario analysis is a process of analyzing possible future events by considering alternative possible outcomes. The analysis is designed to allow improved decision-making by allowing more complete consideration of outcomes and their implications.
Chief financial officer	Chief financial officer refers to executive responsible for overseeing the financial operations of an organization.
Holding	The holding is a court's determination of a matter of law based on the issue presented in the particular case. In other words: under this law, with these facts, this result.
Brief	Brief refers to a statement of a party's case or legal arguments, usually prepared by an attorney. Also used to make legal arguments before appellate courts.
Aid	Assistance provided by countries and by international institutions such as the World Bank to developing countries in the form of monetary grants, loans at low interest rates, in kind, or a combination of these is called aid. Aid can also refer to assistance of any type rendered to benefit some group or individual.
Household	An economic unit that provides the economy with resources and uses the income received to purchase goods and services that satisfy economic wants is called household.
Credit risk	The risk of loss due to a counterparty defaulting on a contract, or more generally the risk of loss due to some "credit event" is called credit risk.
Franchisor	A company that develops a product concept and sells others the rights to make and sell the

Go to **Cram101.com** for the Practice Tests for this Chapter.

products is referred to as a franchisor.

Independent business	In business, an independent business as a term of distinction generally refers to privately-owned companies (as opposed to those companies owned publicly through a distribution of shares on the market).
Preparation	Preparation refers to usually the first stage in the creative process. It includes education and formal training.
Venture capital	Venture capital is capital provided by outside investors for financing of new, growing or struggling businesses. Venture capital investments generally are high risk investments but offer the potential for above average returns.
Recovery	Characterized by rizing output, falling unemployment, rizing profits, and increasing economic activity following a decline is a recovery.
Current account	Current account refers to a country's international transactions arising from current flows, as opposed to changes in stocks which are part of the capital account. Includes trade in goods and services plus inflows and outflows of transfers. A current account is a deposit account in the UK and countries with a UK banking heritage.
Marginal tax rate	The percentage of an additional dollar of earnings that goes to taxes is referred to as the marginal tax rate.
Coupon rate	In bonds, notes or other fixed income securities, the stated percentage rate of interest, usually paid twice a year is the coupon rate.
Coupon	In finance, a coupon is "attached" to a bond, either physically (as with old bonds) or electronically. Each coupon represents a predetermined payment promized to the bond-holder in return for his or her loan of money to the bond-issuer. .
Internally generated funds	Internally generated funds refers to funds generated through the operations of the firm. The principal sources are retained earnings and cash flow added back from depreciation and other noncash deductions.
Depreciate	A nation's currency is said to depreciate when exchange rates change so that a unit of its currency can buy fewer units of foreign currency.
Product mix	The combination of product lines offered by a manufacturer is referred to as product mix.
Management system	A management system is the framework of processes and procedures used to ensure that an organization can fulfill all tasks required to achieve its objectives.

283

Capital structure	Capital Structure refers to the way a corporation finances itself through some combination of equity sales, equity options, bonds, and loans. Optimal capital structure refers to the particular combination that minimizes the cost of capital while maximizing the stock price.
Divestiture	In finance and economics, divestiture is the reduction of some kind of asset, for either financial or social goals. A divestment is the opposite of an investment.
Capital	Capital generally refers to financial wealth, especially that used to start or maintain a business. In classical economics, capital is one of four factors of production, the others being land and labor and entrepreneurship.
Asset	An item of property, such as land, capital, money, a share in ownership, or a claim on others for future payment, such as a bond or a bank deposit is an asset.
Restructuring	Restructuring is the corporate management term for the act of partially dismantling and reorganizing a company for the purpose of making it more efficient and therefore more profitable.
Bankruptcy	Bankruptcy is a legally declared inability or impairment of ability of an individual or organization to pay their creditors.
Merger	Merger refers to the combination of two firms into a single firm.
Mergers and acquisitions	The phrase mergers and acquisitions refers to the aspect of corporate finance strategy and management dealing with the merging and acquiring of different companies as well as other assets. Usually mergers occur in a friendly setting where executives from the respective companies participate in a due diligence process to ensure a successful combination of all parts.
Acquisition	A company's purchase of the property and obligations of another company is an acquisition.
Consolidation	The combination of two or more firms, generally of equal size and market power, to form an entirely new entity is a consolidation.
Business unit	The lowest level of the company which contains the set of functions that carry a product through its life span from concept through manufacture, distribution, sales and service is a business unit.
Controlling	A management function that involves determining whether or not an organization is progressing toward its goals and objectives, and taking corrective action if it is not is called controlling.
Financial management	The job of managing a firm's resources so it can meet its goals and objectives is called financial management.
Management	Management characterizes the process of leading and directing all or part of an organization, often a business, through the deployment and manipulation of resources. Early twentieth-century management writer Mary Parker Follett defined management as "the art of getting things done through people."
Firm	An organization that employs resources to produce a good or service for profit and owns and operates one or more plants is referred to as a firm.
Legal entity	A legal entity is a legal construct through which the law allows a group of natural persons to act as if it were an individual for certain purposes. The most common purposes are lawsuits, property ownership, and contracts.
Stock	In financial terminology, stock is the capital raized by a corporation, through the issuance and sale of shares.
Takeover	A takeover in business refers to one company (the acquirer) purchasing another (the target).

Go to **Cram101.com** for the Practice Tests for this Chapter.

	Such events resemble mergers, but without the formation of a new company.
Holder	A person in possession of a document of title or an instrument payable or indorsed to him, his order, or to bearer is a holder.
Shares	Shares refer to an equity security, representing a shareholder's ownership of a corporation. Shares are one of a finite number of equal portions in the capital of a company, entitling the owner to a proportion of distributed, non-reinvested profits known as dividends and to a portion of the value of the company in case of liquidation.
Shareholder	A shareholder is an individual or company (including a corporation) that legally owns one or more shares of stock in a joined stock company.
Stockholder	A stockholder is an individual or company (including a corporation) that legally owns one or more shares of stock in a joined stock company. The shareholders are the owners of a corporation. Companies listed at the stock market strive to enhance shareholder value.
Corporation	A legal entity chartered by a state or the Federal government that is distinct and separate from the individuals who own it is a corporation. This separation gives the corporation unique powers which other legal entities lack.
Context	The effect of the background under which a message often takes on more and richer meaning is a context. Context is especially important in cross-cultural interactions because some cultures are said to be high context or low context.
Negotiation	Negotiation is the process whereby interested parties resolve disputes, agree upon courses of action, bargain for individual or collective advantage, and/or attempt to craft outcomes which serve their mutual interests.
Interest	In finance and economics, interest is the price paid by a borrower for the use of a lender's money. In other words, interest is the amount of paid to "rent" money for a period of time.
Acquirer	An acquirer is a company offering debit and credit card acceptance services for merchants. Often the company is partially or wholly owned by a bank, sometimes a bank itself offers acquiring services.
Board of directors	The group of individuals elected by the stockholders of a corporation to oversee its operations is a board of directors.
Charter	Charter refers to an instrument or authority from the sovereign power bestowing the right or power to do business under the corporate form of organization. Also, the organic law of a city or town, and representing a portion of the statute law of the state.
Stock certificate	Evidence of stock ownership that specifies the name of the company, the number of shares it represents, and the type of stock being issued is referred to as the stock certificate.
Target firm	The firm that is being studied or benchmarked against is referred to as target firm.
Tender offer	A public offer by a bidder to purchase a subject company's shares directly from its shareholders at a specified price for a fixed period of time is called tender offer.
Tender	An unconditional offer of payment, consisting in the actual production in money or legal tender of a sum not less than the amount due.
Fixed price	Fixed price is a phrase used to mean that no bargaining is allowed over the price of a good or, less commonly, a service.
Gain	In finance, gain is a profit or an increase in value of an investment such as a stock or bond. Gain is calculated by fair market value or the proceeds from the sale of the investment minus the sum of the purchase price and all costs associated with it.
Purchasing	Purchasing refers to the function in a firm that searches for quality material resources,

287

	finds the best suppliers, and negotiates the best price for goods and services.
Investment	Investment refers to spending for the production and accumulation of capital and additions to inventories. In a financial sense, buying an asset with the expectation of making a return.
Market price	Market price is an economic concept with commonplace familiarity; it is the price that a good or service is offered at, or will fetch, in the marketplace; it is of interest mainly in the study of microeconomics.
Argument	The discussion by counsel for the respective parties of their contentions on the law and the facts of the case being tried in order to aid the jury in arriving at a correct and just conclusion is called argument.
Market	A market is, as defined in economics, a social arrangement that allows buyers and sellers to discover information and carry out a voluntary exchange of goods or services.
Raw material	Raw material refers to a good that has not been transformed by production; a primary product.
Production	The creation of finished goods and services using the factors of production: land, labor, capital, entrepreneurship, and knowledge.
Competitor	Other organizations in the same industry or type of business that provide a good or service to the same set of customers is referred to as a competitor.
Conglomerate merger	A conglomerate merger is whereby two companies or organizations which have no common interest and nor competitors or have or could have the same supplier or customers merger.
Conglomerate	A conglomerate is a large company that consists of divisions of often seemingly unrelated businesses.
Investment banks	Investment banks, assist public and private corporations in raising funds in the capital markets (both equity and debt), as well as in providing strategic advisory services for mergers, acquisitions and other types of financial transactions. They also act as intermediaries in trading for clients. Investment banks differ from commercial banks, which take deposits and make commercial and retail loans.
Security	Security refers to a claim on the borrower future income that is sold by the borrower to the lender. A security is a type of transferable interest representing financial value.
Antitrust laws	Legislation that prohibits anticompetitive business activities such as price fixing, bid rigging, monopolization, and tying contracts is referred to as antitrust laws.
Antitrust	Government intervention to alter market structure or prevent abuse of market power is called antitrust.
Industry	A group of firms that produce identical or similar products is an industry. It is also used specifically to refer to an area of economic production focused on manufacturing which involves large amounts of capital investment before any profit can be realized, also called "heavy industry".
Economy	The income, expenditures, and resources that affect the cost of running a business and household are called an economy.
Fair dealing	Fair dealing is a doctrine of limitations and exceptions to copyright which is found in many of the common law jurisdictions of the Commonwealth of Nations.
Horizontal merger	Horizontal merger refers to the merger into a single firm of two firms producing the same product and selling it in the same geographic market.
Federal government	Federal government refers to the government of the United States, as distinct from the state and local governments.

Go to **Cram101.com** for the Practice Tests for this Chapter.

Monopoly	A monopoly is defined as a persistent market situation where there is only one provider of a kind of product or service.
Trust	An arrangement in which shareholders of independent firms agree to give up their stock in exchange for trust certificates that entitle them to a share of the trust's common profits.
Synergy	Corporate synergy occurs when corporations interact congruently. A corporate synergy refers to a financial benefit that a corporation expects to realize when it merges with or acquires another corporation.
Marketing	Promoting and selling products or services to customers, or prospective customers, is referred to as marketing.
Brand	A name, symbol, or design that identifies the goods or services of one seller or group of sellers and distinguishes them from the goods and services of competitors is a brand.
Market share	That fraction of an industry's output accounted for by an individual firm or group of firms is called market share.
Portfolio	In finance, a portfolio is a collection of investments held by an institution or a private individual. Holding but not always a portfolio is part of an investment and risk-limiting strategy called diversification. By owning several assets, certain types of risk (in particular specific risk) can be reduced.
Operation	A standardized method or technique that is performed repetitively, often on different materials resulting in different finished goods is called an operation.
Acquit	To set free or judicially to discharge from an accuzation is to acquit.
Book value	The book value of an asset or group of assets is sometimes the price at which they were originally acquired, in many cases equal to purchase price.
Credit	Credit refers to a recording as positive in the balance of payments, any transaction that gives rise to a payment into the country, such as an export, the sale of an asset, or borrowing from abroad.
Profit	Profit refers to the return to the resource entrepreneurial ability; total revenue minus total cost.
Expense	In accounting, an expense represents an event in which an asset is used up or a liability is incurred. In terms of the accounting equation, expenses reduce owners' equity.
Holding company	A corporation whose purpose or function is to own or otherwise hold the shares of other corporations either for investment or control is called holding company.
Subsidiary	A company that is controlled by another company or corporation is a subsidiary.
Holding	The holding is a court's determination of a matter of law based on the issue presented in the particular case. In other words: under this law, with these facts, this result.
Business operations	Business operations are those activities involved in the running of a business for the purpose of producing value for the stakeholders. The outcome of business operations is the harvesting of value from assets owned by a business.
Tactic	A short-term immediate decision that, in its totality, leads to the achievement of strategic goals is called a tactic.
Stock market	An organized marketplace in which common stocks are traded. In the United States, the largest stock market is the New York Stock Exchange, on which are traded the stocks of the largest U.S. companies.
Oligopoly	A market structure in which there are a small number of sellers, at least some of whose

individual decisions about price or quantity matter to the others is an oligopoly.

Consideration	Consideration in contract law, a basic requirement for an enforceable agreement under traditional contract principles, defined in this text as legal value, bargained for and given in exchange for an act or promise. In corporation law, cash or property contributed to a corporation in exchange for shares, or a promise to contribute such cash or property.
P/E ratio	In finance, the P/E ratio of a stock is used to measure how cheap or expensive share prices are. It is probably the single most consistent red flag to excessive optimism and over-investment.
Investment banker	Investment banker refers to a financial organization that specializes in selling primary offerings of securities. Investment bankers can also perform other financial functions, such as advising clients, negotiating mergers and takeovers, and selling secondary offerings.
Bond market	The bond market refers to people and entities involved in buying and selling of bonds and the quantity and prices of those transactions over time.
Junk bond	In finance, a junk bond is a bond that is rated below investment grade. These bonds have a higher risk of defaulting, but typically pay high yields in order to make them attractive to investors.
Bond	Bond refers to a debt instrument, issued by a borrower and promising a specified stream of payments to the purchaser, usually regular interest payments plus a final repayment of principal.
Cash flow	In finance, cash flow refers to the amounts of cash being received and spent by a business during a defined period of time, sometimes tied to a specific project. Most of the time they are being used to determine gaps in the liquid position of a company.
Capital budgeting	Capital budgeting is the planning process used to determine a firm's long term investments such as new machinery, replacement machinery, new plants, new products, and research and development projects.
Mistake	In contract law a mistake is incorrect understanding by one or more parties to a contract and may be used as grounds to invalidate the agreement. Common law has identified three different types of mistake in contract: unilateral mistake, mutual mistake, and common mistake.
Cost of equity	In finance, the cost of equity is the minimum rate of return a firm must offer shareholders to compensate for waiting for their returns, and for bearing some risk.
Discount rate	Discount rate refers to the rate, per year, at which future values are diminished to make them comparable to values in the present. Can be either subjective or objective .
Discount	The difference between the face value of a bond and its selling price, when a bond is sold for less than its face value it's referred to as a discount.
Equity	Equity is the name given to the set of legal principles, in countries following the English common law tradition, which supplement strict rules of law where their application would operate harshly, so as to achieve what is sometimes referred to as "natural justice."
Fund	Independent accounting entity with a self-balancing set of accounts segregated for the purposes of carrying on specific activities is referred to as a fund.
Yield	The interest rate that equates a future value or an annuity to a given present value is a yield.
Premium	Premium refers to the fee charged by an insurance company for an insurance policy. The rate of losses must be relatively predictable: In order to set the premium (prices) insurers must be able to estimate them accurately.

Go to **Cram101.com** for the Practice Tests for this Chapter.

293

Market value	Market value refers to the price of an asset agreed on between a willing buyer and a willing seller; the price an asset could demand if it is sold on the open market.
Speculation	The purchase or sale of an asset in hopes that its price will rise or fall respectively, in order to make a profit is called speculation.
Remainder	A remainder in property law is a future interest created in a transferee that is capable of becoming possessory upon the natural termination of a prior estate created by the same instrument.
A share	In finance the term A share has two distinct meanings, both relating to securities. The first is a designation for a 'class' of common or preferred stock. A share of common or preferred stock typically has enhanced voting rights or other benefits compared to the other forms of shares that may have been created. The equity structure, or how many types of shares are offered, is determined by the corporate charter.
Present value	The value today of a stream of payments and/or receipts over time in the future and/or the past, converted to the present using an interest rate. If X t is the amount in period t and r the interest rate, then present value at time t=0 is V = ?T /t.
Cash inflow	Cash coming into the company as the result of a previous investment is a cash inflow.
Alpha	Alpha is a risk-adjusted measure of the so-called "excess return" on an investment. It is a common measure of assessing active manager's performance as it is the return in excess of a benchmark index or "risk-free" investment.
Interest rate	The rate of return on bonds, loans, or deposits. When one speaks of 'the' interest rate, it is usually in a model where there is only one.
Depreciation	Depreciation is an accounting and finance term for the method of attributing the cost of an asset across the useful life of the asset. Depreciation is a reduction in the value of a currency in floating exchange rate.
Balance sheet	A statement of the assets, liabilities, and net worth of a firm or individual at some given time often at the end of its "fiscal year," is referred to as a balance sheet.
Balance	In banking and accountancy, the outstanding balance is the amount of money owned, (or due), that remains in a deposit account (or a loan account) at a given date, after all past remittances, payments and withdrawal have been accounted for. It can be positive (then, in the balance sheet of a firm, it is an asset) or negative (a liability).
Treasury bills	Short-term obligations of the federal government are treasury bills. They are like zero coupon bonds in that they do not pay interest prior to maturity; instead they are sold at a discount of the par value to create a positive yield to maturity.
Terminal value	In finance, the terminal value of a security is the present value at a future point in time of all future cash flows. It is most often used in multi-stage discounted cash flow analysis, and allows for the limitation of cash flow projections to a several-year period.
Stock valuation	There are several methods used for stock valuation. They try to give an estimate of their fair value, by using fundamental economic criteria. This theoretical valuation has to be perfected with market criteria, as the final purpose is to determine potential market prices.
Valuation	In finance, valuation is the process of estimating the market value of a financial asset or liability. They can be done on assets (for example, investments in marketable securities such as stocks, options, business enterprises, or intangible assets such as patents and trademarks) or on liabilities (e.g., Bonds issued by a company).
Failure rate	Failure rate is the frequency with an engineered system or component fails, expressed for example in failures per hour. Failure rate is usually time dependent. In the special case

Go to **Cram101.com** for the Practice Tests for this Chapter.

Go to **Cram101.com** for the Practice Tests for this Chapter.
And, **NEVER** highlight a book again!

	when the likelihood of failure remains constant as time passes, failure rate is simply the inverse of the mean time to failure, expressed for example in hours per failure.
Business Week	Business Week is a business magazine published by McGraw-Hill. It was first published in 1929 under the direction of Malcolm Muir, who was serving as president of the McGraw-Hill Publishing company at the time. It is considered to be the standard both in industry and among students.
Strategic management	A philosophy of management that links strategic planning with dayto-day decision making. Strategic management seeks a fit between an organization's external and internal environments.
Wall Street Journal	Dow Jones & Company was founded in 1882 by reporters Charles Dow, Edward Jones and Charles Bergstresser. Jones converted the small Customers' Afternoon Letter into The Wall Street Journal, first published in 1889, and began delivery of the Dow Jones News Service via telegraph. The Journal featured the Jones 'Average', the first of several indexes of stock and bond prices on the New York Stock Exchange.
Journal	Book of original entry, in which transactions are recorded in a general ledger system, is referred to as a journal.
Recession	A significant decline in economic activity. In the U.S., recession is approximately defined as two successive quarters of falling GDP, as judged by NBER.
Service	Service refers to a "non tangible product" that is not embodied in a physical good and that typically effects some change in another product, person, or institution. Contrasts with good.
Leverage	Leverage is using given resources in such a way that the potential positive or negative outcome is magnified. In finance, this generally refers to borrowing.
White knight	White knight refers to a firm that management calls on to help it avoid an unwanted takeover offer. It is an invited suitor.
Greenmail	The purchase by a target corporation of its stock from an actual or perceived tender offeror at a premium is a greenmail.
Anticipation	In finance, anticipation is where debts are paid off early, generally in order to pay less interest.
Bylaw	In corporation law, a document that supplements the articles of incorporation and contains less important rights, powers, and responsibilities of a corporation and its shareholders, officers, and directors is referred to as a bylaw.
Controlling interest	A firm has a controlling interest in another business entity when it owns more than 50 percent of that entity's voting stock.
Poison pill	Poison pill refers to a strategy that makes a firm unattractive as a potential takeover candidate. These are attempts by a potential acquirer to obtain a control block of shares in a target company, and thereby gain control of the board and, through it, the company's management.
Contract	A contract is a "promise" or an "agreement" that is enforced or recognized by the law. In the civil law, a contract is considered to be part of the general law of obligations.
Principal	In agency law, one under whose direction an agent acts and for whose benefit that agent acts is a principal.
Default	In finance, default occurs when a debtor has not met its legal obligations according to the debt contract, e.g. it has not made a scheduled payment, or violated a covenant (condition) of the debt contract.

Go to **Cram101.com** for the Practice Tests for this Chapter.
And, **NEVER** highlight a book again!

Leveraged buyout	An attempt by employees, management, or a group of investors to purchase an organization primarily through borrowing is a leveraged buyout.
Buyout	A buyout is an investment transaction by which the entire or a controlling part of the stock of a company is sold. A firm buysout the stake of the company to strengthen its influence on the company's decision making body. A buyout can take the forms of a leveraged buyout or a management buyout.
Nabisco	In 2000 Philip Morris Companies acquired Nabisco; that acquisition was approved by the Federal Trade Commission subject to the divestiture of products in five areas: three Jell-O and Royal brands types of products (dry-mix gelatin dessert, dry-mix pudding, no-bake desserts), intense mints (such as Altoids), and baking powder. Kraft later purchased the company.
Proxy	Proxy refers to a person who is authorized to vote the shares of another person. Also, the written authorization empowering a person to vote the shares of another person.
Proxy fight	Proxy fight is an event that may occur when opposition develops to a corporation management among its stockholders. Corporate activists may attempt to persuade shareholders to use their proxy votes to install new management for any of a variety of reasons.
Strategic fit	In business planning, the strategic fit is an indication of how well a company's mission and strategies fit its internal capabilities and its external environment.
Liquidation	Liquidation refers to a process whereby the assets of a business are converted to money. The conversion may be coerced by a legal process to pay off the debt of the business, or to satisfy any other business obligation that the business has not voluntarily satisfied.
Reorganization	Reorganization occurs, among other instances, when one corporation acquires another in a merger or acquisition, a single corporation divides into two or more entities, or a corporation makes a substantial change in its capital structure.
Insolvency	Insolvency is a financial condition experienced by a person or business entity when their assets no longer exceed their liabilities or when the person or entity can no longer meet its debt obligations when they come due.
Creditor	A person to whom a debt or legal obligation is owed, and who has the right to enforce payment of that debt or obligation is referred to as creditor.
Liability	A liability is a present obligation of the enterprise arizing from past events, the settlement of which is expected to result in an outflow from the enterprise of resources embodying economic benefits.
Going concern	A going concern describes a business that functions without the intention or threat of liquidation for the foreseeable future. Accountants and auditors may be required to evaluate and disclose whether a company is no longer a going concern, or is at risk of ceasing to be
Petition	A petition is a request to an authority, most commonly a government official or public entity. In the colloquial sense, a petition is a document addressed to some official and signed by numerous individuals.
Involuntary bankruptcy	Involuntary bankruptcy refers to bankruptcy procedures filed by a debtor's creditors.
Shell	One of the original Seven Sisters, Royal Dutch/Shell is the world's third-largest oil company by revenue, and a major player in the petrochemical industry and the solar energy business. Shell has six core businesses: Exploration and Production, Gas and Power, Downstream, Chemicals, Renewables, and Trading/Shipping, and operates in more than 140 countries.
Trustee	An independent party appointed to represent the bondholders is referred to as a trustee.

Business plan	A detailed written statement that describes the nature of the business, the target market, the advantages the business will have in relation to competition, and the resources and qualifications of the owner is referred to as a business plan.
Interest payment	The payment to holders of bonds payable, calculated by multiplying the stated rate on the face of the bond by the par, or face, value of the bond. If bonds are issued at a discount or premium, the interest payment does not equal the interest expense.
Deferral	Deferred is any account where the asset or liability is not realized until a future date, e.g. annuities, charges, taxes, income, etc. The deferred item may be carried, dependent on type of deferral, as either an asset or liability.
Composition	An out-of-court settlement in which creditors agree to accept a fractional settlement on their original claim is referred to as composition.
Conversion	Conversion refers to any distinct act of dominion wrongfully exerted over another's personal property in denial of or inconsistent with his rights therein. That tort committed by a person who deals with chattels not belonging to him in a manner that is inconsistent with the ownership of the lawful owner.
Extension	Extension refers to an out-of-court settlement in which creditors agree to allow the firm more time to meet its financial obligations. A new repayment schedule will be developed, subject to the acceptance of creditors.
Dividend	Amount of corporate profits paid out for each share of stock is referred to as dividend.
Devise	In a will, a gift of real property is called a devise.
Closing	The finalization of a real estate sales transaction that passes title to the property from the seller to the buyer is referred to as a closing. Closing is a sales term which refers to the process of making a sale. It refers to reaching the final step, which may be an exchange of money or acquiring a signature.
Accounting	A system that collects and processes financial information about an organization and reports that information to decision makers is referred to as accounting.
Deception	According to the Federal Trade Commission, a misrepresentation, omission, or practice that is likely to mislead the consumer acting reasonably in the circumstances to the consumer's detriment is referred to as deception.
Fraud	Tax fraud falls into two categories: civil and criminal. Under civil fraud, the IRS may impose as a penalty of an amount equal to as much as 75 percent of the underpayment.
Enron	Enron Corportaion's global reputation was undermined by persistent rumours of bribery and political pressure to secure contracts in Central America, South America, Africa, and the Philippines. Especially controversial was its $3 billion contract with the Maharashtra State Electricity Board in India, where it is alleged that Enron officials used political connections within the Clinton and Bush administrations to exert pressure on the board.
Lender	Suppliers and financial institutions that lend money to companies is referred to as a lender.
WorldCom	WorldCom was the United States' second largest long distance phone company (AT&T was the largest). WorldCom grew largely by acquiring other telecommunications companies, most notably MCI Communications. It also owned the Tier 1 ISP UUNET, a major part of the Internet backbone.
Verizon	Verizon a Dow 30 company, is a broadband and telecommunications provider. The acquisition of GTE by Bell Atlantic, on June 30, 2000, which formed Verizon, was among the largest mergers in United States business history. Verizon, with MCI, is currently the second largest telecommunications company in the United States.

Go to Cram101.com for the Practice Tests for this Chapter.

Go to **Cram101.com** for the Practice Tests for this Chapter.
And, **NEVER** highlight a book again!

Distribution	Distribution in economics, the manner in which total output and income is distributed among individuals or factors.
Secured debt	A general category of debt that indicates the loan was obtained by pledging assets as collateral is secured debt. Secured debt has many forms and usually offers some protective features to a given class of bondholders.
Creditworthiness	Creditworthiness indicates whether a borrower has in the past made loan payments when due.
Unsecured debt	Unsecured debt is a financial term that refers to any type of debt that is not collateralized by any specified assets in the event of default.
Common stockholder	A person who owns common stock is referred to as common stockholder. They elect the members of the board of directors for the company, as well.
Residual value	Residual value is one of the constituents of a leasing calculus or operation. It describes the future value of a good in terms of percentage of depreciation of its initial value.
Contribution	In business organization law, the cash or property contributed to a business by its owners is referred to as contribution.
Residual	Residual payments can refer to an ongoing stream of payments in respect of the completion of past achievements.
Wage	The payment for the service of a unit of labor, per unit time. In trade theory, it is the only payment to labor, usually unskilled labor. In empirical work, wage data may exclude other compenzation, which must be added to get the total cost of employment.
Instrument	Instrument refers to an economic variable that is controlled by policy makers and can be used to influence other variables, called targets. Examples are monetary and fiscal policies used to achieve external and internal balance.
Revenue	Revenue is a U.S. business term for the amount of money that a company receives from its activities, mostly from sales of products and/or services to customers.
Strategic plan	The formal document that presents the ways and means by which a strategic goal will be achieved is a strategic plan. A long-term flexible plan that does not regulate activities but rather outlines the means to achieve certain results, and provides the means to alter the course of action should the desired ends change.
National bank	A National bank refers to federally chartered banks. They are an ordinary private bank which operates nationally (as opposed to regionally or locally or even internationally).
Peak	Peak refers to the point in the business cycle when an economic expansion reaches its highest point before turning down. Contrasts with trough.
Brief	Brief refers to a statement of a party's case or legal arguments, usually prepared by an attorney. Also used to make legal arguments before appellate courts.
Senior executive	Senior executive means a chief executive officer, chief operating officer, chief financial officer and anyone in charge of a principal business unit or function.
Return on equity	Net profit after taxes per dollar of equity capital is referred to as return on equity.
Product line	A group of products that are physically similar or are intended for a similar market are called the product line.
Marginal tax rate	The percentage of an additional dollar of earnings that goes to taxes is referred to as the marginal tax rate.
Common stock	Common stock refers to the basic, normal, voting stock issued by a corporation; called residual equity because it ranks after preferred stock for dividend and liquidation

Go to **Cram101.com** for the Practice Tests for this Chapter.
And, **NEVER** highlight a book again!

distributions.

Perpetuity	A perpetuity is an annuity in which the periodic payments begin on a fixed date and continue indefinitely. Fixed coupon payments on permanently invested (irredeemable) sums of money are prime examples of perpetuities. Scholarships paid perpetually from an endowment fit the definition of perpetuity.
Bid	A bid price is a price offered by a buyer when he/she buys a good. In the context of stock trading on a stock exchange, the bid price is the highest price a buyer of a stock is willing to pay for a share of that given stock.
Venture capitalists	Venture capitalists refer to individuals or companies that invest in new businesses in exchange for partial ownership of those businesses.
Debt to equity ratio	The debt to equity ratio is a financial ratio debt divided by shareholders' equity. The two components are often taken from the firm's balance sheet, but they might also be calulated as market values if both the companiy's debt and equity are publicly traded. It is used to calculate a company's "financial leverage" and indicates what proportion of equity and debt the company is using to finance its assets.
Fixed asset	Fixed asset, also known as property, plant, and equipment (PP&E), is a term used in accountancy for assets and property which cannot easily be converted into cash. This can be compared with current assets such as cash or bank accounts, which are described as liquid assets. In most cases, only tangible assets are referred to as fixed.
Liquidated	Damages made certain by the prior agreement of the parties are called liquidated.
Current asset	A current asset is an asset on the balance sheet which is expected to be sold or otherwise used up in the near future, usually within one year.
Google	As it has grown, Google has found itself the focus of various controversies related to its business practices and services. For example, Google Print's effort to digitize millions of books and make the full text searchable has led to copyright disputes with the Authors Guild, cooperation with the governments of China, France and Germany to filter search results in accordance to regional laws and regulations has led to claims of censorship.
Yahoo	Yahoo is an American computer services company. It operates an Internet portal, the Yahoo Directory and a host of other services including the popular Yahoo Mail. Yahoo is the most visited website on the Internet today with more than 400 million unique users. The global network of Yahoo! websites received 3.4 billion page views per day on average as of October 2005.
Trend	Trend refers to the long-term movement of an economic variable, such as its average rate of increase or decrease over enough years to encompass several business cycles.

Go to **Cram101.com** for the Practice Tests for this Chapter.

Go to **Cram101.com** for the Practice Tests for this Chapter.
And, **NEVER** highlight a book again!

Domestic	From or in one's own country. A domestic producer is one that produces inside the home country. A domestic price is the price inside the home country. Opposite of 'foreign' or 'world.'.
Export	In economics, an export is any good or commodity, shipped or otherwise transported out of a country, province, town to another part of the world in a legitimate fashion, typically for use in trade or sale.
Gross domestic product	Gross domestic product refers to the total value of new goods and services produced in a given year within the borders of a country, regardless of by whom.
International Business	International business refers to any firm that engages in international trade or investment.
Exporting	Selling products to another country is called exporting.
Direct investment	Direct investment refers to a domestic firm actually investing in and owning a foreign subsidiary or division.
Investment	Investment refers to spending for the production and accumulation of capital and additions to inventories. In a financial sense, buying an asset with the expectation of making a return.
Operation	A standardized method or technique that is performed repetitively, often on different materials resulting in different finished goods is called an operation.
Multinational corporations	Firms that own production facilities in two or more countries and produce and sell their products globally are referred to as multinational corporations.
Multinational corporation	An organization that manufactures and markets products in many different countries and has multinational stock ownership and multinational management is referred to as multinational corporation.
Corporation	A legal entity chartered by a state or the Federal government that is distinct and separate from the individuals who own it is a corporation. This separation gives the corporation unique powers which other legal entities lack.
Financial market	In economics, a financial market is a mechanism which allows people to trade money for securities or commodities such as gold or other precious metals. In general, any commodity market might be considered to be a financial market, if the usual purpose of traders is not the immediate consumption of the commodity, but rather as a means of delaying or accelerating consumption over time.
Market	A market is, as defined in economics, a social arrangement that allows buyers and sellers to discover information and carry out a voluntary exchange of goods or services.
Stock	In financial terminology, stock is the capital raized by a corporation, through the issuance and sale of shares.
Portfolio investment	Portfolio investment refers to the acquisition of portfolio capital. Usually refers to such transactions across national borders and/or across currencies.
Portfolio	In finance, a portfolio is a collection of investments held by an institution or a private individual. Holding but not always a portfolio is part of an investment and risk-limiting strategy called diversification. By owning several assets, certain types of risk (in particular specific risk) can be reduced.
Bond	Bond refers to a debt instrument, issued by a borrower and promising a specified stream of payments to the purchaser, usually regular interest payments plus a final repayment of principal.
Developed	A developed country is one that enjoys a relatively high standard of living derived through

Go to **Cram101.com** for the Practice Tests for this Chapter.

country	an industrialized, diversified economy. Countries with a very high Human Development Index are generally considered developed countries.
Financial management	The job of managing a firm's resources so it can meet its goals and objectives is called financial management.
Management	Management characterizes the process of leading and directing all or part of an organization, often a business, through the deployment and manipulation of resources. Early twentieth-century management writer Mary Parker Follett defined management as "the art of getting things done through people."
Exchange	The trade of things of value between buyer and seller so that each is better off after the trade is called the exchange.
Firm	An organization that employs resources to produce a good or service for profit and owns and operates one or more plants is referred to as a firm.
Foreign exchange	In finance, foreign exchange means currencies, such as U.S. Dollars and Euros. These are traded on foreign exchange markets.
Exchange market	Exchange market refers to the market on which national currencies are bought and sold.
Foreign exchange market	A market for converting the currency of one country into that of another country is called foreign exchange market. It is by far the largest market in the world, in terms of cash value traded, and includes trading between large banks, central banks, currency speculators, multinational corporations, governments, and other financial markets and institutions.
Stock exchange	A stock exchange is a corporation or mutual organization which provides facilities for stock brokers and traders, to trade company stocks and other securities.
Commercial bank	A firm that engages in the business of banking is a commercial bank.
Service	Service refers to a "non tangible product" that is not embodied in a physical good and that typically effects some change in another product, person, or institution. Contrasts with good.
Exchange rate	Exchange rate refers to the price at which one country's currency trades for another, typically on the exchange market.
Inverse relationship	The relationship between two variables that change in opposite directions, for example, product price and quantity demanded is an inverse relationship.
Security	Security refers to a claim on the borrower future income that is sold by the borrower to the lender. A security is a type of transferable interest representing financial value.
Buyer	A buyer refers to a role in the buying center with formal authority and responsibility to select the supplier and negotiate the terms of the contract.
Profit	Profit refers to the return to the resource entrepreneurial ability; total revenue minus total cost.
Spot transaction	The predominant type of exchange rate transaction, involving the immediate exchange of bank deposits denominated in different currencies is a spot transaction.
Forward rate	Forward rate refers to the forward exchange rate, this is the exchange rate on a forward market transaction.
Spot rate	Spot rate refers to the rate at which the currency is traded for immediate delivery. It is the existing cash price.
Broker	In commerce, a broker is a party that mediates between a buyer and a seller. A broker who also acts as a seller or as a buyer becomes a principal party to the deal.

Discount	The difference between the face value of a bond and its selling price, when a bond is sold for less than its face value it's referred to as a discount.
Premium	Premium refers to the fee charged by an insurance company for an insurance policy. The rate of losses must be relatively predictable: In order to set the premium (prices) insurers must be able to estimate them accurately.
Forward exchange	When two parties agree to exchange currency and execute a deal at some specific date in the future, we have forward exchange.
Hedging	A technique for avoiding a risk by making a counteracting transaction is referred to as hedging.
Forward exchange rate	The exchange rates governing forward exchange transactions is called the forward exchange rate.
Forward market	A market for exchange of currencies in the future is the forward market. Participants in a forward market enter into a contract to exchange currencies, not today, but at a specified date in the future, typically 30, 60, or 90 days from now, and at a price that is agreed upon.
Foreign exchange risk	Foreign exchange risk refers to a form of risk that refers to the possibility of experiencing a drop in revenue or an increase in cost in an international transaction due to a change in foreign exchange rates. Importers, exporters, investors, and multinational firms alike are exposed to this risk.
Hedge	Hedge refers to a process of offsetting risk. In the foreign exchange market, hedgers use the forward market to cover a transaction or open position and thereby reduce exchange risk. The term applies most commonly to trade.
Contract	A contract is a "promise" or an "agreement" that is enforced or recognized by the law. In the civil law, a contract is considered to be part of the general law of obligations.
Common currency	A situation where several countries form a monetary union with a single currency and a unified central bank is referred to as common currency.
Euro	The common currency of a subset of the countries of the EU, adopted January 1, 1999 is called euro.
Supply and demand	The partial equilibrium supply and demand economic model originally developed by Alfred Marshall attempts to describe, explain, and predict changes in the price and quantity of goods sold in competitive markets.
Supply	Supply is the aggregate amount of any material good that can be called into being at a certain price point; it comprises one half of the equation of supply and demand. In classical economic theory, a curve representing supply is one of the factors that produce price.
Demand curve	Demand curve refers to the graph of quantity demanded as a function of price, normally downward sloping, straight or curved, and drawn with quantity on the horizontal axis and price on the vertical axis.
Market price	Market price is an economic concept with commonplace familiarity; it is the price that a good or service is offered at, or will fetch, in the marketplace; it is of interest mainly in the study of microeconomics.
Commodity	Could refer to any good, but in trade a commodity is usually a raw material or primary product that enters into international trade, such as metals or basic agricultural products.
Capital	Capital generally refers to financial wealth, especially that used to start or maintain a business. In classical economics, capital is one of four factors of production, the others being land and labor and entrepreneurship.

Go to **Cram101.com** for the Practice Tests for this Chapter.

Consumption	In Keynesian economics consumption refers to personal consumption expenditure, i.e., the purchase of currently produced goods and services out of income, out of savings (net worth), or from borrowed funds. It refers to that part of disposable income that does not go to saving.
Preference	The act of a debtor in paying or securing one or more of his creditors in a manner more favorable to them than to other creditors or to the exclusion of such other creditors is a preference. In the absence of statute, a preference is perfectly good, but to be legal it must be bona fide, and not a mere subterfuge of the debtor to secure a future benefit to himself or to prevent the application of his property to his debts.
License	A license in the sphere of Intellectual Property Rights (IPR) is a document, contract or agreement giving permission or the 'right' to a legally-definable entity to do something (such as manufacture a product or to use a service), or to apply something (such as a trademark), with the objective of achieving commercial gain.
Tariff	A tax imposed by a nation on an imported good is called a tariff.
Policy	Similar to a script in that a policy can be a less than completely rational decision-making method. Involves the use of a pre-existing set of decision steps for any problem that presents itself.
Quota	A government-imposed restriction on quantity, or sometimes on total value, used to restrict the import of something to a specific quantity is called a quota.
Foreign direct investment	Foreign direct investment refers to the buying of permanent property and businesses in foreign nations.
Recession	A significant decline in economic activity. In the U.S., recession is approximately defined as two successive quarters of falling GDP, as judged by NBER.
Economy	The income, expenditures, and resources that affect the cost of running a business and household are called an economy.
Financial assets	Financial assets refer to monetary claims or obligations by one party against another party. Examples are bonds, mortgages, bank loans, and equities.
Inflation rate	The percentage increase in the price level per year is an inflation rate. Alternatively, the inflation rate is the rate of decrease in the purchasing power of money.
Interest rate	The rate of return on bonds, loans, or deposits. When one speaks of 'the' interest rate, it is usually in a model where there is only one.
Inflation	An increase in the overall price level of an economy, usually as measured by the CPI or by the implicit price deflator is called inflation.
Interest	In finance and economics, interest is the price paid by a borrower for the use of a lender's money. In other words, interest is the amount of paid to "rent" money for a period of time.
Asset	An item of property, such as land, capital, money, a share in ownership, or a claim on others for future payment, such as a bond or a bank deposit is an asset.
Holding	The holding is a court's determination of a matter of law based on the issue presented in the particular case. In other words: under this law, with these facts, this result.
Gain	In finance, gain is a profit or an increase in value of an investment such as a stock or bond. Gain is calculated by fair market value or the proceeds from the sale of the investment minus the sum of the purchase price and all costs associated with it.
Intervention	Intervention refers to an activity in which a government buys or sells its currency in the foreign exchange market in order to affect its currency's exchange rate.

Go to **Cram101.com** for the Practice Tests for this Chapter.

Go to **Cram101.com** for the Practice Tests for this Chapter.
And, **NEVER** highlight a book again!

International monetary system	International monetary system is a network of international commercial and government institutions that determine currency exchange rates.
Domestic price	The price of a good or service within a country, determined by domestic demand and supply is referred to as domestic price.
Balance	In banking and accountancy, the outstanding balance is the amount of money owned, (or due), that remains in a deposit account (or a loan account) at a given date, after all past remittances, payments and withdrawal have been accounted for. It can be positive (then, in the balance sheet of a firm, it is an asset) or negative (a liability).
Cost of living	The amount of money it takes to buy the goods and services that a typical family consumes is the cost of living.
Floating exchange rate	A system under which the exchange rate for converting one currency into another is continuously adjusted depending on the laws of supply and demand is referred to as a floating exchange rate.
Free market	A free market is a market where price is determined by the unregulated interchange of supply and demand rather than set by artificial means.
International Monetary Fund	The International Monetary Fund is the international organization entrusted with overseeing the global financial system by monitoring exchange rates and balance of payments, as well as offering technical and financial assistance when asked.
Fixed exchange rate	A fixed exchange rate, sometimes is a type of exchange rate regime wherein a currency's value is matched to the value of another single currency or to a basket of other currencies, or to another measure of value, such as gold.
Fund	Independent accounting entity with a self-balancing set of accounts segregated for the purposes of carrying on specific activities is referred to as a fund.
Revaluation	Revaluation means a rise of a price of goods or products. This term is specially used as revaluation of a currency, where it means a rise of currency to the relation with a foreign currency in a fixed exchange rate.
Investing activities	Investing activities refers to cash flow activities that include purchasing and disposing of investments and productive long-lived assets using cash and lending money and collecting on those loans.
Aid	Assistance provided by countries and by international institutions such as the World Bank to developing countries in the form of monetary grants, loans at low interest rates, in kind, or a combination of these is called aid. Aid can also refer to assistance of any type rendered to benefit some group or individual.
Balance of trade	Balance of trade refers to the sum of the money gained by a given economy by selling exports, minus the cost of buying imports. They form part of the balance of payments, which also includes other transactions such as the international investment position.
Trade deficit	The amount by which imports exceed exports of goods and services is referred to as trade deficit.
Deficit	The deficit is the amount by which expenditure exceed revenue.
Trade surplus	A positive balance of trade is known as a trade surplus and consists of exporting more (in financial capital terms) than one imports.
Accumulation	The acquisition of an increasing quantity of something. The accumulation of factors, especially capital, is a primary mechanism for economic growth.
Supply curve	Supply curve refers to the graph of quantity supplied as a function of price, normally upward

Go to **Cram101.com** for the Practice Tests for this Chapter.
And, **NEVER** highlight a book again!

	sloping, straight or curved, and drawn with quantity on the horizontal axis and price on the vertical axis.
Trade balance	Balance of trade in terms of exports versus imports is called trade balance.
Capital market	A financial market in which long-term debt and equity instruments are traded is referred to as a capital market. The capital market includes the stock market and the bond market.
Eurodollars	Eurodollars refers to u.S. dollars that are deposited in foreign banks outside the United States or in foreign branches of U.S. banks.
Medium of exchange	Medium of exchange refers to any item sellers generally accept and buyers generally use to pay for a good or service; money; a convenient means of exchanging goods and services without engaging in barter.
Securities and exchange commission	Securities and exchange commission refers to U.S. government agency that determines the financial statements that public companies must provide to stockholders and the measurement rules that they must use in producing those statements.
Disclosure	Disclosure means the giving out of information, either voluntarily or to be in compliance with legal regulations or workplace rules.
Eurobond	A bond that is issued outside of the jurisdiction of any single country, denominated in a eurocurrency is referred to as eurobond.
Political risk	Refers to the many different actions of people, subgroups, and whole countries that have the potential to affect the financial status of a firm is called political risk.
Authority	Authority in agency law, refers to an agent's ability to affect his principal's legal relations with third parties. Also used to refer to an actor's legal power or ability to do something. In addition, sometimes used to refer to a statute, case, or other legal source that justifies a particular result.
Sovereignty	A country or region's power and ability to rule itself and manage its own affairs. Some feel that membership in international organizations such as the WTO is a threat to their sovereignty.
Property	Assets defined in the broadest legal sense. Property includes the unrealized receivables of a cash basis taxpayer, but not services rendered.
Government units	The federal, state, and local agencies that buy goods and services for the constituents they serve is a government units.
Expropriation	Expropriation is the act of removing from control the owner of an item of property. The term is used to both refer to acts by a government or by any group of people.
Conversion	Conversion refers to any distinct act of dominion wrongfully exerted over another's personal property in denial of or inconsistent with his rights therein. That tort committed by a person who deals with chattels not belonging to him in a manner that is inconsistent with the ownership of the lawful owner.
Inputs	The inputs used by a firm or an economy are the labor, raw materials, electricity and other resources it uses to produce its outputs.
Host country	The country in which the parent-country organization seeks to locate or has already located a facility is a host country.
Foreign Corrupt Practices Act	The Foreign Corrupt Practices Act of 1977 is a United States federal law requiring any company that has publicly-traded stock to maintain records that accurately and fairly represent the company's transactions; additionally, requires any publicly-traded company to have an adequate system of internal accounting controls.

Go to **Cram101.com** for the Practice Tests for this Chapter.

Go to **Cram101.com** for the Practice Tests for this Chapter.
And, **NEVER** highlight a book again!

Free enterprise	Free enterprise refers to a system in which economic agents are free to own property and engage in commercial transactions.
Corruption	The unauthorized use of public office for private gain. The most common forms of corruption are bribery, extortion, and the misuse of inside information.
Enterprise	Enterprise refers to another name for a business organization. Other similar terms are business firm, sometimes simply business, sometimes simply firm, as well as company, and entity.
Financial perspective	Financial perspective is one of the four standard perspectives used with the Balanced Scorecard. Financial perspective measures inform an organization whether strategy execution, which is detailed through measures in the other three perspectives, is leading to improved bottom line results.
Capitalism	Capitalism refers to an economic system in which capital is mostly owned by private individuals and corporations. Contrasts with communism.
Union	A worker association that bargains with employers over wages and working conditions is called a union.
Cash flow	In finance, cash flow refers to the amounts of cash being received and spent by a business during a defined period of time, sometimes tied to a specific project. Most of the time they are being used to determine gaps in the liquid position of a company.
Balance sheet	A statement of the assets, liabilities, and net worth of a firm or individual at some given time often at the end of its "fiscal year," is referred to as a balance sheet.
Foreign subsidiary	A company owned in a foreign country by another company is referred to as foreign subsidiary.
Parent company	Parent company refers to the entity that has a controlling influence over another company. It may have its own operations, or it may have been set up solely for the purpose of owning the Subject Company.
Subsidiary	A company that is controlled by another company or corporation is a subsidiary.
Consolidation	The combination of two or more firms, generally of equal size and market power, to form an entirely new entity is a consolidation.
Abstraction	Abstraction is a model building simplification process that refers to retaining only the essential facts, and the elimination of irrelevant and non-economic facts, to obtain an economic principle.
Accounting	A system that collects and processes financial information about an organization and reports that information to decision makers is referred to as accounting.
Financial statement	Financial statement refers to a summary of all the transactions that have occurred over a particular period.
Equity	Equity is the name given to the set of legal principles, in countries following the English common law tradition, which supplement strict rules of law where their application would operate harshly, so as to achieve what is sometimes referred to as "natural justice."
Liability	A liability is a present obligation of the enterprise arizing from past events, the settlement of which is expected to result in an outflow from the enterprise of resources embodying economic benefits.
Production	The creation of finished goods and services using the factors of production: land, labor, capital, entrepreneurship, and knowledge.
Business	Business analysis is a structured methodology that is focused on completely understanding the

Go to **Cram101.com** for the Practice Tests for this Chapter.
And, **NEVER** highlight a book again!

analysis	customer's needs, identifying how best to meet those needs, and then "reinventing" the stream of processes to meet those needs.
Treasurer	In many governments, a treasurer is the person responsible for running the treasury. Treasurers are also employed by organizations to look after funds.
Marketing	Promoting and selling products or services to customers, or prospective customers, is referred to as marketing.
Purchasing	Purchasing refers to the function in a firm that searches for quality material resources, finds the best suppliers, and negotiates the best price for goods and services.
Exporter	A firm that sells its product in another country is an exporter.
Markup	Markup is a term used in marketing to indicate how much the price of a product is above the cost of producing and distributing the product.
Marginal tax rate	The percentage of an additional dollar of earnings that goes to taxes is referred to as the marginal tax rate.
Manufacturing	Production of goods primarily by the application of labor and capital to raw materials and other intermediate inputs, in contrast to agriculture, mining, forestry, fishing, and services a manufacturing.
Spot exchange rate	The exchange rate at which a foreign exchange dealer will convert one currency into another that particular day is the spot exchange rate.

Go to **Cram101.com** for the Practice Tests for this Chapter.

LaVergne, TN USA
26 August 2009
156010LV00001B/32/A

9 781428 811386